THE EDUCATION OF BETSEY STOCKTON

The Education of Betsey Stockton

AN ODYSSEY OF SLAVERY AND FREEDOM

Gregory Nobles

THE UNIVERSITY OF CHICAGO PRESS
Chicago and London

The University of Chicago Press, Chicago 60637
The University of Chicago Press, Ltd., London

Published 2022
Printed in the United States of America

31 30 29 28 27 26 25 24 23 22   1 2 3 4 5

ISBN-13: 978-0-226-69772-7 (cloth)
ISBN-13: 978-0-226-69786-4 (e-book)
DOI: https://doi.org/10.7208/chicago/9780226697864.001.0001

Library of Congress Cataloging-in-Publication Data

Names: Nobles, Gregory H., author.
Title: The education of Betsey Stockton : an odyssey of slavery and freedom / Gregory Nobles.
Description: Chicago : The University of Chicago Press, 2022. | Includes bibliographical references and index.
Identifiers: LCCN 2021040707 | ISBN 9780226697727 (cloth) | ISBN 9780226697864 (ebook)
Subjects: LCSH: Stockton, Betsey, 1798?–1865. | African American women—New Jersey—Princeton—Biography. | Slaves—United States—Biography. | Freedmen—United States—Biography. | Women missionaries—United States—Biography. | Missionaries—United States—Biography. | Missionaries—Hawaii—Biography. | Women teachers—United States—Biography. | Presbyterians—Biography. | Princeton (N.J.)—Biography. | LCGFT: Biographies.
Classification: LCC E185.97.S86 N63 2022 | DDC 974.9/65 [B]—dc23
LC record available at https://lccn.loc.gov/2021040707

⊗ This paper meets the requirements of ANSI/NISO Z39.48-1992 (Permanence of Paper).

To Anne

Contents

Prologue

BETSEY STOCKTON HAD made up her mind to get out of Princeton and never come back. She would be leaving everyone and everything she had known, including the institution of slavery, into which she had been born. Now in her early twenties and a free woman, she would be making the biggest step in her life so far—going to the Sandwich Islands as a missionary. She would be the first single woman, the first Black woman, to do that; she would be making history.

But she had to make one last stop—to say good-bye to the Reverend Ashbel Green, a man with whom she had had a long and complicated relationship. As an enslaved child, she had been given to Green's wife, and she had grown up under Green's authority, first in slavery and then in indentured servitude, until her teenaged years, when she became emancipated. Even then, she stayed in his household, working for wages, saving her money until she had enough to leave. This would be an emotional farewell.

That evening, she stood in the downstairs hallway in Green's house, outside his study, waiting for him to usher her in. Like Green, she had come to live in that house in October 1812, when he became president of the College of New Jersey. She had cooked and cleaned and done all sorts of chores, and when she could find time, she immersed herself in the books in Green's study. Betsey Stockton had never been to school, but she had become an eager reader, even of the ponderous volumes that lined Green's shelves. When she came into his study now, she was at home.

She didn't come alone. Joining her was a thin, sharp-featured young man about her age named Charles Samuel Stewart, who had been one of Green's students at the college and later had graduated from the nearby Princeton Theological Seminary. Stewart was white, Stockton was Black, and they had determined to work together as part of a larger "missionary family"—including Stewart's young bride Harriet and fifteen others—heading for the Pacific under the auspices of the American Board of Commissioners for Foreign Missions (ABCFM).

When Betsey Stockton had applied to the ABCFM a year earlier, Ashbel Green wrote a letter of recommendation that covered, to use Green's terms, her life from the time she was "given, as a slave" to Green's wife, through her "wild and thoughtless" early teenage years, and coming to her "saving change of heart" a little later. Now, she was about to start the next chapter of her life, leaving for New Haven to board a whale ship, sailing to the Pacific with her own sense of purpose.

By contrast, Ashbel Green was old, just past his sixtieth birthday, white-haired and tired, worn down by the decade of his college presidency. In that time he had suffered the deaths of two wives and one son, he had been derided and defied by unruly students, and he had lost the favor of the college trustees. He was in fact about to resign, leaving Princeton himself, for Philadelphia.

Betsey Stockton and Charles Stewart and Ashbel Green talked, prayed, and finally took leave of each other. "The next day they went East and I West," Green would write in his diary, "probably to meet no more on earth."

But they would meet again, and in time, Betsey Stockton would return to Princeton. She would become a leader in the town's Black community, a woman who helped build institutions of resistance to racism over the decades until she died, in 1865, the year slavery came to a legal end in the United States.

SEARCHING FOR BETSEY STOCKTON

Today, it's still possible to find markers honoring Betsey Stockton in Princeton, some old, some very new. The newest is a plaque that stands in front of the old President's House (now called Maclean House, home of the university's Alumni Association), which lists her as one of at least sixteen enslaved people who lived there in the eighteenth and nineteenth centuries. But to see the older—and more personal—memorials to her, you have to leave the campus, cross Nassau Street, the town's main thoroughfare, then head down Witherspoon Street, the center of the town's small business district. The shopping area fades away after only two blocks, at the Paul Robeson Center for the Arts, named for the famous actor, athlete, and activist, who was born in Princeton. A block or so more takes you to the town's old cemetery on the right side of the street and the historic Witherspoon Street Presbyterian Church on the left, a modest white frame church building. It's just a few blocks from the campus—but in a historically different world.

Outside the church is a sign, part of the New Jersey Women's Heritage Trail. "Betsey Stockton (1798–1865) began life as a slave for the prominent Stockton family in Princeton," it reads, going on to give the basic outline of her life—becoming free, going to Hawai'i as a missionary, coming back to teach in Philadelphia and Canada, then returning to Princeton in 1835. There she "spent the rest of her life working to enrich the lives of members of her local community," as one of the founding members of the First Presbyterian Church of Colour and teaching in the Witherspoon School for Colored Children. "When Betsey Stockton died in Princeton at the age of 67," the sign concludes, "she was memorialized by former students who donated a stained glass window in her honor to the church."

And inside the church there's the window, an orderly ensemble of geometric shapes in reds, blues, purples, and yellows, that contains only seven words: "Presented by the Scholars of Elizabeth Stockton." There's also a brass plaque, installed in 1906 on the same wall as the window, that notes her long life of service in Princeton, where she became a "powerful influence for good in the community." Since then, she has lived in the collective memory of the town's Black community, particularly in the Witherspoon Street Presbyterian Church, and in the recent work of the Witherspoon-Jackson Historical and Cultural Society to tell the larger history of African American people in Princeton.[1]

A few years ago, when I first read the sign and saw the window and plaque, Betsey Stockton's story struck me as a remarkable saga—a journey from slavery to freedom, from Princeton to the Pacific, all the way around the world, and eventually back to Princeton. I've written this book to tell that story as fully as I can.[2]

DIGGING FOR HER HISTORY

It hasn't been easy: there's no Betsey Stockton archive, no treasure trove of collected documents, especially for her early years. She left no childhood diaries or collections of correspondence or any other record of her youth written in her own hand or rendered in her own voice. Essentially everything we know about the first two decades of her life comes from Ashbel Green. But Green gives us only a few fleeting entries in the thousand-plus pages of his diary and only two brief references in the 628 pages of his autobiography. The most Green ever wrote about her came in 1821, when he offered the brief overview of her early life in his letter to the ABCFM. This document is the most comprehensive contemporaneous statement we have about Betsey Stockton's early life, but it's one I've come to read with caution, even skepticism.

There's a little more from her adult life, but not much. In making out her will, in 1862, she left "all my library, books, letters & other papers" to Charles Samuel Stewart, but unfortunately, almost all of that is gone. There are a couple of her letters to Stewart from the 1840s, but otherwise no correspondence of substance. There's only one known volume from her library, a book now owned by a rare book specialist in Princeton, who let me see it. Holding that book in my hands—one she held in hers some two centuries ago, one in which she wrote her name as an act of personal possession—gave me a moment of direct connection, an almost spiritual experience. But it also made me aware of all that was missing. What else did she read, what else did she keep? How could a twenty-first-century historian get a deeper look into her mind, her motivations, her emotions?

The best place to start seemed to be the journal she kept during her five-month voyage to the Pacific, in 1822–23, on a whaling vessel, the *Thames*. The original manuscript apparently doesn't still exist, but the published version first appeared in a Philadelphia religious paper, the *Christian Advocate*, in three installments in 1824–25. But there again, the record of her experience passed through the hands of Ashbel Green, who edited it. He claimed to have done little: "Some of her letters to me after her arrival at the island," he wrote, "were so well written, that, with very few corrections, I inserted them in the Christian Advocate, . . . and they were greatly admired." Greatly admired they still are, the longest and most readily available source for Stockton's own writing—even if we allow for Green's "very few corrections." In her journal she wrote about her various pleasures, frustrations, and fears, revealing not just the quality of her mind—she was not just literate, but intellectual, a well-read woman who could quote Milton from memory—but the state of her soul. On the *Thames*, Betsey Stockton was the only unmarried woman, the only Black woman, living among her "missionary family" and the men of the crew, almost all of them in their late teens or twenties. Several of the other missionaries wrote journals, but Betsey Stockton's stands out, both for its eloquence and for the exceptional situation of its author. Still, it's almost all there is.

There's almost no personal record for the rest of her life, nothing she wrote that gives us similar insight into her mind or emotions, especially about some of the most basic aspects of her experience. She was born into slavery, but we don't have any statements about her stance on the most important issues of the era, whether colonization or abolition or the pervasive racism in America. She never married, but there's nothing to tell us why that was the case, whether her sexuality or spirituality or commitment to her calling. If Betsey Stockton ever wrote about such things, the documents apparently no longer exist, and there is no evidence from others to support conclusions in one direction or another.

Other historians have faced similar challenges in studying people who didn't leave extensive writings—or didn't even know how to write. I have been especially impressed by recent biographies of Black people in antebellum America, formerly obscure, even unlettered figures who had been all but invisible in the historical record. Telling the stories, writing the lives of ordinary people requires rethinking our relationship with the normal archival sources, which most often reflect the perspective of the historically articulate, people in positions of power who wrote the documents we have traditionally relied on—people like Ashbel Green. Trying to know Betsey Stockton on her own terms has involved the detective work of history, digging for shards of evidence from a variety of sources, exploring the physical environment and sensory experiences of her world, finding what other people wrote about her, occasionally reading against the grain of their beliefs and biases, trying to fill the empty spaces and silences in the archival record by judiciously engaging in some measure of historical speculation. It's been suggested to me, more than once, that I might have had an easier time writing a novel, putting into Betsey Stockton's mouth the words I wish she had said, the feelings and opinions I wish she had expressed. But I remain a writer of history, not fiction, and I have based this book on the available evidence, even while realizing it can never be enough. I have limited my use of terms like "no doubt," "most likely," and "probably," but they do appear here. They do not, however, preclude imagining other possibilities, and readers may certainly do so.[3]

FOLLOWING HER AROUND THE WORLD

Betsey Stockton traveled the world. After her birth in Princeton, probably in 1798, she spent her childhood in Philadelphia, until 1812, and from then until 1822, she was back in New Jersey—Princeton, Woodbury, and Princeton again. In 1822, she left to go to New Haven, Connecticut, to sail to the Sandwich Islands, then sailed back, in 1825, with a stopover in England, before arriving back in the United States in 1826. She went to Cooperstown, New York, and then to Philadelphia again, 1828–30, with a brief interlude on Grape Island, in Canada, before returning to Cooperstown, 1830–33, and then back to Princeton again, to stay.

The itinerary is almost exhausting to read, and probably even more exhausting to have lived. Betsey Stockton was periodically ill throughout her adult life, perhaps due to the rigors of travel and certainly due to the effects of racial hostility. But for a child born into slavery, she lived a life of remarkable mobility, seeing more of the world than most Americans of her era ever would, making her mark in more places than anyone would have expected. Three of those places have special resonance.

She lived in Philadelphia twice. Philadelphia is arguably the best-studied American city, particularly its Black community, in the era between the American Revolution and the Civil War. The only thing missing from the research picture, I was surprised to find, was much awareness about infant schools, where Betsey Stockton worked; for that I was on my own.

Philadelphia is a historic walking town. Ashbel Green's Second Presbyterian Church, at Third and Arch, was less than a mile north of Richard Allen's Mother Bethel African Methodist Episcopal (AME) Church on Sixth Street. (The social distance was quite another matter.) I could use city directories, maps, and other sources to recreate Betsey Stockton's neighborhood, to imagine what and who she might have seen as she ran errands as a child, or as she later walked to work at her infant school on Gaskill Street, near the corner of Fourth. The building is no longer there, but I could try to visualize the daily scene at the school, as Black parents left their toddlers in the morning and picked them up in the afternoon, talking with each other, as parents always do, about their children and their community. And even though I couldn't actually put myself inside her classroom, I could try to visualize that scene as well, with Stockton and sometimes an assistant teacher surrounded by fifty or seventy or more children between the ages of two and five, doing their best to bring some form of order to what must have been the chaos of toddlers' needs.

Hawai'i was likewise an important place to experience Betsey Stockton's world, but it also posed some problems. In Honolulu, I visited the house where she and her fellow missionaries lived when they first arrived, the buildings and grounds now well preserved. Inside, it's possible to imagine the close social connections of the missionaries, the communal meals and meetings and other daily interactions. Outside, it's a different story. The grounds are still lush with shade trees, but they're surrounded by a cityscape of busy streets and office buildings. The same is true in Lahaina, on Maui, where Betsey Stockton spent the bulk of her time as a teacher. A few buildings from the missionary era still stand, but they too are surrounded by restaurants, bars, T-shirt shops, and other amenities of the tourist trade.

There's nothing too surprising about that, of course: no place stays the same after two centuries of economic development. But it's an ironic reminder that the missionary movement was embedded in a larger process of historical change, not just the spread of Christianity, but the spread of capitalism, both of which brought—or certainly accelerated—a remarkable cultural transformation on the islands. From the time of their arrival to today, Christian missionaries have come in for considerable criticism about the consequences, both intended and unintended, of their presence in the Pacific. For a brief time and in her own way, Betsey Stockton contributed to this historical process. She was certainly not an architect of missionary policy, nor was she an aggressive agent of cultural change. She was the first among the missionaries to focus her work not solely on

Hawaiian elites but on ordinary farmers and their families. Teaching them Christianity and literacy may have been a form of social transformation, even social control, but Betsey Stockton saw it as a step toward greater social equality among island people. It was also a significant first step for her, helping define the path she would pursue throughout the rest of her life.

Most of her life she spent in Princeton. Today, Princeton may seem like an upscale, placid place, and so it did in the antebellum era. But the town's veneer of gentility glossed over the deep racism suffusing all of American society, the North as well as the South. Today, in fact, far too many people still think of the antebellum South as the land of slavery and the North as the land of freedom. But slavery died a slow death in the nineteenth-century North, gradually and most often grudgingly. New Jersey was the last northern state to endorse gradual abolition, in 1804, but the institution did not end until 1865: in Princeton alone, twelve Black people remained enslaved as late as 1840. And in Princeton, as elsewhere in the North, free Blacks did not enjoy the right to vote or other forms of citizenship and equal rights. They generally worshipped in segregated churches, and they sent their children to segregated schools—if such schools existed at all.

The school that mattered most in Princeton was the college, and I've become a student of its history in the antebellum era. I've been fortunate to do so at the right time, joining other recent inquiries into the role of colleges in shaping the racial history of the United States. These have begun to dissolve the shadows that had long covered the economic contribution of slavery to the self-satisfied success of elite white colleges, like Princeton. Since 2013, the Princeton & Slavery Project, a collaborative effort of students, faculty, and other contributors, has generated some nine hundred pages of online essays and primary source documents, several of which have figured into my fuller picture of Princeton, both the college and the community.[4]

It's important to see the connections between the two. From the late eighteenth century onward, the College of New Jersey had the reputation of being the most southern college in the North, sometimes with a majority of its students coming from the South. The first nine presidents and several other members of the faculty not only held people in slavery but crafted intellectual arguments that undergirded racism. Many of the students went beyond intellectual debate, turning to violence against African American people and opponents of slavery. Throughout the antebellum era, the college and the town's white community reflected and reinforced one another. That had a profound effect on the town's Black community, which had to deal with the sometimes veiled, sometimes vicious racism that emanated from the other side of Nassau Street. But given its size—six-hundred-plus people, as much as 20 percent of the town's population in the 1840s and 1850s—Princeton's Black community in Betsey Stockton's era was a community with its own institutions and history.

GETTING TO KNOW HER

Yet for all the emphasis on Princeton and other places, this book is about Betsey Stockton. Finding traces of her in the archives or imagining her where she lived is not the same as knowing her, or knowing what to make of her. That's been an ongoing process of living with her in my mind, thinking about her in different ways, trying to get to know her better, and ultimately coming to terms with the critical historical question—So what? What is it about Betsey Stockton that deserves our attention, that makes a place for her in American history?

When I started work on this book, I discussed the project over a sandwich with someone who claimed to know something about Betsey Stockton. "Oh, she was just a well-mannered schoolmarm," my lunch companion sniffed. I probably bristled a little, but I kept that patronizing description in mind as I worked.

Ashbel Green didn't consider the teenage Betsey Stockton well mannered at all. Teenagers can be like that, or at least seem so to a beleaguered, bookish, middle-aged, Presbyterian pastor and college president. So he sent her away, selling three years of her labor to another Presbyterian clergyman some fifty miles away. When she came back to Princeton, she seemed a different person, apparently pious enough to be entered into the records of Green's church as "Betsey Stockton—a coloured woman living in the family of the Revd. Dr. Green." Green would soon come to admit that "Her manners, as well as her mind, are above her station." The elders of the Princeton Presbyterian session, "being satisfied as to her experimental acquaintance with religion, and her good conduct—agreed to receive her."

Religion proved to be much more than a passing acquaintance, staying with Betsey Stockton throughout her life. Like many Christians, she found in it both support and uncertainty. Soon after setting sail for Hawai'i in 1822, for instance, she reassured herself that "my heart was still rejoicing in the strength of my God," but over the course of the voyage, she wrote several times about fearing a loss of faith: "I was declining in the spiritual life. . . . I find a void within my breast that is painful." Such doubts dogged her for years. In 1845, feeling low both spiritually and physically, she would write that "I thank God there is yet balm in Gilead," but "it is good for me to be afflicted, already the grave is strip[p]ed of much of its gloom to me."

Such doubts did not overcome her determination, her sense of direction, even destiny. As a young woman, she knew her own mind. In writing her recommendation for missionary service, Ashbel Green noted that "she has been, for a good while, exceedingly desirous to go on a mission." Another recommender cited her "active, persevering, self-sacrificing spirit," adding that "she loves to teach children . . . and has appropriated a part of every week to the instruction of a number of coloured children." Some forty years after she died, another admirer would write about the strength of her character, describing her as "the most influential person in the colored community" of Princeton. "Among her own people she moved a queen and her word was law. . . . Her manner was deliberate and dignified and by the younger people she was both loved and feared." Betsey Stockton might have become well mannered, but she was certainly not weak willed.

Nor was she simply a schoolmarm, a priggish disciplinarian who could be easily laughed off as an intellectual lightweight. Becoming an educator requires becoming educated, and Betsey Stockton did that the hard way. She didn't attend the College of New Jersey or the Princeton Theological Seminary, and neither did anyone else in Princeton's antebellum Black community. But she made the most of her connections to several white men who studied and taught at those institutions, learning from them and, above all, gaining access to their books—especially Ashbel Green's. By the time she was in her early twenties, a student at the Princeton Theological Seminary marveled at her academic achievements, and not just in the basic areas of geography, grammar, and arithmetic: "I am of opinion," he concluded, "that few pious young ladies of her age can be found to equal her in knowledge of the Bible and general theology." Even one of the mariners on the *Thames* emphasized her intellect, recalling over fifty years later that she was "as well educated as any" of the other missionaries. She continued her education until late in life, learning Latin and studying Caesar's Commentaries with a young seminary student when she was in her sixties. In a college town where so many people prided themselves on their intellectual attainments, Betsey Stockton could hold her own. In that sense, her lifetime of learning gives a broader and subtler meaning to the term "Princeton education."

Above all, her stature in Princeton's Black community stemmed from the importance of her sharing that education. Living just blocks from Princeton's elite, white male college, Betsey Stockton committed her life to working for the "other" Princeton. Whether in her Sunday school class or in her day-to-day position as sole teacher at Princeton's sole school for Black students, she spent thirty years promoting literacy and learning—critical tools of survival that could hardly be taken for granted, especially because they had been so often denied. At a time when the education of Black people was outlawed or kept extremely limited, she took on a role that could generate disapproval in white society, perhaps even danger.

It's also a role that needs to be put into the context of the resistance to racism in her era. Teaching was not a dramatic act, certainly not in comparison to other forms of protest; we might be inclined to locate Betsey Stockton on the spectrum of struggle by acknowledging who and what she was not. She was not the leader of an armed insurrection, like Nat Turner. She was not an African American "Moses," like Harriet Tubman, repeatedly leading enslaved people to freedom. She was not an eloquent public orator, like Frederick Douglass, denouncing slavery and inequality. These and other famous figures have earned their rightful places in the pantheon of antebellum protest, and many, if not most, modern-day Americans have come, albeit slowly, to know them for their courageous work.

But sometimes we seem to know them so well that we don't know them at all. Such heroic and principled people can become historical symbols, legendary giants more than actual people. Sojourner Truth, for instance, became famous in the nineteenth century as an outspoken advocate for abolition and women's rights, and since then, she has been memorialized many times on plaques, statues, even a postage stamp. She remains best known for one thing she reportedly said: "Ar'n't I a woman?" But her biographer, Nell Irvin Painter, has noted that such cultural notoriety can distort historical reality, describing Sojourner Truth as one of the "invented greats" in American history, "beloved for what we need her to have said," now best known as a symbol that is "stronger and more essential in our culture than the complicated historic person." We need such symbols, of course, accessible inspirations. But we also need other stories, about people who engaged in the struggle in less dramatic ways, not ostensibly heroic but essentially human, working at the local level over a long period of time, staying rooted and committed, carrying on the day-to-day business of making a difference in the lives of others, struggling, like Betsey Stockton, to keep a community together in a nation coming apart. There are hundreds, perhaps thousands, of those stories that haven't yet been written, much less read.[5]

Betsey Stockton's is one of those stories. Her persistence was a form of resistance.

A NOTE ON HER NAME

"Presented by the Scholars of Elizabeth Stockton"—the formal "Elizabeth" in the church window is a rare version of her name: throughout her life, from her first surviving signature to her last will and testament, even to her gravestone, she always went by "Betsey."

So what do I call her? During the course of researching and writing, I often adopted "Betsey" as a shorthand name. But I can't indulge in such familiarity. I've developed a deep sense of deference and respect for her as a woman, and since I don't refer to men only by first names—"Ashbel," for instance—I generally use the same standard for her, using "Stockton" in the same way I would "Green." The exceptions come in describing her childhood years, when I do call her "Betsey." Like many people born into slavery, she probably hadn't been given a last name at birth. It's only when she came back to Princeton, in 1816, that her full name, Betsey Stockton, appears in the records of Princeton's Presbyterian church. I don't think anybody gave her that last name; she must have taken it for herself, laying claim to her birth identity in Princeton's most prominent family. A few years later, Ashbel Green concluded his recommendation for missionary work by noting that "She calls herself Betsey Stockton." And so do I.

But I begin her story on a difficult day in her early childhood, when an unhappy Ashbel Green called her simply "Bet."

1

Given, as a Slave

"BET PLAYED THE MISCHIEF." With that brief note in the diary of the Reverend Ashbel Green, on September 20, 1804, Betsey Stockton first entered the historical record, when she was about six years old. Green said no more, nothing about what sort of "mischief" she got into. Whatever it was, Green probably shouldn't have been too surprised: that's what children do. But something about her behavior must have stayed with him, because he wrote about her again the next day, on a morning that got off to a bad start. "Puked up my breakfast," Green wrote. Then: "Corrected Bet." Again, he said no more; "corrected" could cover a wide range of responses, from verbal admonition to physical abuse. Neither did he say anything about Bet's reaction, whether she resisted or cried. But with those two terse entries, Ashbel Green offered the first glimpse we get of Betsey Stockton.[1]

Throughout her early years, glimpses are all we get. Green wrote about her in his diary a handful of other times, but without much elaboration about what work she did, how she fit in with other members of the household, or who she was as a person. The most he ever wrote about her came later, in 1821, when he offered the two-page overview of her early life for her application to become a missionary. But even that contains enough gaps, silences, and occasional evasions that it needs to be read with questions, even skepticism, about its many missing pieces, sometimes the result of weak memory, sometimes of self-serving motive.

In the first sentence of that document, Green gave a matter-of-fact account of a defining moment in Betsey Stockton's life: "A coloured woman, by the name of Betsy, was given, as a slave, by Robert Stockton, Esqr., of this place, to my first wife, his daughter." He never indicated exactly when or why this transaction took place, or what role he played in it. Still, there Betsey was, suddenly a human presence in his household.[2]

She was also his human property. Even though Betsey came into the household "given, as a slave" to Green's wife, the gift also became Green's: according to the laws of coverture, a British legal inheritance still in place in the United States after the Revolution, a married woman's rights and obligations, including her possessions, would be incorporated into those of her husband's household. As head of that household, Green apparently assumed responsibility for maintaining order. But by the time Green "corrected Bet" because she had "played the mischief," he himself had gotten into something much more serious than mere mischief—human slavery.

"By my wife and me she was never intended to be held as a slave," Green explained, and eventually she wasn't—but not immediately. Betsey Stockton gained her emancipation from slavery while living as a minor in Green's household—although again, Green doesn't say exactly when—but she remained subject to his authority for several years afterward. No one had a greater influence on—or certainly control over—the first two decades of Betsey Stockton's life than Ashbel Green. To know the story of her enslavement, we begin with the story of his path to slaveholding.

ASHBEL GREEN ASCENDANT

By the time "Bet" came into his household, Ashbel Green had lived four decades of upwardly mobile success, and he was well on his way to being one of the most prominent Presbyterian clergymen of his era. When he wrote that Betsey "was never intended to be held as a slave," he might just as well have written that he never intended to become a slaveholder.

He inherited a legacy of liberty. Born in 1762, the son of a Presbyterian pastor and grandson of another, Green grew up in an antislavery household. His father, the Reverend Jacob Green, a Harvard-trained clergyman in Hanover, New Jersey, had become an ardent advocate for American independence by the early 1770s, and an ardent opponent of slavery as well. Although he had once bought an enslaved man in the 1750s, he soon came to regret that; by the Revolutionary era, he decried slavery as "one of the great and crying evils among us," a source of political and moral hypocrisy that undermined the American cause. In 1781, he barred slaveholders from membership in his congregation, making it the only Presbyterian church to do so during the Revolution. Still, for all his commitment to radical religious and political principles, Jacob Green also had to deal with the less lofty aspects of his calling, sometimes taking on side jobs to supplement his meager ministerial salary. Knowing well enough the financial problems of being a pastor, Jacob Green wanted young Ashbel to do something a little more lucrative, like farming.[3]

But the boy followed his father's path. During the American Revolution, the teenaged Green served as an enlisted man in the Morris County militia, occasionally alternating military duty in northern New Jersey with school teaching (a role his father promoted to protect his son with a deferment of sorts). He saw enough of war to question its human cost and moral consequences, but still, he concluded, "My tour of service in the militia during our revolutionary war, had, I think, little if any unfriendly influence on my religious principles and moral conduct." With his principles and conduct thus intact, Green matriculated at the College of New Jersey as a junior in 1782, and the following year he graduated as valedictorian of the class of 1783—first in a class of fourteen, the shining exemplar of the student body.[4]

On September 24, Green delivered his valedictory address to the most illustrious crowd ever assembled for a Princeton commencement, with the US Congress, several members of the foreign diplomatic corps, and George Washington himself in attendance. (The Congress had recently arrived in Princeton, having wisely decided to vacate Philadelphia in the face of menacing demonstrations by unpaid soldiers.[5]) Toward the end of his speech, Green addressed George Washington directly, laying on the literary effusion as only a college student could: "Some future bard," the twenty-one-year-old Green intoned, "shall tell in all the majesty of epic song the man whose gallant sword taught the tyrants of the earth to fear oppression and opened an asylum for the virtuous and free." The commander-in-chief blushed in embarrassment (although whether for himself or for Green is not clear).[6] Still, they made a connection, and the two would encounter each other many times again.

Green's graduation turned out to be just the first step on a rapid climb. John Witherspoon, the college's president and a great admirer of his much-esteemed student, asked Green to stay on as tutor. Little more than two years later, in 1785, Green assumed the position of professor of mathematics and natural philosophy, and he also studied divinity with Witherspoon; in early 1786, he became a licensed member of the clergy. Equally important, he became a husband, taking Elizabeth Stockton as his wife in November 1785.[7]

By doing so, he married into one of the most significant families in Revolutionary-era America, and by far the most prominent in Princeton. He also married into a slaveholding family that would make him a slaveholder too.

THE STOCKTONS OF PRINCETON

The Stockton family preceded Princeton itself. The first Stockton to come to North America, Richard (1606–1707), settled on Flushing, Long Island, before 1656, and then moved to New Jersey by 1692. One of his sons, also named Richard (d. 1709), purchased some six thousand acres of land in New Jersey from William Penn between 1696 and 1701 and became one of the first white settlers of what would eventually become the town of Princeton. This younger Richard Stockton was a Quaker, but he was also a slaveholder—not of hundreds, or even dozens, of human beings, but enough to make slavery part of his legacy. At his death, he left each of his six sons between three hundred and five hundred acres in the vicinity of Princeton, and, as a local historian later noted, "Every one of his sons, as they came of age, was to have a slave." The Stocktons of Princeton assumed the gift of human property to be their right, and it defined an early rite of passage from one generation to the next, across the eighteenth century.[8]

By the time of the American Revolution, the extended Stockton family dominated Princeton, both the community and the still-new college. The most famous member of the family, yet another Richard (1730–81), was a member of the College of New Jersey's first graduating class, in 1748, when it was still located in Elizabeth. (Stockton family influence helped move the college south to Princeton in 1756.) This Richard Stockton served in a number of lofty positions and finally, when the Revolution came, as a member of the Continental Congress, arriving in Philadelphia just in time to sign his name to the Declaration of Independence—and thus became distinguished from all the other Richard Stocktons by the moniker "the Signer." But he died in 1781, and in his will, he provided for a posthumous gesture to the growing Quaker call for abolition: "My wife may free what slaves she wishes."[9]

Richard's cousin, Robert Stockton (1730?–1805), also did significant service during the war. During the New Jersey campaign of 1776–77, George Washington selected Stockton as quartermaster to his army. Robert Stockton also offered his house in Princeton as the site of the drafting of the New Jersey's Revolutionary-era constitution, in 1776, and the estate came to be known as Constitution Hill.[10] Just over two decades later, Constitution Hill would also be the birthplace of the enslaved baby Robert Stockton would give to his daughter—both of them known as Betsey.

Just as the Stocktons used the name Richard over and over, so they did with Elizabeth, along with its diminutive form, Betsey: for several generations, Stockton women had been called by both. The most notable, perhaps, was the Betsey Stockton celebrated as "The Belle of Princeton" in a pair of poems written by William Paterson (1745–1806) in 1772, while he served as law clerk to the Signer. (Paterson later became a member of the Constitutional Convention and then served as New Jersey's governor; he is now better remembered, perhaps mercifully, for his political rather than poetical works.) The gushing tribute Paterson paid that Betsey Stockton spread the name in print, giving another dimension to the family's visibility.

When Green married into the family, in 1785, his brother Calvin wrote, "This year my brother Ashbel was married to Betsey Stockton." Over the next two decades, when Ashbel Green wrote letters to his wife, he always addressed her as "Betsey." Betsey was not just any name, and no one in the Stockton family—including son-in-law Ashbel Green—could take it for granted.[11]

Neither could Green take his profession for granted, especially if he wanted to keep his new wife happy with the standard of living she had known. At first, Elizabeth Stockton Green urged her husband to become a lawyer, and her cousin, Richard Stockton Jr., offered to give him free lessons in the law. But for Green, the spiritual calling of the ministry seemed stronger. In 1786, while still teaching at the College of New Jersey, he received a job offer from the Second Presbyterian Church in Philadelphia, and in May 1787 he and his wife moved to the Quaker City, where he would serve as co-pastor with the elderly Reverend James Sproat. Setting aside both the limited prospects of the professorial life and the more likely fortune as a lawyer, the young Reverend Green immediately found himself on the Presbyterian fast track.[12]

PASTOR GREEN'S PHILADELPHIA

Second Presbyterian was not just any church, but a top spot for a young man not yet twenty-five years old. Founded in 1743, in the wake of the Great Awakening and particularly after the powerful preaching of the evangelist George Whitefield in Philadelphia,

Second Presbyterian stood as the "new light" center of the city; the Reverend Gilbert Tennent, Whitefield's evangelical protégé, served as the church's first pastor. But Second Presbyterian came to enjoy more worldly benefits. Its location, at the northeast corner of Third and Arch Streets, was only a half mile from the Pennsylvania State House, where the Continental Congress sat in the early days of the American Revolution, and the adjacent Congress Hall, which housed the Congress when Philadelphia again became the seat of the US government in 1790. The church's 1794 seating plan showed a special section set aside for "Presidents & Governors" straight down the main aisle, with an unobstructed view of the pulpit. By the 1790s, Second Presbyterian "drew to its organization and worship the highest families of the City," its nineteenth-century historian proudly wrote. "It was a power in political circles and social life."[13]

Ashbel Green moved easily into those circles when he assumed his co-pastorship, and he soon added to his personal profile. In 1792, he was elected, "without my knowledge, or even suspicion," one of the two chaplains to the US Congress, a largely ceremonial post that still gave him frequent contact with the leaders of the new nation. He dined with George Washington and John Adams, and he got on surprisingly well with Thomas Jefferson ("Infidel though he was, he was more courteous to the chaplains than his predecessor had been"). By the time the government moved on to Washington, DC, in 1800, Ashbel Green had known—and become known to—the most famous men of the founding era. He had not yet turned forty.[14]

He was lucky to have lived that long. Throughout much of the 1790s, Philadelphia became a pestilential city, first beset by influenza and then yellow fever, and Green struggled with protecting his family while still performing his pastoral duties for his congregation. When yellow fever first swept the city in 1793, both Green and his wife became ill, then recovered, then watched as hundreds of other Philadelphians succumbed to a horrible death. At first, people didn't know where the disease came from (it was a mosquito) or what to do about it. They tried a variety of cures—bleeding, drinking, resting, doing anything that might seem to help—but nothing much worked. The best way to avoid dying from the disease was to get out of town. President Washington and most of the members of Congress evacuated the city, and the federal government, such as it was, all but shut down. The Pennsylvania government did likewise, and state officials and other people with adequate means fled in growing numbers, eventually up to half the city's population. Yellow fever made no distinction as to identity but cut across the lines of race and class. It did, however, become especially deadly among Philadelphia's "lower sort," Black and white, the men and women and children of the working classes who lived in overcrowded and unsanitary housing, ate inferior food, and, above all, had no way out of town. People who had to stay behind had to suffer the consequences, and in 1793, one in five of them succumbed to the fever.[15]

The Greens had a way out, heading forty-two miles northeast to Princeton, where they would find refuge at Constitution Hill. When the fever struck again, in 1797 and 1798 and 1799, Green wrestled with his sense of pastoral responsibility, which kept him in Philadelphia at times, but his sense of self-preservation often led him to the relative safety of Princeton. In the country, he kept track of the daily death toll in the city: "more than 40 have died of a day on an average," he wrote in August 1798, and in September he recorded the rising number of deaths—48 one day, then 73 a week later, 86 a week after that, and eventually 106 on the last day of the month. At the height of the 1798 epidemic, he wrote to those in his much-diminished congregation who remained behind, "From a conviction of duty, I remain absent from you in body, but my heart is truly with you." Those who had stayed in Philadelphia might well have been hard-pressed to measure whatever benefit Green's heart might be in the face of yellow fever. For his own part, Green had a better benefit: "God has been pleased to grant me freedom to leave town."[16]

That freedom didn't apply to everyone in Green's household, however. When Green and his family went to Princeton in 1797, he left behind a man named Paul, an "old black servant from Carolina [who] had the charge of our house and did the marketing." Green failed to say what sort of servant Paul was, enslaved or indentured, but because Paul was Black, he was designated to stay in the sick city. Green apparently subscribed to the common (although erroneous) notion in the white community that people of African descent had an innate immunity to yellow fever, thus making them better able ride out an epidemic and, in the process, provide valuable assistance to white people. So Green assumed to be the case with Paul—although he never wrote about how Paul fared thereafter.[17]

Green did write repeatedly about his frequent visits to his father-in-law's estate throughout the 1790s, which gave him exposure not just to Robert Stockton and his family, but also to the enslaved people the Stocktons kept at Constitution Hill—one of whom gave birth to the child that would soon be given into Green's own household.

QUESTIONS ABOUT BETSEY'S BIRTH

Betsey probably never knew all the details of her origins. Slaveholders did not issue birth certificates for babies born into slavery, and Robert Stockton didn't provide any written record for Betsey, even something as basic as the year she was born. Other documents that do exist offer inconsistent information about her birth year, usually estimating it around the turn of the century. In 1824, for instance, Ashbel Green wrote that "her present age is about twenty-five," which would suggest that she was born in 1799 or so. Two years later, a New York customs report listed her as thirty-one, implying a birth year of 1795. The federal censuses for 1850 and 1860 indicated that she was born in 1800, but that was probably just a guess she gave the census-taker. Her tombstone said she died "aged 67 years," making her birth around 1798. That now seems to be the most commonly accepted year.[18]

But the tombstone also recorded the most critical issue of her origins—that she was "of African blood and born into slavery." The African blood came from her mother. Throughout her life, Betsey was identified in both personal and official documents as "mulatto," almost certainly, given the racial and power dynamics of her time, the mixed-race result of a white man's impregnating a Black woman, either by rape or some other form of sexual coercion.[19] Frederick Douglass famously speculated about such circumstances surrounding his own birth:

> The whisper that my master was my father, may or may not be true; . . . the fact remains, in all its glaring odiousness, that slaveholders have ordained, and by law established, that the children of slave women shall in all cases follow the condition of their mothers; and this is done too obviously to administer to their own lusts, and make a gratification of their wicked desires profitable as well as pleasurable; for by this cunning arrangement, the slaveholder, in cases not a few, sustains to his slaves the double relation of master and father.[20]

In recent years, there have been occasional "whispers" about Betsey's father's identity. One brief biography has suggested that because she and Ashbel Green had similar physical features and a long personal relationship, "we puzzle over the question as to whether or not Stockton was Green's natural daughter." Some of Green's modern-day descendants have echoed this assumption, noting a long-standing family conjecture that Ashbel was Betsey's biological father. Stockton descendants have likewise entertained conjectures about their ancestors—perhaps Robert Stockton himself, who would have been around sixty-eight in 1798, or maybe one of his three sons, forty-nine-year-old Job, forty-four-year-old James, or thirty-eight-year-old Ebenezer, all of whom lived near the family estate. The evidence for any of these men remains circumstantial at best. Ashbel Green's numerous visits to Constitution Hill during the late 1790s put him, at least occasionally, in the right place at the right time, and he can't be given a pass just for being a Presbyterian pastor. One of the Stockton men, however, might be the more likely candidate: father and sons had a consistent presence at Constitution Hill and, more important, the power as slaveholders to, as Douglass put it, "administer to their own lusts" with one of the enslaved women on the estate.[21]

But which woman? The possibilities appear to be limited in number, but elusive in the historical record. In 1801, when Robert Stockton drew up his will, he noted by name only one enslaved woman in his household, Phebe, whom he left to his wife, Helen, "to wait upon her and serve her" after his death. Stockton also noted that if Phebe didn't satisfy his wife, then "I do hereby direct my said Executor to procure another wench or negro girl to serve her during her life as aforesaid." That order suggests that he might not have had a suitable substitute available in his household.

He did have one only a few years earlier, a woman named Sealy (or Celia), who became the focus of his anger and frustration in 1797, when she ran away from Constitution Hill. Sealy made her way to Philadelphia, no doubt trying to find freedom by blending into the sizable free African American population there. When she got to Philadelphia, she also made contact with Ashbel and Elizabeth Green, whom she apparently knew, perhaps hoping they could provide some measure of refuge or support. When Robert Stockton got wind of her whereabouts, he sent an agitated letter to Green: "please to Inform her that I wish her to Return, and that I shall treat her as usal [*sic*] looking over what has pasd [*sic*] She conducting her self as she ought to." What had passed, he did not say, and perhaps he assumed Green already knew what it was. But in the next line Stockton let go of any implied leniency and took a harsher stance: "if she will not Return I wish you to take Such Steps as proper to secure her so that she cannot make her escape, and if Nessary [*sic*] I shall come to Phild."[22]

In ordering Green to "secure her," Stockton had the law of the new nation on his side. The Fugitive Slave Act of 1793 held that slaveholders had a right to the return of enslaved people who sought freedom. Stockton didn't explicitly mention the act, but he didn't have to: Ashbel Green had served as chaplain to the Congress when the law had been passed. Still, the increasing sense of urgency in Robert Stockton's letter suggests that his concern was not just a legal matter, but a much more personal one, stemming from "what has pasd."[23]

Green didn't try to defy his father-in-law's insistence or intervene on the woman's behalf. Instead, he apparently exerted some influence on her to return: in June 1797 he wrote in his diary that "Celia came here and agreed to go to Princeton."[24] Two months later, making his escape from the onset of that year's yellow fever epidemic, Green traveled between Philadelphia and Princeton several times. If he saw Sealy at Constitution Hill, he never said so. In fact, he never recorded another word about her again.

Neither did Robert Stockton. There's no mention of her in his 1801 will or, when he died, in 1805, in the inventory of his estate. Sealy may have again gone away—or been sold away—from the Stockton household.[25] Yet brief and incomplete though it is, Sealy's story suggests circumstantial connections to Betsey Stockton's. The timing certainly seems significant. At the time Sealy fled Constitution Hill in the spring of 1797, it is possible—and *only* possible—that she was pregnant, and that she might have been Betsey's birth mother. The evidence is, again, circumstantial, and neither Robert Stockton nor Ashbel Green ever identified the birth mother by name.

Neither did Betsey Stockton. When she was in her midtwenties, she wrote to Green and requested that he "Ask Dr. J—— to tell my mother that I am well and happy."[26] That is the only surviving reference she made to her mother, and it is as tantalizing as it is brief. Does "my mother" refer to Betsey's birth mother and imply that Betsey knew who and perhaps where she was? Might the term instead refer to a woman who had shown Betsey some form of maternal feeling, and who would still want to know she was "well and happy"? And given the limited reference to "Dr. J——," it is impossible to know who Betsey might intend to deliver her wishes in the first place. The letter invites speculation, but it doesn't offer an answer.

EARLY DAYS WITH THE GREENS

Given the uncertainty surrounding Betsey's birth, her story perhaps better begins when Robert Stockton gave Betsey to his daughter,

Elizabeth Stockton Green—and therefore to Ashbel Green. Even there, however, the record has as many questions as answers. In writing about the transaction, Green didn't say exactly when or why it took place. It almost certainly occurred before September 1804—when he "corrected" her for "playing the mischief"—but otherwise, there remains no written record. When Robert Stockton made out his will, in 1801, he gave all his children shares in his estate—land for the three sons, the "residue" for his three daughters, including Elizabeth. But except for the provision concerning Phebe, Stockton's will said nothing about other enslaved people in his household. It's quite likely he had already given young Betsey to Elizabeth by then.

The question is what Elizabeth and Ashbel Green would get from the gift. Some people might have seen an enslaved child as a status symbol, but human baubles had no place in the household of a prominent Presbyterian pastor. The Green household wasn't large—Ashbel, Elizabeth, and their three sons, Robert Stockton Green (b. 1787), Jacob Green (b. 1790), and James Sproat Green (b. 1792), all the boys at least six years older than Betsey, presumably old enough to take care of themselves without much help. The one member of the household who did need help was Elizabeth. In 1802, during yet another yellow fever outbreak, Elizabeth came down with what her husband described as "hydrothorax or water in the chest," and she remained in poor health for four years. Throughout that period, Green always noted the attention he gave her, never mentioning help from anyone else—including Betsey. But even though she was still a young child, Betsey must have been increasingly involved in Elizabeth's care, doing more to prepare and serve meals, bringing water or tea to her bedside, helping change her clothes and bedding, assisting her with bathing and even more delicate details of personal hygiene. Being a domestic servant was never easy work, but when the lady of the house was ill or frequently weakened, it would be even less so.[27]

In writing about that difficult time, Ashbel Green never gave Betsey any credit, much less gratitude. Instead, the picture that emerges from his later account of Betsey's early years is that he found the girl to be a problem, both behavioral and moral, and he and his wife didn't know quite what to do with her: "We deliberated seriously on the subject of dedicating her to God in baptism," Green wrote, "But on the whole concluded not to do it." They didn't consider her spiritually fit—"Betsey gave no evidence of piety"—but troublesome: "she was, at least till the age of thirteen or fourteen, wild and thoughtless, if not vicious."[28]

Green never said what he did about such behavior, except for the one instance in 1804. He did, however, offer clues about his disciplinary approach elsewhere in his diary, as he handled his own boys. Green often found himself torn between affection and correction. In May 1797, for instance, he noted that his eldest son, Robert, had gone to see the launching of the frigate *United States* on the Philadelphia docks—an exciting experience for a ten-year-old boy, but an adventure that violated his father's orders. "I had to correct him," Green wrote. A little over a year later, Robert again did something that bothered his father, and Green confessed that he "Corrected Robert in a way for which I am sorry. I have again condemned myself for this fault. Oh God, keep me from evil." The deity apparently didn't do that, and within a few months Green again lost control in correcting his son: "my passion got the better of me and I struck Robert in the face." The boy "deserved correction," Green asserted, but he also chastised himself for failing to adhere to "my repeated resolutions to strike not in anger."[29] Green's reference to his "repeated resolutions" suggests that this instance had not been the only time he struck in anger—nor would it be the last by any means—but he understood the need to keep better control of his emotions.

If so, being wary of the way "my passion got the better of me" with his son may well explain his behavior when he "Corrected Bet" six years later, in 1804. He became aware of her "mischief" one day, then waited until the next morning to do anything about it. Perhaps he didn't want to act immediately or precipitously or passionately, but instead exercise some self-restraint. Perhaps he intended to take a more measured approach, separating the infraction from the punishment, letting the little girl fret about her fate for a day. Or perhaps he was simply uneasy with the notion of having to discipline her at all, even to the point of puking.

Betsey posed a bigger issue than mere mischief. She had come into the Green household as a gift, and by accepting her on those terms, they accepted being slaveholders—but apparently uncomfortably. "By my wife and me she was never intended to be held as a slave," Green wrote in 1821, and they certainly hadn't paid for her, probably didn't ask for her, and perhaps didn't even want her. Still, they had her. What they chose to do about her would be, on one level, a decision they would make about an individual child, but it would also be located within a larger moral and political context. The landscape of slavery had begun to change in the North, and the Greens' experience would reflect that change—and eventually affect young Betsey.

THE PACE OF EMANCIPATION

The two states where the Greens divided their time, Pennsylvania and New Jersey, had been the first and last of the northern states to pass laws providing for the gradual abolition of slavery, Pennsylvania in 1780 and New Jersey in 1804. The states' embrace of emancipation proved to be tentative in the beginning, and slavery certainly did not disappear overnight; it just evolved into new forms of unfreedom, creating what one historian has called a "hodgepodge of labor arrangements." Still, the post-Revolutionary abolition laws did create a new context for relationships between slaveholders and enslaved people.[30]

In Pennsylvania, where Quaker influence promoted antislavery pressure, the language of the 1780 statute made the natural rights argument that the enslavement of Black people had "deprived them of the common blessings that they were by nature entitled to." The letter of the law, however, did not immediately set any enslaved person free. Instead, the statute required slaveholders to register the people they considered their property; those who complied would be able to keep in bondage any enslaved person born before March 1,

1780. Children born into slavery after that date would still have to wait twenty-eight years before gaining the legal right to be free—a two-generation grace period for slaveholders.[31]

New Jersey, where the number of people held in bondage had actually risen by 20 percent in the years after the American Revolution, waited almost a quarter century before taking a similar step. The state's 1804 Act for the Gradual Abolition of Slavery provided that a child born to an enslaved parent on or after July 4, 1804, would become free over two decades later—at age twenty-five for males, twenty-one for females—but in the meantime would remain bound to the mother's slaveholder. Clearly, the date cutoff would not help any enslaved person born before Independence Day of 1804—including Betsey—nor did the passage of the statute require slaveholders to reduce the number of enslaved people in the state.[32]

The implications of the gradual abolition laws did, however, cause both slaveholders and the enslaved to look to a farther historical horizon and, in the process, to think anew about what the future might mean. The passage of these laws led to subtle but significant changes that would accelerate the process of emancipation: the number of freedom seekers rose considerably, especially among males, and enslaved people who remained in the slaveholders' household quite often made life difficult for them, shirking work and otherwise refusing to be obedient servants. Many slaveholders likewise began to realize the need to adjust to the prospect of eventual abolition, however gradual: a combination of moral opposition to slavery, changing labor needs, and frustration with the inefficiencies of the system led them to divest themselves of the people they kept in bondage, either by manumission or, more often, sale. Despite the glacial-seeming pace of state-mandated emancipation, the prospect of eventual abolition created a period of transition, in which slaveholders and the enslaved negotiated, either implicitly or explicitly, the conditions of labor, the duration of servitude, and the prospects for freedom.[33]

That notion of negotiation helps explain Ashbel Green's relationship with an enslaved man named George, who was held by the Stockton family in Princeton, but whose situation seemed to be at least partially subject to Green's influence. In 1803, George "was taken suddenly ill," and Green apparently felt some measure of concern for the man's health, at least enough to pay him a personal visit. But Green still felt unable or unwilling to offer George a bigger benefit—his freedom. It was not until several years later, in September 1806, that Green talked with his mother-in-law, Helen Stockton, "on the subject of mandating negro George which I find I cannot do." This reference to "mandating," or manumitting, raises questions about the nature of the constraints Green seems to have felt. They may have stemmed from reservations of his own or, more likely, they may have come from Helen Stockton, who did not want to surrender control of labor in the household. Several weeks later, Green told George if he would continue in his current status a while longer, "then I would do something better for him." George apparently acquiesced, no doubt taking the prospect of delayed freedom to be his best option, and Green eventually made good on his promise. On the morning of March 24, 1807, Green began the day "praying to God that he would not suffer me to be deceived in regard to the state of my soul." Later in the day, he "Wrote a manumission for George at Princeton and enclosed it in a letter for Dr. Stockton." It's not clear whether Green himself had the authority to grant George his emancipation, or if, as is more likely, he simply drafted the document for the Stocktons. In any event, George seems to have gained his freedom: he did not appear again in Green's written account.[34]

But Betsey was still on the scene, and 1807 might have been an important year for her as well. Green's involvement in George's slowly unfolding freedom may have influenced his thinking about the enslaved girl in his own household. Unfortunately, Ashbel Green never said much about his thinking at the time, however, so the evidence for Betsey's emancipation relies on a handful of often ill-fitting shards in the sources.

FREEDOM, TO A DEGREE

Elizabeth Stockton Green's long illness absorbed her husband's attentions. "Principally occupied with attending on and nursing my sick wife," Green wrote in his diary in December 1806. "Yesterday the Dr. told me that she might go off suddenly." Then she did: "My wife died January 15, 1807." As Green would tell it forty years later, "I lost the wife of my youth, after having lived with her in the marriage state twenty-one years, two months, and twelve days."[35]

Elizabeth's death may have given new life to Betsey. Betsey had come into the household as a gift to Elizabeth, Green wrote in the late 1840s, "and with her concurrence was freed by myself." That concurrence had to have come no later than the first two weeks of 1807, when Betsey would have been no older than nine or ten. In that case, Green may have technically emancipated her from slavery, but he would still have kept her in some other sort of servitude. At the time, he didn't write about her status in his diary, nor did he apparently record it with the Pennsylvania Abolition Society, which listed manumissions and indentures in Philadelphia. In 1821, when he wrote about Betsey's early life, he muddied the story even more, alluding to her emancipation in a surprisingly imprecise way: "At the age of twenty, as near as I can judge, I gave her her freedom." If Betsey were indeed twenty when Green granted her freedom, that would put the timing somewhere around 1818, give or take a year or so. But questions remain: freedom when (perhaps 1807, perhaps a decade or so later?) and freedom from what (slavery, indentured servitude, or some other form of unfreedom?).[36] Perhaps the differences didn't matter enough for Green to make clear.

There's a clue, however, in the federal census for Philadelphia in 1810, which listed Green with a family of four white people—Green and his wife (his second, whom he had married in October 1809) and two sons. The household also included a man and a woman under the age twenty-five simply categorized as "All Other Free Persons," neither of them named, but the female presumably Betsey. The census document's column for enslaved people was empty. If the census is correct—and there is no good reason to doubt that it is—Green's household reflected a larger change in society. The number of people kept enslaved in Pennsylvania fell from 3,760 in 1790 to 795 in 1810, most of them held in the rural regions south and west of Philadelphia. Philadelphia experienced an even more dramatic decline in the same period, with the number of enslaved people going from 301 to only two. According to the census records, neither lived with Ashbel Green.[37]

Betsey did, though, and she would continue to do so for more than a decade—perhaps no longer enslaved, but not yet free—still part of Green's household, still under his control.

BETSEY'S PHILADELPHIA

In the years just after Elizabeth's death, Betsey made more frequent appearances in Green's diary, showing her growing role in the household. Understandably, Ashbel Green needed more help, and he recorded instances of Betsey doing occasional errands outside the house. In December 1807, Green wrote that "Betsy returned from the country where she has been since Saturday." A few months later, he noted that he had five dollars for a financially needy woman, "which I sent her by Betsy."[38] The young girl had been granted some measure of movement around the city.

The city had much to show her. In the first decade of the nineteenth century, Philadelphia was the second-largest city in the new nation—in 1810, a population of almost ninety-two thousand, with just over 10 percent Black people—but still physically compact and easily walkable. Lombardy poplars provided pleasant shade for many of the streets. "Within the improved parts of the city," an 1802 travelers' guide noted, "the streets are paved with pebbles for carriages, &c. and have a brick foot way on each side, very commodious." People of different races lived in comparatively close proximity and constantly passed each other in those streets.[39]

As Betsey ran errands for Green, she briefly experienced the freedom of being part of that scene. She lived in Green's home very near his church, a three-story brick house at 79 Mulberry (or Arch) Street. When she ventured out, she might be wary about walking the few blocks eastward to the city's bustling docks, the most likely site where kidnappers could steal Black people and spirit them away to slavery in the South. In 1799, some leading figures in Philadelphia's Black community had petitioned the state legislature for better protection against kidnapping, to help prevent "the sad separation of the dearest ties in nature, husband from wife, and Parents from children," but the plea went nowhere. A decade later, children remained vulnerable targets, and Betsey no doubt knew of the danger. Still, wherever she went, she could encounter free Black people who pursued of all sorts of occupations. A stroll southward, for instance, would take her past the homes of several laborers and laundresses, a few mariners, waiters, and barbers, and a grocer, a cheesemonger, a confectioner, an oysterman, a fruiterer, a carter, a carpenter, a shoemaker, and a shingle-shaver—in short, a cross section of Philadelphia's Black community. The neighborhood became an outdoor classroom where she could see society—and perhaps begin to think about her place in it.[40]

Black people occasionally came into Green's house, too, seeking spiritual guidance and other forms of support. Betsey had the opportunity to meet them, perhaps even to talk with them as she showed them in or served refreshments. One in particular became an important repeat visitor. In May 1807, Green first recorded the arrival of "John Gloucester, a black man, who has been with me for several days past and who is a candidate for being a missionary." Gloucester had been born into slavery in Blount County, Tennessee, in 1776, but had become free when a Presbyterian missionary to the region, the Reverend Gideon Blackburn, converted him to Christianity and then purchased him in order to manumit him. Then, in 1807, Gloucester accompanied Blackburn to Philadelphia, where he met the most prominent Presbyterian clergymen in the city, among them Ashbel Green. Green became a valuable ally, welcoming Gloucester into his home several times, going to hear him preach, and writing at least two letters of recommendation to support his formal ordination. With Green's support, the Presbyterian General Assembly looked upon Gloucester as a promising candidate: given "the evidence of unusual talents, discretion, and piety, possessed by John Gloucester," it found "good reason . . . to believe that he may be highly useful in preaching the gospel among those of his own colour." In 1810, Ashbel Green and other members of the Philadelphia Evangelical Society provided the financial support that helped Gloucester form the African Presbyterian Church. Gloucester's church became one of the important religious institutions in the Black community, and by the time of his death, in 1822, Gloucester had taken his place as one of the city's leading African American clergymen.[41]

Living and serving in Green's house, Betsey knew John Gloucester from his first days in Philadelphia, and she might well have been captivated by his story. She did not, however, become a member of his church—or of Absalom Jones's African Episcopal Church of St. Thomas or Richard Allen's Bethel AME Church, for that matter. She was still a child in Ashbel Green's household and under his authority, and he no doubt expected her to attend Second Presbyterian (where she and other people of color sat upstairs in the gallery and took communion apart from the white parishioners). Yet her familiarity with the Black congregations from her first years in Philadelphia would later provide a memory—and a model.[42]

Betsey lived in Green's household as it went through several significant changes. In 1809, he married Christiana Anderson, who in 1811 bore him a son, Ashbel. Green offered no insight in his diary about how his new wife got along with Betsey or how the birth of the new baby affected Betsey's work routine, which no doubt had more chores and childcare. He did indicate that he needed additional help. In August 1811, he "Went down to see John Gloucester and to try to get a black boy to live with me." A few days later, he seemed to have been successful: "Asbury, my black boy, came to live with me today." Asbury may not have lasted long, however, because in April 1812 Green wrote that he "Called at Brother J's and to look for a black boy," and in July, he repeated his earlier note, "Went to see Gloucester to get a black boy to live with me."[43] It's not clear exactly how many young Black men Green recruited, what they did, or how long they stayed. But Betsey stayed, and she had more than enough work to do.

Whatever the workload, she somehow made time for one task for herself—learning to read, one of the most critical steps she would take in her life. She did so with no direct help from Ashbel Green: as an acquaintance of Betsey's would recall, "Dr. Green did not favor educating his servants in books." His sons apparently didn't adhere to their father's strict position, but "appreciated her natural intelligence and her merit [and] helped her in her study." Green said much the same thing: "by the instruction received in my family, principally from my son James, [she] had made laudable improvements in knowledge." And those improvements came principally through Green's own houseful of volumes, newspapers, pamphlets, all manner of reading material—and none of it fluff. There's no record of exactly what she read while she lived with Green, or exactly when she read it, but by the time she was preparing to leave his household for good, in 1821, one of Green's students would write that "She has a larger acquaintance with sacred and the Mosaic Institutions, than almost any ordinary person, old or young, I have ever known." Green's sons may have given her helpful lessons in literacy at the outset, but she went well beyond the basics to a much higher intellectual level, eventually developing a voracious and sophisticated appetite for reading.[44]

DEPARTING FOR PRINCETON

On August 14, 1812, Green received news that would take him and his family and Betsey—and his books—back to Princeton: "It was on the morning of this day that I was elected president of the college."[45] He would be the eighth president of the College of New Jersey, not just his alma mater but the most prominent spot for a Presbyterian in academia. He would also be the eighth president who, at some point, had been a slaveholder. Green never wrote any-

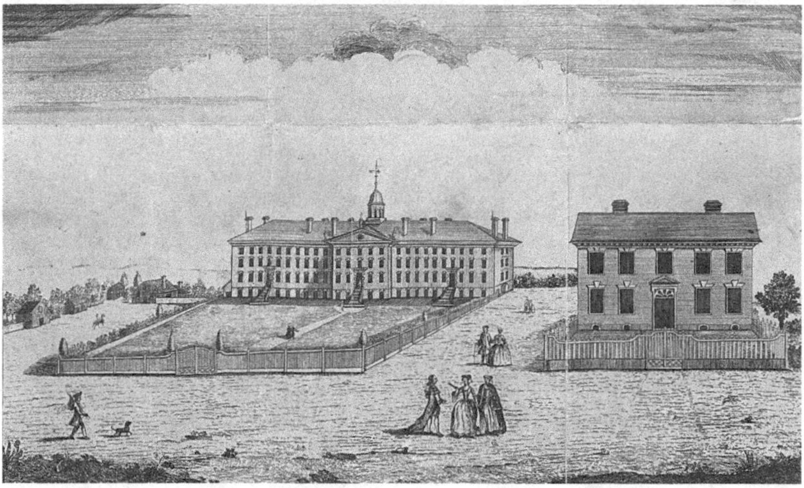

FIGURE 1.1. Nassau Hall and President's House, College of New Jersey, 1764.

thing about the place of slavery in the college's past, but instead looked forward to his own future there. The next couple of months would be a time of transition for him, writing a farewell address to his congregation in Philadelphia, and "a short Latin address to be spoken at my inauguration." By October, he had become "so consistently occupied in preparing to go to Princeton that I could not keep a regular diary." There was nothing regular about life in the household, as everyone, perhaps especially Betsey, had to get on with packing up possessions. Finally, on October 29, the time came: "Left the city for Princeton with my wife and child and servant maid and black boy and Miss Hannah Haskill," Green wrote. "We arrived at Princeton safely in the evening."[46] After a day-long, forty-two-mile journey in a crowded carriage, Betsey, now described as a "servant maid," would likewise have been grateful for a safe arrival.

What she felt about coming back to the place of her birth might be quite another matter—if, indeed, she remembered it at all. Spending most of her childhood in Philadelphia, she had grown increasingly accustomed to the bustle of the city streets and the mix of people, white and Black. By comparison, Princeton must have seemed a placid backwater, a small college town with one main thoroughfare, Nassau Street, little more than a wide dirt road that turned into a muddy mess in the rain. Most of the town's inhabitants—around two thousand, a few hundred of them Black—lived on one side of Nassau Street, and the college occupied a stretch of the other. The main campus building, Nassau Hall, was by far the most impressive edifice in town, but the one that would matter most to Betsey stood next to it—the President's House, a handsome Georgian-style structure that had been built in the same year, 1756. A decade later, in 1766, following the death of one of Green's predecessors, Samuel Finley, the house had been the site of the sale of "two negro women, a negro man, and three Negro children," who had been part of Finley's estate.[47] But at the time she arrived there, Betsey had no reason to care about its architecture or know about its history. It was simply the place where she would live and work, still under the authority of its newest occupant, Ashbel Green.

She wouldn't be there long, though: less than eight months later, in June 1813, Ashbel Green would assert his authority over her in a new way, selling three years of her time to another man, sending her away to another household in another town.

2

She Calls Herself Betsey Stockton

"SOLD TO MR. TODD 3 YEARS of the time of Betty to commence from July 30th." With that short note in June 1813, Ashbel Green recorded the first half of a transaction for teenage labor. The other part came just a few lines later: "Purchased the time of a black boy and black girl of the estate of the late Mrs. Little"—twelve-year-old John and seventeen-year-old Phoebe—noting that both would serve him until the age of twenty-five. Green didn't say whether John and Phoebe were enslaved or indentured, but like Betsey, they clearly lived under some form of unfreedom. He also didn't say anything about how much money he got for Betsey's time, but he did note the monetary value of his purchases, $150 for John's time and $140 for Phoebe's, presumably more for John because he was younger and would be in service longer. Green apparently hoped to gain some leverage over them by offering a slim and distant chance for future freedom: "I told them that if they served me to my entire satisfaction and that of my wife, I would give to each of them a year of their time. Otherwise I would not give them any." Neither John nor Phoebe—nor Betsey, for that matter—had any opportunity to shape the terms of servitude to their own "entire satisfaction," but the situation was set. On paper, it appeared to work well enough—at least for Ashbel Green.[1]

At the time, he didn't explain his reasons for sending Betsey away; writing in his diary, he probably didn't feel the need to. Eight years later, though, he provided a fuller account, but one that relied on a fading, even flawed, memory. First, he claimed that he did it for her own good: "To save her from the snares and temptations of the city, which I feared threatened her ruin, I sent her to live in the country." That might have made sense if Betsey had still been in Philadelphia, but by mid-1813 she had been living for the better part of a year in Green's household in bucolic Princeton. But behind this concern lay another, about Betsey herself. His emphasis that John and Phoebe serve to "my entire satisfaction and that of my wife" might have stemmed from his feeling that Betsey did not. In 1821, he wrote explicitly that in her early teenage years, Betsey had gone bad and become "wild and thoughtless, if not vicious."[2] Whatever Ashbel Green said about wanting to save her from possible ruin, he apparently wanted to save himself from her.

Ashbel Green would not be the first (or last) adult to want to banish a teenager from his household, and he had considerable legal and cultural precedent for doing so. As far back as the seventeenth century, people on both sides of the Atlantic often bound teenaged children out to apprenticeships in other households, sending them to learn a trade and, in the process, perhaps be subject to stricter discipline. Moreover, in the post-Revolutionary North, with the increasing shift from enslaved labor to extended terms of indentured servitude, white householders engaged in a lively trade in unfree labor, selling off the time, if not the lives, of Black people they deemed unwanted, unruly, or otherwise undesirable.[3] Green could thus sell Betsey's time in the knowledge that it was within his legal right. In the meantime, thanks to the demise of "the late Mrs. Little," he could replace her with John and Phoebe, a two-for-one labor exchange he expected to fulfill his needs at home. And so, on July 12, 1813, Green brought the issue to a close: "Betsy left us this morning."

TIME WITH THE TODDS

As it turned out, Betsey's departure gave her a chance for a fresh start in Woodbury, New Jersey, a small town fifty miles south of Princeton. Woodbury rested on a "high, airy and healthy spot," nine miles east of the Delaware River, across from Philadelphia. It would have been a healthy spot for Betsey in another way, as Gloucester County had long had a strong Quaker influence and, as a result, a comparatively small number of people still held in slavery. In 1790, New Jersey as a whole had had just under 11,500 enslaved people, most of them in its northern half; Gloucester County had only 191, and that number would steadily decline, to 61 in 1800 and 37 in 1820. When Betsey lived in Woodbury, the free Black population in Gloucester County was around a thousand people, or 4 percent of the total population.[4] Still, like Philadelphia, the Woodbury area gave Betsey some measure of exposure to the future of freedom.

But she was not yet completely free herself. She was bound for three years to the Reverend Nathaniel Todd (1780–1867), a Presbyterian pastor and schoolmaster. Todd had arrived in the town only a few years before. A graduate of Brown in 1800, he studied under Ashbel Green in Philadelphia in 1803, and when he applied for the ministry the following year, Green wrote a useful, if tepid, letter of recommendation: "His whole character & deportment is unexceptionable & amiable, & his pulpit performances have been very acceptable among us." In late 1805, Todd took a post as pastor in Schenectady, New York, and the following year he married Green's niece, Elizabeth Green Bradford, both of which events may have boosted him in Green's estimation. But by the end of 1806, Todd and his new wife had to leave Schenectady; according to one account, his departure was "owing to the bursting of a blood vessel," while another explained that "the congregation were unable to support him." In 1808, Todd accepted the call to another struggling congregation, in Woodbury. While Nathaniel Todd didn't seem destined for Presbyterian prominence, Ashbel Green still thought well enough of him by then to attend his installation. He later engaged in at least one preaching exchange, leading worship in Todd's Woodbury church one Sunday while Todd filled the pulpit in his. Green also had the Todds as guests in his Philadelphia home a time or two, where Betsey got to meet them, and she once went to Woodbury for a short visit.[5] The Todds were not complete strangers to Betsey, then, and Green no doubt determined them to be acceptable buyers of her time.

That purchase coincided with the birth of the Todds' twin daughters, Elizabeth and Mary, in mid-August, 1813, barely two weeks after Betsey arrived. She had done childcare before, but now she faced it twofold, beyond her day-to-day duties—fetching water, making fires, preparing and cooking meals, mending and sewing clothes, making soap and doing the wash, now increased by the constant-seeming need to clean two sets of soiled baby clothes. Helping take care of the Todds and their toddlers would be enough of a full-time job, but there was even more to it. In the year before Betsey arrived, Nathaniel Todd had begun to supplement his meager ministerial salary by serving as the principal of a private academy in Woodbury, and the school advertised that "Mr. Todd will take in boarders"—yet another domestic concern for Betsey.[6] As a teenager, she was getting another crash course in all aspects of household service, and she could certainly see the limited occupational prospects available to Black women in the North.

Yet despite her burdens, she found a modest bonus in her situation. Above all, Nathaniel Todd's dual roles gave Betsey an opportunity to benefit from the academic ambience around her. Todd taught the whole range of grammar school subjects—"English, Latin and Greek languages, Reading Writing and Arithmetic, Geography, the use of Globes"—and for that he had books. Betsey could continue her self-education whenever she could get away from her work.[7]

But Betsey's time in Woodbury came to an end in 1815, along with Nathaniel Todd's pastoral position. Once again, he had to give up his ministry, as the church's history would later explain, "for the usual reason—inadequate support." Todd struggled to find a few short-term schoolmaster positions in Pennsylvania, while preaching and performing weddings when he could.[8] Given his uncertain prospects, he couldn't afford to keep Betsey, so sometime in early 1816, she was sent back to Princeton—and to Ashbel Green.

PRINCETON AGAIN

In mid-July, 1816, Princeton resident Elijah Slack placed an ad in the newspapers, offering for sale "A Negro Girl, Near 19 years of age." Slack played up her domestic skills—"good in all kinds of housework, and is likewise an excellent spinster . . . she will particularly suit a farmer"—and he also made sure any potential purchaser understood the unnamed woman's status: "She is a slave."[9] In the time Betsey had been away, some things about Princeton hadn't changed.

But Betsey had. "Near 19 years of age" herself, she came back a different person, and certainly in different circumstances. She took an important step by applying for admission to the town's main church, Princeton Presbyterian, and the session agreed to receive her as a full, communion-taking member. In September 1816, she was entered in the church book as "Betsey Stockton—a coloured woman living in the family of the Revd. Dr. Green."[10] Brief though it is, that note reveals important evidence about Betsey's situation, both what it says and what it doesn't say.

While it says that she was "living in the family" of Ashbel Green, it doesn't specify her status—enslaved, indentured, or emancipated. That omission becomes meaningful in light of the identification of other Black people in the church. Princeton Presbyterian's church book for the years 1792–1822 included thirty-six names in a "List of Black Communicants," specifying seventeen as "Slave," fifteen of them by first name only, with no surname. The church records also noted the names of the men who held them in slavery (including two members of the extended Stockton family). The absence of any such designation would indicate that a Black member was a free person. Betsey Stockton was one of them, listed as neither servant nor slave, but simply as "a coloured woman living in the family of the Revd. Dr. Green."[11]

The church records also indicate that she had apparently become spiritually transformed. The church ascertained "her experimental acquaintance with religion, and her good conduct." In his 1821 narrative, Green himself also acknowledged a change. If he had once considered her a "wild and thoughtless, if not vicious" young girl, he acknowledged her in 1816 as possessed of the piety he said had been so lacking: "This woman, as I hope and she believes, met with a saving change of heart while she lived in my family." Putting the burden on Betsey for her unruly childhood behavior, Green took more than his share of spiritual credit for her transformation "while she lived in my family," when in fact that might just as well have happened while she lived in the Todd family. Still, Green's vicious-to-religious narrative created a comforting (if self-serving) Christian parable about the path to salvation. He did, though, insert a subtle qualifier: the distinction between "I hope" and "she believes" might well imply a measure of reservation on Green's part.[12]

But Betsey's salvation aside, Green had good reason to worry about his own spiritual situation. Just before she returned, he moaned in his diary that "It seems as if family and college troubles come together"—and indeed they had for several years.

THE PRESIDENT'S PROBLEMS

When he assumed the presidency, in 1812, Ashbel Green made no secret of his disdain for the intellectual laxity that had crept into the curriculum under his predecessor, Samuel Stanhope Smith. Juniors and seniors no longer had to study the Greek and Latin classics, and Green sniffed that "The majority of those who have received degrees from us for a number of years past, could not possibly have translated their own diplomas into [E]nglish." He would change that, embracing the classical past and redoubling the emphasis on religious instruction, requiring Bible study for the first time. His students were equally disdainful of their new president, and they gave him the rudest of awakenings.[13]

He had been at the college barely two months when he wrote despairingly that December 1812 had been "one of the most trying periods of my life. I was almost entirely employed in the exercise of watching and disciplining the college." On the fourteenth, students got into the belfry in Nassau Hall and decommissioned the college bell, and on the next night "there was an unusual explosion of gun powder." Setting off "crackers"—not just standard fireworks, but gunpowder packed into larger containers, sometimes even hollowed logs—had been a common student prank, but Green faced an especially serious outbreak of cracker attacks and other forms of defiance. In February 1813, he discovered that a Bible used in the college hall had been "abused in a most profane and shocking manner," with a square cut out of the pages, a deck of cards placed in the hole and, worse still, a "horrid sentence on one of the cards." A horrified Green set out to do something. As his first academic year came to an end in the summer of 1813, "the session closed triumphantly in favour of the authority of the College," as he and his faculty colleagues "dismissed seven or eight of the principal offenders, and admonished three or four."[14]

But that was hardly the end of Green's troubles. In late September 1813, soon after he had sent Betsey to the Todds, Green's beloved first son, twenty-six-year-old Robert, died while on a trip to Boston. Robert had graduated from Princeton in 1807 and had become a young man "free from vice, and a constant and reverential attendant on public worship." The contrast between him and the current crop of rebellious college boys must have been especially grievous to Green: "I have had some searchings of heart in regard to my afflictions since Sept. last when my son died." Then came another tragedy in the household. In March 1814, his second wife, Christiana Anderson Green, fell ill during a second pregnancy, her infant was stillborn, and "after suffering greatly she expired."[15]

In early 1815, things began looking better, but only briefly. A sudden surge of religious revival started to stir the students; instead of setting off "crackers," they came to Green for counsel "on the state of their minds relative to religion." Soon enough, he counted forty or so students with "favorable hopes . . . that they have been made the subjects of renewing grace," and perhaps another twelve to fifteen getting close. In his report to the trustees, Green took pains to emphasize the orderly course of the revival, assuring them that "There has been no neglect of study," that academic concerns had "probably never been pursued with more diligence and success." Green gave himself an implicit compliment for his recent addition of Bible study: "For more than two years, the Holy Scripture has been made the subject of regular study and examination as the classics, the mathematics, or philosophy."[16] On the whole, Green's report made the revival seem a heartfelt, well-ordered, almost studious phenomenon.

It didn't last. Most of the "renewing grace" of 1815 departed with that year's graduates, and by the following year, the college's students would again be setting off explosives, burning the campus privy, insulting their elders, and straying from the way of piety. By July 1816, Green would find himself "employed with the faculty all morning examining into charges against the students for being concerned with a harlot."[17] The woman had apparently said who, and some of the boys were soon sent on their way—just about the time Betsey came back.

Betsey's return came amid this dark time in Ashbel Green's life. He soon faced yet another death in his family—his third wife, Mary McCulloch, whom he had married in October 1815. Mary, like Christiana before her, became sick, her condition apparently worsening while her husband was again dealing with student disorder. "In the evening between 9 and 10 o'clock there was a cracker in the college," Green wrote on November 18, 1817. "My wife's bowels were affected." Five days later, she would be dead.[18] This marriage was Green's last.

While Ashbel Green had been suffering, Betsey had been flourishing and maturing, now pious enough to be accepted as a professing Presbyterian, and more experienced at managing household affairs. She also had a new relationship with Green. "I gave her her freedom," he recalled several years later, "and have since paid her wages as a hired woman." She now earned her own money and exercised some degree of freedom in her mobility. For a few months in 1817, Green noted, "she chose to go to service in Philadelphia"—with "she chose" suggesting increasing independence. On December 16, 1817, Green noted that "Betsy returned to Princeton and came to live with us."[19] His wife had died just three weeks earlier, and Ashbel Green must have seen Betsey as a welcome ray of relief.

"SHE CALLS HERSELF"—AND FEELS A CALLING

The more important question is how she saw herself. Her return to Princeton sheds light on a significant development: she used the surname Stockton. She may have begun to do so at some earlier point in her life, but the 1816 entry in the Presbyterian church book is the first written record of both a first name and surname. Throughout all of Ashbel Green's diary entries about young Betsey, he used only her first name or some variant—Betsy, Betty, Bet—never a last name. Even in the opening line of his 1821 narrative, he referred to her as a "coloured woman, by the name of Betsy." At the end of that document, however, he concluded with a single sentence, on its own line: "She calls herself Betsey Stockton."[20]

"She calls herself," not "Her name is" or "She is named." Green's locution may have been inadvertent, but it is nonetheless worthy of note as an indication of the linguistic distance between the names enslaved people were given and the ones they took for themselves. Throughout the history of Atlantic slavery, enslavers took it upon themselves to assign names—and almost always only first names—as an expression of possession of the people they enslaved, sometimes with an added note of racial insult. But enslaved people often resisted that given identity, renaming themselves as a form of self-identity. They also took surnames, especially as they anticipated or achieved emancipation.[21] In that sense, Betsey's self-naming would indicate an important step in her emerging notion of her future—and its connection to her past. She could have called herself almost anything—Betsey Green, perhaps—but she chose a different identity. Both Betsey and Stockton associated her with the people into whose household she had been born into slavery. She may not have known all the details of her birth or the identities of her parents, but she no doubt knew that she had been given to another woman named Betsey Stockton—Elizabeth Stockton Green, Ashbel Green's first wife. Whatever her sentiments about individual Stocktons, Betsey acknowledged the circumstances of her birth and claimed a connection to that family. And so she called herself Betsey Stockton.

One of the most striking signs of her new sense of self comes from another example of her full name, written in her own hand: "Betsey Stockton, Princeton New Jersey," boldly inscribed on the flyleaf of a book. Just below her signature, another inscription, in a different hand (and misspelling her first name), helps locate her in time as well as space: "Betsy Stockton, at Dr. Green's, Princeton, New Jersey."[22] Although she lived in Green's Princeton household for nine months in 1812–13, the note most likely refers to the time after she came back to Princeton, in 1816, or maybe a year or so later. That was a time of transition for Betsey Stockton, from her late teenaged years to early adulthood, from servitude to emancipation, from having her time sold to earning her own wages. How the volume came into her hands is unclear—perhaps a gift, perhaps her own purchase—but it stands as a symbol of that transition. Putting her signature on the flyleaf clearly indicated that she considered the book hers, an act of possession by a young woman who had once been kept as a possession herself.

That book was *The Flowers of Literature*, by Thomas Branagan. Born in Dublin in 1774, Branagan ran away from home as a young man, first working on slave ships and eventually becoming the manager of a sugar plantation in Antigua. In his early twenties, though, he experienced a conversion to religion and antislavery as well. After immigrating to the United States in 1798, he took up street preaching in Philadelphia and New York. Then, instead of giving away his

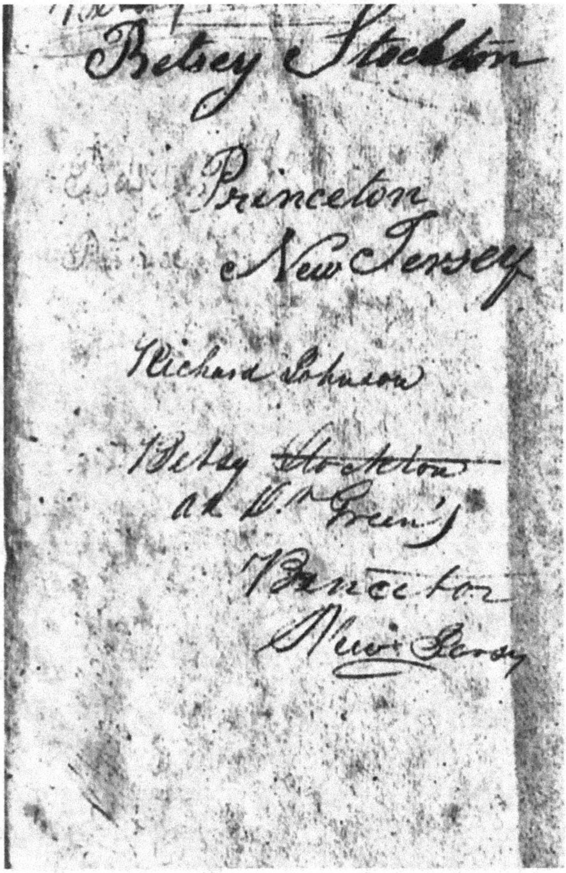

FIGURE 2.1. Betsey Stockton's signature on flyleaf of Thomas Branagan, *The Flowers of Literature; Being an Exhibition of the Most Interesting Geographical, Historical, Miscellaneous and Theological Subjects, in Miniature. To Which Are Prefixed, Preliminary Addresses, to Parents, Teachers and Their Pupils* (Trenton NJ, 1810), Collection of Joseph J. Felcone, Princeton, NJ.

words on the street for free, he started writing them in books to sell. Although largely forgotten now, Branagan's works were quite popular at the time, particularly several long poems and polemics about human rights, including the rights of women and the evils of slavery.[23]

The Flowers of Literature did not deal directly with either of those pertinent topics. Instead, it offered a three-hundred-plus-page compendium of geographical, historical, and poetical information, what Branagan called his "best endeavours to entertain as well as instruct my readers," concluding with a brief but earnest overview of religious history, from the fall of Adam to the gates of Eternity.[24] The book might be considered, at best, a useful reference work, but hardly a polemical page-turner.

Branagan provided a prefatory section that no doubt caught Betsey Stockton's attention. In the book's "Preliminary Addresses, to Parents, Teachers and Their Pupils," Branagan laid straightforward exhortations before all three groups. Of parents, he asked "Can any duty be of greater weight to families, and of more importance to society than the duty of parents to their children?" He gave an emphatic answer—"No!"—and he warned parents of the need for a moral reformation to instill the virtues of economy, modesty, and prudence in their offspring. "Parents!" he seemed to shout, "remember your children are entrusted to your care by the God of Nature, not as animal machines, but as immortal spirits." To children, the message was simpler still: "YOU ARE BORN TO DIE." Such a thought "perhaps seldom occurs to your minds," Branagan warned, but the young person's time on earth began and ended with the choice between virtue and vice: "from the moment of your existence, you are travelling to your graves—to endless misery, or everlasting happiness and joy."[25]

Betsey Stockton was not a parent, nor was she any longer a child. But by the late 1810s—the time she most likely acquired Branagan's book—she was just beginning to see herself in the third role Branagan discussed. Sandwiched between his stern words for parents and the threat of death for children, he added a gentle interlude intended for teachers. The challenges of the job might be many, he acknowledged, but the mission could be critical: "by turning one young person from the error of his ways you will save a soul from death, and hide a multitude of sins." In that sense, Branagan's book contained a meaningful message for Betsey Stockton. Michael Osborn, a student at Princeton Theological Seminary who had taught her in his Sabbath school class, wrote approvingly that "She loves to teach children." She had on occasion led a Sabbath school class of her own and had "appropriated a part of every week to the instruction of a number of coloured children." Betsey Stockton had even bigger plans, Osborn continued: "For a considerable time, she has been studying with the ultimate view of taking charge of a day school for coloured children."[26] Given Stockton's nascent commitment to teaching, Branagan's insistence that "YOUR employment is truly important" would inspire a young woman looking for a future calling.[27]

Michael Osborn's observation of Betsey Stockton's studiousness suggests the strong self-direction inherent in her education and, above all, her embrace of literacy in making her way from enslaved child to adult teacher. Branagan's *Flowers of Literature* may have been the only book Betsey Stockton owned at the time, but it was by no means the only one she read. Osborn highlighted her skill in a wide range of subject areas: "Her knowledge of geography is respectable, she has conquered the larger part of Murray's English grammar, writes a legible hand, and is now cyphering in compound multiplication." Noting his own role in working with her, Osborn wrote that he had "questioned her about some facts in biblical history, or some minute point in Jewish antiquities, and have immediately received a correct answer." But rather than claim more for his own efforts, Osborn gave credit to the opportunity that stemmed from her "unrestrained access to the private library of the Revd. President of Nassau Hall," in whose household "I am persuaded [she] has improved the privilege."[28]

The "Revd. President" himself echoed Osborn's observations. Ashbel Green noted that Stockton had "manifested a great degree of natural sensibility . . . and a great aptitude for mental improvement":

> She reads extremely well, and few of her age and sex have read more books on religion than she; or can give a better account of them. She has no small share of miscellaneous reading, and has a real taste for literature. She understands Geography and English grammar, pretty

> well. She composes in English, in a manner very uncommon for one of her standing in society. She is tolerably skilled in arithmetick.

Whatever the drawbacks of her personal situation, "her age and sex . . . [and] standing in society," Green acknowledged Betsey's effort at educating herself "without ever going to school at all."[29] Like Osborn, Green said nothing about the time she had spent with Nathaniel Todd, but instead pointed to the effect of "improving her time and privilege" in the intellectual environment of his own household.

LESSONS LEARNED FROM ASHBEL GREEN

Green himself was an inescapable part of that environment, of course, and while his books were one thing, his behavior could be another. What did it mean for Betsey Stockton to be in such frequent proximity to such a prominent man as Ashbel Green? In the close confines of the eight-room President's House, Green and Stockton had almost constant exposure to each other. While she would busy herself with household tasks in every room, he could seal himself off in his downstairs study to attend to the business of education and religion, writing letters and longer pieces and meeting visitors. But Green and Stockton inevitably interacted many times a day, and she could easily hear and see almost everything that happened in the house. What she saw and heard of Ashbel Green, what she learned from him beyond what she read in his books, poses a question neither of them answered directly, but one that invites speculation.

Most of the speculation to date has been exceedingly kind to Green, giving him credit for providing the "privilege" of his household and portraying him as a progressive and supportive authority figure. One profile of Green from the 1950s asserted that "The Negro race considered Ashbel its sincere friend since he fought against discrimination wherever it existed." A handful of subsequent articles about Betsey Stockton also reflect a similarly benign view of Green. One stated that Green "took an interest in his precocious servant and became concerned for her future welfare." Another likewise described Green as a man "keenly interested in the education of children and the conversion of African Americans," so that "he could not ignore the academic and spiritual growth of the naughty and bright mulatto girl in his household." So the story goes in other coverage of Stockton's early life, culminating with an entry for her in the *American National Biography*: having a place in the "affectionate, indulgent Green household," she lived among "reform-minded people who supported the abolition of slavery and believed she was prepared for freedom."[30]

Flattering though they may be to Ashbel Green, such descriptions of his benevolence claim more than the evidence would warrant, whether about his opposition to slavery or his assistance to Black people. The notion that he "supported the abolition of slavery" makes a linguistic reach beyond its historical grasp. Throughout the era leading up to the Civil War, many people found it possible to look askance at slavery as an unjust, even immoral institution, but still not endorse its immediate eradication. Ashbel Green was one of those people. He was a complicated character, a man of mixed messages: he could be both self-assured and fretful, generous and vengeful, benign and violent, a man who could at once write of the evils of slavery and engage in cruel behavior toward the Black people under his own control.

No one would have known that better than John, the Black teenager whose time Green purchased in the summer of 1813, just before sending Betsey away to the Todds. On May 2, 1815, Green noted tersely, "Whipped John." In early December 1816, Green again "Had a most uncomfortable time with my servant John," he wrote, and once again, he whipped him. Although the law prohibited the physical abuse of enslaved and indentured people, enforcement remained lax to nonexistent. And anyway, prominent and godly Ashbel Green had nothing to worry about. "On the whole," he concluded after whipping John the second time, "I desire to be thankful that I was carried through it with as little to regret as I have."[31] A similar description appeared in January 1821: "Last night John, my servant, was out all night and did not appear until late in the afternoon. Prayed for him and dealt with him." Green did not indicate what "dealt with him" meant, but he did note that "I hope it will be for his good."

The latter two punishments occurred soon after Betsey Stockton had come back to Green's household. There is no record, however, of how the abuse of John's body affected her. But witnessing a whipping, or even seeing the victim soon after, had to leave a profound impression about power. It made visible the ultimate means of control. It reminded Black people, whatever their legal status—enslaved, indentured, or even free—about their vulnerability in a society where slaveholding and its associated violence still held sway. Among all the lessons Betsey Stockton might have learned in the allegedly "affectionate, indulgent Green household," that could be a lasting one.

"THE MINUTE ABOUT SLAVERY"

She would also witness the playing out of a more complicated relationship between Ashbel Green and the larger question of slavery. In May 1818, Green found himself in the spotlight for an important performance before one of his most important professional organizations, the General Assembly of the Presbyterian Church of the United States, meeting in Philadelphia. (He had been a member of the General Assembly since 1790, and he never missed a meeting.) "I was busily employed during the sitting of the Assembly," he noted. "I wrote the minute about slavery." He didn't say anything more about it at the time, but his "minute" became an influential position paper for the church, and it now bears scrutiny not just for what it said about slavery, but also for what it suggested about both the Presbyterian church and Green himself.[32]

Green never intended to be the Presbyterian point man. He had long been a prominent player in the General Assembly, however, and now his colleagues called on him to address an especially vexing question about the fundamental sinfulness of slavery.[33] Pressure had come from one outspoken member, the Reverend George Bourne, a young, British-born pastor in Virginia, who, in 1815, had attracted attention with an attack on slavery and, perhaps more important, on slaveholding Presbyterians. He refused to allow slaveholders into his small congregation in the Shenandoah Valley, questioning whether people who kept other people enslaved could truly qualify as Christians. (Bourne was taking the same stance as Ashbel Green's father, Jacob, had in the Revolutionary era.) When Bourne brought his attack before the General Assembly, he met immediate resistance, particularly from those members who held people in bondage. For his own part, Bourne never named names but simply let slaveholding pastors squirm in uneasy silence.

In turn, they tried to silence him. When Bourne continued his attack—against the fundamental sinfulness of slavery as a form of man-stealing, against the hypocrisy of clergymen who were slaveholders, against the much-too-temperate position of the whole church on the slavery question—Presbyterians pushed back with force. By May 1818, the leadership had become more hostile to this dissident pastor than to slavery itself. To get at Bourne, they turned to Green.[34]

The assembly agreed to consider one particular aspect of slavery—a lesser charge, so to speak—"That a person who shall sell as a slave a member of the Church, who shall be at the time of sale in good standing in the Church, and unwilling to be sold, acts inconsistently with the spirit of Christianity, and ought to be debarred from the communion of the Church." One might think that the evil of selling enslaved Presbyterians would be a self-evident truth, but the assembly needed further study, duly passing the question on to a committee of three. One of the committee members had long been a staunch opponent of George Bourne's position, while another had followed Bourne's practice of barring slaveholders from communion in his congregation; the third, Ashbel Green, stood in the proverbial middle, the man most likely to balance moral principle with more practical politics. Green assumed the role of lead author—"I wrote the minute about slavery"—and then presented the report to the assembly on June 2.[35]

It opened with promising words of opposition to the institution of slavery: "We consider the voluntary enslaving of one part of the human race by another, as a gross violation of the most precious and sacred rights of human nature; as utterly inconsistent with the law of God." Having established the fundamental unfitness of slavery in the divine order of things, the document went on to assert that "it is manifestly the duty of all Christians . . . to correct the errors of former times, and as speedily as possible to efface this blot on our holy religion, and to obtain the complete abolition of slavery throughout Christendom, and if possible throughout the world."[36] So far, the call for "complete abolition" seemed ready to lay slavery to rest.

But then, Green gave slaveholding Presbyterians a bit of breathing room. By locating the original "errors of former times" somewhere in some distant-seeming past, the report made slaveholding seem an unfortunate historical inheritance, not an immediate social imperative. By leaving the correction of such errors for some point in the future, it also lessened the pressure for immediate action. (The phrase employed, "as speedily as possible," was as imprecise as "with all deliberate speed" would be a little over a century later.) Looking at the present, the report veered away from assigning guilt to anyone but made a victim of seemingly everyone, white as well as Black: "We do, indeed, tenderly sympathize with those portions of our church and our country where the evil of slavery has been entailed upon them; where a great, and the most virtuous part of the community abhor slavery." The reference to the collective—"those portions of our church and our country"—deflected attention away from the individual slaveholder as a sinner and instead sought pity for "the most virtuous part of the community," those who may have opposed slavery but who seemed unable or unwilling to do more than abhor it.[37]

Finally, the report suggested that ending slavery "as speedily as possible" might actually be too soon: "the number of slaves, their ignorance, and their vicious habits generally," it concluded, would "render an immediate and universal emancipation inconsistent alike with the safety and happiness of the master and the slave."[38] Enslaved people would have to wait until they became fit for freedom—again, whenever that might be. For years, Green had divided his time between Pennsylvania and New Jersey, two states that promoted gradual abolition, and that slow approach became embedded in Presbyterian policy. Ultimately, for all its invocation of the "sacred rights of human nature," Green's "minute" left the property rights of slaveholders essentially intact.

But there might yet be a better approach: "We recommend to all our people to patronize and encourage the society lately formed, for colonizing in Africa, the land of their ancestors, the free people of colour in our country." The American Colonization Society had barely come into existence at the time, first organized in Washington, DC, in 1816, but already much popularized throughout the country. The ostensibly benign intent of colonization—sending Black people to West Africa as an alternative to living in a white society that would never fully accept them as equals—would become a thin veneer of racism: it covered whites' underlying desire to be rid of Black people altogether. At the outset, though, the initial appeal of colonization proved alluring to many people, both white and Black, providing a seemingly positive approach and reaching across the regions, both South and North, and encompassing both Philadelphia and Princeton.[39]

The roots of the American Colonization Society grew partly out of Princeton, in fact, its seeds planted by someone very close to Ashbel Green, both geographically and intellectually. Robert Finley—a Princeton-born, Princeton-educated, Presbyterian pastor in Basking Ridge, New Jersey—knew Ashbel Green quite well. Finley had attended the College of New Jersey from 1783 to 1787, under Green's personal tutelage. He later served on the college's board of trustees from 1806 to 1817, overlapping the first five years of Green's presidency. When Finley resigned his position as pastor to pursue a college presidency of his own, at the University of Georgia, Ashbel Green signed the local presbytery letter to "dismiss him with many fervent prayers for his comfort and usefulness."[40] Finley died just three months after taking office in Georgia, but the American Colonization Society lived on for several decades more, becoming a source of increasing contention throughout the antebellum era—and prominent perhaps nowhere more than in Princeton.

In 1818, though, the ACS was still new, Robert Finley only recently deceased. Ashbel Green may have put the colonization proposal before the General Assembly as much as a personal tribute to Finley as an institutional endorsement of his organization. Still, there could hardly have been a more powerful recommendation than Green's that Presbyterians "patronize and encourage the society." In the end, the General Assembly adopted Green's entire report unanimously. Presbyterians from the South as well as the North could acknowledge the moral problem posed by slavery, but still temporize on taking any significant steps to abolish it. Instead, the alternative of colonization allowed them to see another way out altogether.

A SENSE OF MISSION

Betsey Stockton, another Presbyterian much influenced by Ashbel Green, was beginning to see her own way out—out of Green's household, out of Princeton, out of the United States. While Green was working on his "minute" about slavery, she was working on her household tasks, never far away from his downstairs study, always close enough to speak to him in passing. What did she make of the opportunity? Did she seek to engage him in a discussion about slavery as a doctrinal problem in the Presbyterian church? Did she share her own feelings about having been born into slavery, given into his household as an enslaved child, emancipated from slavery but kept in servitude for several years? Did she see hopeful possibilities in the prospect of colonization, as some other Black people in the North did? Green never mentioned any of that in his diary at the time, but he would soon attest to her emerging awareness of the role she might play as a free woman. She had begun to build on her commitment to being a teacher by looking beyond the limits imposed by Princeton and following a calling to the far side of the world.

"She has been, for a good while, exceedingly desirous to go on a mission," Green wrote of Betsey Stockton in 1821, "and I am willing that she should. I think her, in many respects, well qualified for this." His words came in his letter of recommendation to the American Board of Commissioners for Foreign Missions (ABCFM), and they carried considerable weight; were he not agreeable to her going, the matter probably would have ended right there. But he could not deny Stockton's apparent passion for mission, a point also underscored by Michael Osborn. "From my first acquaintance with her she had expressed a decided wish to go to the heathens," Osborn wrote of the "young mulattoe woman." He also knew her preferred destination: "Africa was the place of her choice."[41]

With the rise of the ACS, Africa had become very much a subject of attention among many Americans, and an obvious focus for a young Black woman "exceedingly desirous to go on a mission." There were other places to go, of course, other "heathens" to save. The ABCFM had established missions among the Cherokee people in the South, much closer to home. But for a young, unmarried Black woman like Betsey Stockton, it would have been unsafe, perhaps even insane, to try to be a missionary there. Even in the North, the hostile racial context constrained the sorts of work she could do. "She loves to teach children," Osborn observed, but to do so she would best look beyond the bounds of the slaveholding nation where she had been born—and born into bondage. Africa would offer the most likely spot. But Africa also offered dangers, and Osborn noted that "the opposition of her friends" had kept her from going—so far.

As it happened, another young Princeton seminarian offered another option for foreign mission. Charles Samuel Stewart had been a student of Ashbel Green's, and he came to know Betsey Stockton as a member of Green's household. Like Osborn, Stewart must have been struck by Stockton's quality of mind and commitment to mission. When he made his own plans to become a missionary in the

Sandwich Islands and applied to the ABCFM, he added a request that she accompany him as an assistant.[42] Stewart would become not just the immediate means of her leaving the United States, but one of her most valuable allies for life.

Stewart was just a few years older than Stockton, born in 1795 in Flemington, New Jersey, a little over twenty miles northwest of Princeton. He entered the College of New Jersey in 1813 and became swept up in the 1815 religious revival that Ashbel Green had so happily welcomed. The fervor of the time fed his intention was to become a minister, but soon after graduation, his spiritual intensity began to fade, leaving him to wonder if he had indeed experienced religious regeneration. Instead, he studied law, a choice that occasioned a slide toward sin: "I became more and more attached to the things of this world & entered very fully into its amusements & pleasures whilst I almost entirely neglected the concerns of my soul." But once again, he got religion, when "it pleased a God of infinite grace to arouse me from the slumber of death into which I had fallen." Newly recommitted to the ministry, Stewart entered the Princeton Theological Seminary in 1819, where he began to read about missionary work: "as I learned more & more of the real state of the world & the wretchedness of by far the greater portion of it, the suggestion was often made to my mind whether it might be my duty to go & preach the Gospel where it was unknown."[43]

At the time, the Gospel was just becoming known in the Sandwich Islands, where the first band of ABCFM missionaries had arrived in 1820. Stewart wanted to be part of the second group. He secured all the necessary letters of recommendation, including a strong one from his "respected and beloved instructor" and "venerated Preceptor," Ashbel Green, who wrote hopefully that Stewart would become "the happy instrument of diffusing among the Heathen the knowledge of our precious Redeemer."[44] Stewart also did the necessary fund-raising to support his work, collecting well over a thousand dollars from various friends, colleagues, and congregations.

In the midst of all that preparatory effort, he also found time to marry "the chosen of my heart," Harriet Bradford Tiffany, a pious young woman from Cooperstown, New York, who declared herself game for the missionary venture: "Even tho' missionaries should labour without the shadow of success," she wrote in her own ABCFM application, "tho' they meet with every discouragement, sow the good seed in a barren soil, or die as it shows itself in the tender blade, still we have reason for joy and rejoicing." She would have reason for pain and difficulty too, but that would come later. For now, she threw herself into her new husband's work. Her favorite uncle, Nathan Whiting of New Haven, Connecticut, also helped. He told Stewart about a ship, the whaling vessel *Thames*, that sat in the harbor there, ready to head for the Pacific.[45]

By the fall of 1822, then, Stewart had the support, the spouse, and the ship—everything he needed for a trip with his extended "missionary family," one of whom would be Betsey Stockton.

LAST WORDS

But first would come the last meeting with the man both Stockton and Stewart knew so well, Ashbel Green. In late September, Green recorded in his diary "a very solemn and affecting time in my study with Mr. Stewart and my coloured woman, Betsy Stockton." His use of the possessive "my" might suggest that he had never fully freed her in his mind. Still, he had written her a letter of recommendation, and he knew that she had long ago decided to leave. Now, Green produced another document. In a striking written agreement signed by himself, Stockton, and Stewart and sent to the ABCFM, Green offered a combination of direction and protection for Betsey Stockton's future.[46]

As this "colored young woman brought up in the family of the Revd. Ashbel Green" moved on to become a member of Charles Stewart's missionary family, Green made clear that "family" could not be taken as just a loose metaphorical expression: the terms of her relationships needed to be carefully spelled out, "as there is something peculiar in her case." First, "she is to be considered, as at all times, under the entire direction and control of the American Board of Commissioners for Foreign Missions." In the immediate mission at hand, she would be "specially attached to the family of the Rev. Charles S. Stewart, and as constituting a member of his family." But then, in a curious turn of phrase, the document specified that "she is to be regarded and treated neither as an equal or as a servant, but as an humble Christian friend." Neither equal nor servant, perhaps family or friend—Betsey Stockton's missionary identity seemed ambiguous at best.

But the rest of the document read much like a labor contract, defining her basic duties and the terms of her work. She would be expected to "lighten the burden of Mr. and Mrs. Stewart's family care . . . especially to relieve Mrs. Stewart in the more laborious parts of domestic concerns." Looking to the Stewarts as "particular friends, patrons, & protectors," Stockton was to "regard their opinions and wishes as the guide of her conduct." Beyond assisting the Stewarts, she would also serve the larger mission cause, but with the critical caveat that she should not be expected to provide "any menial services . . . as this might manifestly render her life servile, and prevent her being employed as a teacher of a school, for which it is hoped that she will be found qualified." Finally, if the Stewarts or Stockton ever decided to terminate the arrangement, "all the parties concerned will be at full liberty to do so," and Stockton would still "remain under the care and Superintendence of the Board, like any other missionary." For a young woman born into slavery and kept in some form of servitude for the first two decades of her life, such a labor agreement provided more flexibility, if not freedom, than she had ever known.

Green could have wished as much for himself. By the early 1820s, his professional life was in shambles. For all his prominence in the church, his influence as president of the College of New Jersey had been steadily on the wane. Students expressed open disrespect toward him, and he even received a warning "that violence would be attempted on me." But Green had even more trouble with the trustees, whose disenchantment with Green stemmed from a variety of issues—his apparent predilection for the theological seminary over the college, his recurrent failure to maintain better disciplinary control over the student body, his transparent attempt to install his son Jacob in a new chaired professorship—and he met their disenchantment with his own. On September 25, 1822, the day after college commencement—also the day after he and Stewart and Stockton signed the ABCFM document—Green delivered his letter of resignation to the trustees. Citing his "age and infirmities," he also noted, with indirect language that had a very direct meaning, "some other considerations not necessary to be specified." The trustees responded with an equally circumspect letter. They assured him that they remained his "affectionate friends" in the last sentence, but only after they had already accepted his resignation in the first. Thus ended Green's ten-year term as the eighth president of the College of New Jersey, part of a chapter in the institution's history that one historian of the college would later call "Princeton's Nadir."[47]

Green's own spirits seemed to have reached a nadir as well. He had felt the sting of death in his family, and as he entered his seventh decade, he had to contemplate the approach of his own. He knew his professional success lay behind him, and in giving up the college presidency, he had no similarly prominent position in sight. It was in the depressing process of packing to depart Princeton that he met with Betsey Stockton just before her own departure. It was "a very solemn and affecting time" for him, indeed.

It was such a time for Betsey Stockton as well. She had lived in his household for most of her life, and she had experienced him as both high-minded and hypocritical; an academician who allowed her access to education in his home, but also a disciplinarian who sold her time and sent her away; a leading figure in the Presbyterian church's debate over slavery, but one who ultimately let slaveholding Presbyterians off the ethical hook. She knew his flaws, but she also felt his influence. Now that she was going off on a new life of her own choosing, she had to assume that she would never see him again.

Green ruefully assumed the same thing: "I counselled and encouraged and prayed with them and charged them to remember me in their prayers," he wrote, and then he closed the account on a final-sounding note: "The next day they went East and I West—probably to meet no more on earth."[48]

Despite Green's grim prediction, the two would yet meet again on earth, but by the time they did, Betsey Stockton had become a woman with a very clear notion of her larger mission in life.

3

A Long Adieu

ON NOVEMBER 19, 1822, Betsey Stockton stepped carefully onto the deck of the *Thames*, a whaling ship anchored at New Haven, Connecticut. It was the first step in a five-month voyage that would take her halfway around the world: down the Atlantic and around Cape Horn, into the Pacific and up the coast of Chile, then eventually westward to the Sandwich Islands (or Hawai'i). Now a free woman, she saw her future on the far side of the world, doing the work she felt called to do.

She shared that sense of calling with the other seventeen members of her new "missionary family": six recently married couples and five unmarried men, one a New Englander and the other four Pacific Islanders. The captain and crew of the *Thames* would account for another twenty-three, making a total of forty-one people aboard, all but five of them younger than thirty.[1] They would live together on the ship, voyaging thousands of miles, through brilliant sunshine and battering storms, with long and enervating days occasionally punctuated by the thrilling chase of whales. Such an extensive voyage would have been a remarkable experience for anyone, but particularly for this young woman, whose life had largely been defined by enslavement and servitude. Sailing away from American shores would be the watershed experience of Betsey Stockton's life.

GETTING A SHIP

The missionaries almost missed the boat. Charles Samuel Stewart, who had invited Stockton to join the expedition, arrived in New Haven in early November, confident he had made all the necessary arrangements, only to have the ship's owners tell him that he was too late, and the *Thames* would soon be sailing. Seeing Stewart's dejection, they agreed to meet and reconsider. Stewart went to his own meeting—a prayer meeting—and came out to find that the shipowners had agreed to wait ten days.[2] If Charles Stewart ever needed reassurance about the power of prayer, he had it.

Stewart hurried to New York City to get his wife and Betsey Stockton and hustled them by boat back to New Haven. "It will be all hurry and confusion from the time we get to New Haven until we sail," Stockton wrote.[3] But the hurry seemed worth it, because the *Thames* seemed to be a perfect ship for the missionary family. Whaling ships didn't often carry passengers, but this one was special. It had been built in 1818, a 350-ton vessel just over 101 feet long, with three masts, two decks, and a female figurehead, all in all a ship "admired for her stately appearance and for her great sailing qualities." Originally outfitted as a passenger packet between New York and England, the *Thames* had become a whaling ship in 1820, when a group of New Haven merchants purchased it. Still, it retained its passenger-packet appeal. The missionaries had a large cabin with seven windows, a space both roomy and discreet: they would hang curtains to provide privacy between the berths, especially for the married couples. On first inspection, Betsey Stockton seemed impressed with "doors made of mahogany, and everything in her elegant."[4] Soon enough, the less elegant reality of the *Thames* would become evident—a creaking, stinking, crowded wooden box, with cold saltwater washing over everything below, people and possessions alike. But at least it was a ship.

At the outset, the mariners and the missionaries had good reason to look at each other with curiosity. Sailors hardly had a reputation for piety, and they certainly had little experience sailing with women on long voyages. In turn, the missionaries had to be wary of the mariners' world, where they would encounter rough seas and even rougher language. Yet these people shared in the historical convergence of two global ventures—killing whales and saving souls. Perhaps they didn't fully grasp it, but their voyage symbolized the connection between American economic and religious expansion, and New Haven had lately become a jumping-off point for both.

NEW HAVEN, NEW VENTURES

As soon as she arrived in New Haven, Betsey Stockton could see it was not like Princeton, though it did have Yale College, an older and bigger institution than the College of New Jersey. Princeton consisted of a straggling collection of "taverns, stores, and a few good dwelling-houses," but otherwise had "little besides the college to recommend it," said a contemporary travelers' guide. New Haven, by contrast, was "one of the most agreeable towns in the United States," where "the public square and the principal streets are finely ornamented with trees, and a great part of the houses have gardens in the rear, filled with forest trees, giving the city a rural and delightful appearance."[5]

New Haven's larger population, which the 1820 federal census put at 7,147, made it the largest city in Connecticut, and more than twice the size of Princeton. Some 624 residents were African American, only two of whom, a generation after the passage of the state's 1784 gradual abolition law, remained enslaved. Freedom did not mean social acceptance, however. New Haven's Black people suffered the standard insults. As one white writer put it, "many of them are thieves, liars, profane, drunkards, sabbath-breakers, quarrelsome, idle, and prodigal, the last in the extreme," only to relent a bit by adding that "A number of the females are well behaved." Looking to the future, the author also noted the recent creation of two schools for Black children, one for boys, one for girls: "These institutions furnish the first rational hope of a reformation among the people."[6] Betsey Stockton had heard racial slurs before, but she also understood the uplifting power of education: she had experienced that in her own life, and she had made a commitment to bring it to others.

Another feature that distinguished New Haven from Princeton was its robust economic growth—various forms of production, ranging from leather goods (shoes, boots, and saddles) to home furnishings (candles, clocks, and chairs) to reading materials (printing presses, newspapers, and bookstores), along with many sorts of consumer goods available in forty-one dry goods stores and forty-two grocery stores. Only one thing seemed to be missing: "We have no *breweries*," a surveyor of the city's economy wrote—surely a surprising absence in a community with so many working people, not to mention sailors and college boys.[7]

But by far, the biggest single economic asset in New Haven was its four-mile-wide harbor, formed by the confluence of the Quinnipiac, Mill, and West rivers as they emptied into Long Island Sound. The harbor had long provided a shared space for oysters and clams at the bottom, all manner of fish in the middle, and sailing ships on the surface. In the first two decades after the American Revolution, New Haven had received between forty and one hundred ships a year, most of them American, with a few British, Danish, and Spanish vessels, too. Most of the export trade went to other states, though, not across the Atlantic. Yet by the late 1790s, New Haven merchants had sought a larger overseas reach, extending to the Pacific, all the way to China.[8]

In the post-Revolutionary era, the China trade offered American merchants a new opportunity for global economic expansion, getting into a complex market that their European counterparts had been working for decades. Carrying a combination of manufactured goods (glass, cloth, rum, and guns, among others) and animal pelts (fur seals from the South Atlantic and sea otters from the Pacific Northwest), ships plied the Pacific to the Chinese port of Canton, where they traded for silk, ceramics, lacquered woods products, and other consumer goods much desired in the West. Midway, many of the ships stopped in the Sandwich Islands, for rest, repairs, and replenishing. There they could take on another valuable trade good—

sandalwood, which the Chinese valued highly as a ceremonial incense. Like other Americans, New Haven merchants came late to the game, but it seemed that almost anyone could play—and win big.[9]

They also came late to whaling. The entrepreneurs who established the New Haven Whalefishery Company in 1820 started small, with only two ships, the *Henry* and the *Thames*. Whales migrated along the New England coast in the winter months, and inhabitants had long made the most of the bounty. Before the arrival of Europeans, Native people went out after whales in canoes, using harpoons and bows and arrows to make the kill. Later, European settlers on Long Island, Cape Cod, and the islands of Martha's Vineyard and Nantucket engaged in shore-whaling expeditions, typically staying well within sight of land. Many of these coastal voyages were cultural joint ventures, as an early historian, the Melvillean-named Alexander Starbuck, has noted: "Indians were usually employed by the English, with the whites furnishing all the implements, and the Indians receiving a stipulated portion of oil in payment." By the eighteenth century, New England merchants and shipowners sought to make the whaling industry bigger on both sides of the Atlantic. Whale oil became an important product for lighting, but it also went into soap, candles, lamps, and lubrication, while whale baleen (or bone) gave form to umbrellas, canes, and corsets. On the eve of the American Revolution, well over one hundred New England whaling ships ranged from Labrador to the coasts of Africa and Brazil. But the coming of Revolution brought the whaling enterprise all but to a halt. From the Revolution to the Quasi-War with France in the late 1790s to the Embargo of 1807 to the War of 1812, global politics repeatedly constricted American whaling ventures. When peace eventually came, however, New England whalemen resumed the rapacious pursuit of whales on an unprecedented scale.[10]

Bigger ambitions meant bigger ships going farther for longer periods of time: "The sperm-whale being of the most value," Starbuck explains, "the effort to encompass his capture was greater; and he was pursued, as he fled from his old haunts, till the Pacific Ocean was obtained." The cetacean flight eventually extended as far as the waters off China and Japan. On a return trip a Massachusetts mariner, one Captain Winship, reported seeing sperm whales in abundance off the Sandwich Islands. That news set off a rush of whaling vessels to the region, first one in 1819, then six in 1821, then fifty in 1823—forty-three of them American, one of them the *Thames*.[11] The missionaries aboard thus owed the timing of their arrival to global economic and environmental forces that had been unfolding for decades.[12]

Still, the destination was hardly happenstance. British missionaries had established a foothold in Tahiti in 1797, and the islands of the Pacific offered a vast opportunity for further work. Evangelical New Englanders had begun looking that way as well. In 1810, a handful of Williams College students established the American Board of Commissioners for Foreign Missions (ABCFM), chartered "for promoting the spread of the Gospel in heathen lands." The first of those was India, where the first batch of ABCFM missionaries went in 1812, but the organization also had its eye on the wider world, from the Mediterranean to the Pacific.[13] In the 1820s, the ABCFM would focus its attention on the Sandwich Islands, sending successive groups of missionaries—including Betsey Stockton's—to spread Christianity there.

But to do so, they had to gain some sense of what "there" was like.

PACIFIC PEOPLE IN NEW HAVEN

By the time Betsey Stockton and her fellow missionaries were set to depart for the Sandwich Islands, information about both the place and its people was still scarce in New Haven, and sometimes scary. Yale had over seven thousand volumes in its library, with just over a hundred titles in the category of "Geography, Voyages and Travels," including specific studies of the United States, Europe, Russia, Asia, and even Africa. The sole work that dealt specifically with the Pacific, however, was Captain James Cook's A *Voyage Towards the South Pole, and Round the World*, published in 1777, a year before Cook actually visited (and gave an English name to) the Sandwich

Islands. In 1822, the most relevant publication in Yale's library was the 1819 edition of Jedediah Morse's *American Universal Geography*, which contained a two-page section on "the Sandwich Isles." Morse offered descriptions of the people's physical appearance, dress, diet, and ceremonial and political practices, but his characterization of the islands' inhabitants might have given a prospective missionary a mixed message: they were "mild and affectionate" people who "still sacrifice human victims, but do not eat them."[14]

Books were not the only resource, however. Beginning in the 1790s, American mariners brought back information about the inhabitants, some of it fanciful and exaggerated. When the original ABCFM group arrived, in the spring of 1820, the missionaries tried to send out more systematic reports, but those still lacked geographic and ethnographic detail. The *Religious Intelligencer*, a New Haven–based periodical devoted largely to missionary news from all parts, carried a letter from a female member of that mission, who declared: "The field which is here opened, is entirely new. It is even now a spiritual desert." Still, she quickly took a more positive-seeming approach: "But let it not be supposed, that this is a wild expedition," pointing to the recent "abolition of idolatry in these islands" as a particularly promising development. Another correspondent who had visited the ABCFM mission in 1820–21 also wrote a hopeful appraisal, saying that the missionaries "have every prospect of succeeding in their arduous undertaking" and that "the reception they received from the natives of these islands were the most flattering." Already, he noted, a "commodious church was erected on the island of Waohoo," and the mission schools had begun to teach some "100 scholars, old and young." He, too, reported that "Idolatrous worship is nearly abolished, and not an instance of the immolation of a human being has happened during the missionaries' residence there."[15]

But the best local source for information came from Pacific Islanders, who could provide a direct cultural connection between the American missionaries and the people they intended to convert. American ships that stopped in the Sandwich Islands often took on native inhabitants as additional crewmen, and a handful of them eventually wound up at the Foreign Mission School in Cornwall, Connecticut. The school had opened in 1817, designed to be both an innovative training ground for the missionary movement and a showcase of consciousness-raising and fund-raising among the Protestant public. To promote future mission work, the ABCFM would bring to the school promising young men from different parts of the world—and they were all men, and most of them men of color—who could then go back as models of cross-cultural conversion. The first cohort started small, with seven men from the Sandwich Islands, two from India, one from Canada, and two native-born New Englanders. Given their disparate, and mostly distant, origins, most of the students no doubt had fascinating stories to tell about how and why they came to Cornwall.[16]

But one student and one story stood out from all the rest—a Sandwich Islander named Ōpūkahaʻia (or Henry Obookiah, as he became known in the United States). Short though his life was—he died in 1818, probably at age thirty—he became just the sort of legendary character the missionary movement needed.[17]

It started in violence and tragedy. Born on the island of Hawaiʻi, Ōpūkahaʻia became a captive as a child when his parents and infant brother were killed during a period of civil warfare among chieftains. An uncle eventually redeemed the boy, intending to make him a priest, but then Ōpūkahaʻia's life turned in a seemingly providential direction toward another form of religion. In 1807, an American ship, the *Triumph*, appeared in a nearby harbor, and while it lay at anchor, the captain, Caleb Brintnall, arranged to make Ōpūkahaʻia a member of his crew, joining another young native man named Thomas Hopoo (Hopu) already on board—even though neither one spoke any English. Brintnall eventually took both young men to his own home, in New Haven, in 1809. There the Ōpūkahaʻia legend moved to a new level.[18]

One of the most important allies Ōpūkahaʻia met in New Haven was Edwin W. Dwight. Dwight had been born and raised in Stockbridge, Massachusetts, a mission town for Native Americans since the middle of the eighteenth century, and unlike most white

New Englanders, Dwight seemed to accept nonwhite converts as worthy of education. Ōpūkaha'ia was apparently an eager learner and a quick study, and he told Dwight that he "wished to live where I could have an opportunity to get in some school, and work in part of the time." Dwight arranged for Ōpūkaha'ia to move into the household of his distant relative, the Reverend Timothy Dwight, president of Yale. There could be no loftier spot in New Haven.[19]

Ōpūkaha'ia made the most of his time at Yale, engaging with many faculty members and students. Samuel J. Mills Jr., one of the driving forces behind the founding of the ABCFM in 1810, met Ōpūkaha'ia that same year. Like Edwin Dwight, Mills saw the missionary potential inherent in the young man, and he soon took him into his care and eventually to the Andover Theological Seminary. After Andover, Ōpūkaha'ia went to live with several other Protestant families in New England, impressing everyone with his intelligence and industriousness, furthering his education through book work and farmwork—both of which would be useful in the calling he had begun to see in his future, as a missionary returning to the Pacific. He used his newfound literacy to create an extensive correspondence network throughout New England and, above all, to begin working on a translation of biblical texts, in some instances directly from Hebrew into his native language. By the time he came to Cornwall as one of the first students in May 1817, Ōpūkaha'ia had become a religious celebrity in the region, a young man who seemed to be on the Protestant path to a shining life of missionary service.[20]

But then, in February 1818, he died, taken away by typhus. In death, his life took on new vitality, his story more meaning. Within a few months, a missionary press in New Haven published the *Memoirs of Henry Obookiah*, which offered him up as the perfect figure for the cause, a young and pious native of the Pacific, just as the ABCFM was beginning to prepare for a Pacific mission.[21] Ōpūkaha'ia proved that the people of the region offered rich new opportunities for religious conversion, that so-called heathens could indeed become Christians, that one convert in Cornwall might well return to the Pacific islands to make thousands more. His legend took on a valuable life of its own: Ōpūkahaʻia had actually existed, so the ABCFM didn't have to invent him.

Given the timing of the book's publication and Betsey Stockton's own preparation for missionary work, it's hard to imagine that she didn't read the *Memoirs of Henry Obookiah* sometime between 1818 and 1822.[22] If she did, she could have seen several striking parallels between Ōpūkahaʻia's story and her own. Born about ten years before she was, he had been separated from his parents, confined to a form of unfreedom, emancipated, largely self-educated in the household of a celebrated (and slaveholding) college president, and converted to Christianity and accepted into membership in a Protestant church.[23] But he represented something more as a missionary model—a young person of color who would never be fully accepted as an equal in American society, but who could hope for success in the Sandwich Islands. Betsey Stockton could hope for the same.

THE FINAL FAREWELL

The missionaries' departure fell on Wednesday, November 20, but as one might expect, several rounds of sermons preceded the leave-taking, all of them offering exhortation tinged with warning. On the preceding Sunday, the "mission family and an unusually large concourse" came together in New Haven's North Church, where the Reverend Horatio Bardwell, recently returned from missionary work in India, preached "with much solemnity and affection" about the challenges missionaries would face. Their labors "could not be entirely directed to the communication of religious instruction," he observed, but also to the more down-to-earth enterprise of "Agriculture and the arts of life." The next evening, the missionaries and a large crowd of well-wishers packed the Centre Brick Church, where the main message came from Jeremiah Evarts, the corresponding secretary of the ABCFM. His official charge (which ran to fourteen pages in print) stressed the need for friendship, unity, commitment, and hard work: "The conversion and salvation of the islanders to whom you are sent . . . furnishes an object of sufficient magnitude

FIGURE 3.1. "Departure of the Missionaries," from John Warner Barber, *New England Scenes . . . Principally of a Religious Nature* (New Haven, CT, 1833).

to claim your greatest exertions." In doing that work, however, he warned the missionaries of what he took to be one basic fact about "heathen people" everywhere: "However they may differ as to temperament, habits, and manners . . . in regard to spiritual objects they are all *crooked* and *perverse*." Evarts spewed out the problems he saw in Pacific island people: "their minds are still in utter darkness as to religion; their hearts are under the influence of depraved passion; and their lives are deformed by gross vices." Yet Evarts intended his exhortation to strengthen his missionary listeners, reminding them to hold fast to their solemn obligation: "The missionary vows are upon you; and you cannot go back."[24] No one wavered, though, and the next afternoon, November 19, they all showed up to board the ship.

The people assembled on the wharf sang a hymn, then heard yet another sermon dedicating them to their work, then finished by singing three verses of one last tear-inducing song, "Blest Be the Tie That Binds." With that and a few final words of benediction, the missionaries boarded the *Thames* for what everyone assumed would be a one-way trip to eternity. One account said the missionaries had all "bidden adieu forever to all that is dear to them on earth, and gone, without the expectation of return, to proclaim the Gospel of Peace in the benighted Islands of the Pacific." Another noted that they "had devoted themselves to this arduous work *for life* . . . [in] those far distant isles—there to live—there to labour—there to die—and that there their bones must rest till the archangel's trump shall summon them to judgment."[25] That seemed sufficiently final.

The *Thames* would set sail the following day, and the farewells shared at Tomlinson's Wharf would begin to drift quietly into memory.

LIVING ON THE SHIP

Betsey Stockton had been right when she wrote about the "hurry and confusion" of getting ready, and the bustle went right up to boarding time. Beyond making room for themselves, the passengers had to find space for the belongings they would need for years to come. For the voyage itself, the recommended wardrobe for women included clothing for both cold Atlantic and warmer Pacific weather: a dozen or so dresses, two dozen changes of linens, three pairs of shoes, stockings, sun bonnet, hood, cloak, and shawl, plus any other personal necessities. Once in the islands, women would need even more: lightweight dresses, more stockings, sturdy shoes, handkerchiefs, fans, a parasol, and enough cloth and sewing supplies to make additional dresses and such. Small wonder, then, that Betsey Stockton would note that "arranging our births [*sic*], clothes, &c." would take all the first day on board the *Thames*.[26]

And these were but a tiny fraction of all the goods that would be loaded onto the *Thames*. A whaling ship had to be essentially self-sufficient, carrying enough goods and gear, as Herman Melville put it, for "a three-years' housekeeping upon the wide ocean, far from all grocers, costermongers, doctors, bakers, and bankers." The list of necessary supplies seemed endless: barrels of food and drink, staves for making more barrels, carpenters' and blacksmiths' tools, along with the many tools of the whaling trade, including harpoons, lances, blubber hooks, cutting spades, pikes, knives, buckets, try pots, chains, and a host of other items. Anything lost could not be easily replaced. "Hence," Melville added, "the spare boats, spare spars, and spare lines and harpoons, and spare everythings, almost, but a spare Captain and duplicate ship."[27]

The captain in this case was Reuben Clasby, a thirty-one-year-old Nantucketer who already had three whaling voyages to his credit. The missionaries found much to like in him. Betsey Stockton offered a positive picture of Clasby, "a well disposed man and does every thing in his power to render the family happy." Charles Stewart seemed equally pleased, noting that Clasby had "none of the sailor's peculiarity in his manner or conversation [and] would pass for an ordinary citizen anywhere." Always concerned about spiritual attributes, Stewart found Clasby to be "not a pious man, but kind and affable, moral and polite," noting that "I am rather of opinion that his religious principles are more in conformity with those of the Friends than any other denomination." Still, Stewart commended Clasby for being "very respectful at our devotions & has never missed being present at them." As the voyage progressed, the missionary family came to appreciate even more Clasby's nautical skill and good judgment, not to mention his indulgent approach to regular religious services.[28]

Immediately under Clasby were the first, second, and third mates, who had charge of the whale boats; then three boat steerers, who had the critical job of harpooning whales; other crewmen who took on specific tasks, as sailmaker, cooper, carpenter, blacksmith, boatswain, and cook; and finally the remainder, listed simply as "seaman." Clasby and the three mates enjoyed the privileges of their positions, living in small but separate cabins, dining on decent food together—and with the missionaries—in Clasby's cabin. The boat steerers and the skilled artisans had only bunks, but they ate essentially the same food as their superiors. The common seamen lived in comparative squalor, sleeping in the cramped and dank quarters of the forecastle, eating monotonous and often miserable meals that one source has described as "unpleasant to revolting."[29] The *Thames* was no floating democracy.

Yet everyone in the crew would share in the typical tedium of the trip, staring out at a seemingly endless sea, enduring weeks with no land in sight, having to put up with each other for months at a time. But then, when someone spied spouts on the horizon, the men occasionally got to do what they set out to do, surging with the excitement and danger of lowering their boats to go after whales and putting their harpoons to use. The crew of the *Thames* did well enough at the hunt, and the ship eventually returned to New Haven with almost two thousand barrels of oil.[30] But that would be several years later, and whale oil was not the missionaries' business anyway.

WRITING ON THE WAVES

If the missionaries didn't expect to come back in person, they did hope to come back on paper—and soon. Charles Stewart observed that by the evening of the first day, everyone in the missionary family had been "busily employed at his writing desk finishing and sealing letters to be sent ashore," carried back by the pilot who had guided the ship into Long Island Sound.[31] A week later, Betsey Stockton reported that a Philadelphia-bound ship, the *Penn*, sailed near, but "the sea was too rough to permit us to send letters." Over the weeks that came, every encounter with a homebound vessel became an opportunity to send mail, but always a very hit-or-miss process. In mid-December 1822, after four weeks at sea, Stockton drafted a long letter to Ashbel Green, but because the *Thames* could not make land at Cape Verde, "I gave up all hopes of being able to send my letter." Three weeks later, however, she penned a hasty postscript to the original correspondence, adding that "A ship has just appeared in sight, and I have scarcely more time than to tell you we are all well."[32] So went mail service at sea.

Stockton's mail eventually arrived in Green's hands, and he began publishing her writings in his new role as editor of a Philadelphia religious periodical, the *Christian Advocate*. Green took pains to assure his readers that Stockton's writings were indeed in her own voice, and he praised the power of her pen. In May 1824, Green wrote that "Within the month past a short letter, and part of a journal, has been received by the Editor from Betsey Stockton, a coloured young woman." Stockton's writings, Green continued, "appear interesting and instructive; especially when we consider that the writer is a young woman of African descent, who was never sent to school a day in her life." Twenty years later, in his autobiography, Green would again underscore Stockton's skill as a writer: "Some of her letters to me after her arrival at the island . . . were so well written, that, with very few corrections, I inserted them in the Christian Advocate . . . and they were greatly admired."[33] Stockton's is only one of four surviving journals kept by the missionaries on the *Thames*. "Betsey and myself have both kept regular journals," Stewart wrote to Green, "copies of which we design, according to our engagement, to transmit to you." Two other journals—by Levi Chamberlain, the superintendent of secular affairs, and by Louisa Everest Ely, a teacher and the wife of James Ely, one of the missionary preachers—did not appear in print. Yet taken together, these four journals make it possible to see the shared shipboard experience.[34]

In a few instances, those shared experiences were rendered in shared wording. The most notable example came in the opening pages of Stockton's and Stewart's journals. The engaging first sentence in the published version of Stockton's journal—"Here begins the history of things known only to those who have bid the American shores a long adieu"—also appears almost verbatim on the second page of the handwritten journal kept by Stewart: "Here then begins the history of things & circumstances known only to those who like ourselves have bid the American shores a long adieu."[35] Unfortunately, there is no surviving copy of Stockton's original journal, and therefore no way to know who used the wording first. In any event, the similarity of language seems less a case of plagiarism and much more likely an instance of ad hoc editing: Stewart and Stockton may have discussed the wording of their respective journals, deciding who would get the "long adieu" line before sending their work to Green. In that regard, the *Thames* journals are not just personal works by individual authors, but representations of a broader conversation among members of an enclosed community, revealing both the relationships among the members of the missionary family and, equally important, the missionaries' relationships with the crewmen.

They quickly learned that this foreign and frightening world was ruled almost entirely by the weather. On the second day out, when they had barely lost sight of land, "The weather became stormy," Betsey Stockton wrote, "and the sea-sickness commenced." So it went for four days, with conditions "still squally, and our family still in bad health," too sick and shaken to organize on-deck Sabbath services, most of the missionaries spending time leaning over the leeward side of the ship.[36]

It was no better down below. "The cabin presented a truly gloomy & desolate aspect," Charles Stewart wrote, and his part of it must have seemed especially so. Stewart was the only member of the missionary family not to become seasick, but his wife, Harriet, suffered enough for both of them. At departure she was around five months pregnant, making her especially vulnerable to the pitching of the ship. Without mentioning anything so delicate as her pregnancy, Charles Stewart wrote that she was "very ill but not the least affected by fear." Stewart himself did fear for her, though, wondering about his responsibility for putting her in danger: "Could it have been my duty thus to expose one so delicate & tender, so unaccustomed to fatigue & hardship? All human within me says no!" But he took heart in the help Betsey Stockton would give: "She proves herself more and more the kind affectionate & faithfull attendant . . . assiduous & thoughtful in every kindness since Harriet has been sick."[37] Harriet would remain weakened for the rest of the trip, and Betsey Stockton would serve as her near-constant caretaker.

For all the early suffering, though, Stockton could still delight in the new world of the ocean. In the midst of the first storm, when she was "so weak that I was almost unable to help myself," she managed to get herself onto the deck to behold the power of the wind and water in its fullest: "the scene that presented itself was, to me, the most sublime that I ever witnessed." Her use of the term "sublime" might have been formulaic, a product of her learning, and she struggled to find fresh words for the wonders she saw. "Just as the sun was setting," she wrote one evening, "we were called to witness one of the most sublime scenes that ever the eyes of mortals beheld—no language could paint it." Another time, she admitted that "If it were in my power I would like to describe the Phosphorescence of the sea," and she turned to her intellectual background to express the difficulty: "But to do this would require the pen of a Milton, and he, I think, would fail, were he to attempt it." Using her own pen, Stockton found a suitable image: "I never saw any display of Fireworks that equaled it for beauty . . . it appeared one sheet of fire, and exhibited figures of which you can form no idea."[38] Throughout the five months of the voyage, she never lost her appreciation for the grandeur of the sea, and she kept seeking the voice to express it:

> I stayed on deck one evening until 12 o'clock, looking at the waves breaking over the ship: it was one of the most beautiful sights I ever beheld. The water would foam up like mountains of snow around us, and break over the deck; while below it sounded like thunder, or like rivers running over us. I could compare our sailing when going before the wind to nothing but flying.[39]

But such moments would be only episodic; far more frequent and immediate were the details of daily life—sleeping, eating, and being part of the shipboard community. Betsey Stockton found that sleeping could be an adventure all its own, especially when the ship pitched in rough weather. "As my birth was abaft the beam," she wrote, using newly acquired nautical language, "whenever my head went to leeward and my feet to windward, which was the case every five minutes, it made me very sick." Captain Clasby arranged a hammock over the table in the missionaries' cabin, and Stockton tried sleeping in that—but without much luck. On the second night, the ship rolled, and she was "thrown back and forth as fast as I could go," until a bed fell down and hit a corner of her hammock, throwing her "first up against the ceiling and then on the dining table." When her fellow missionaries determined she was all right, they started "laughing heartily behind their curtains," and once she got settled again, she could laugh at the situation herself: "It was fine sport for them and the captain, for a few days."[40]

Beyond being the temporary butt of shipboard humor, Stockton had a larger identity within the missionary community, taking her place at the table in that most communal of activities, daily meals. Like sleeping, eating could be a challenge on board a rolling ship. "Our table makes a curious appearance," Stockton wrote. "It is spread over with frames; every plate, dish, and cup, is fastened; and even thus we cannot get a meal, at times, without holding with one hand, while helping ourselves to eat with the other." The ship's cook, she noted, "is a dirty man, and we are obliged to eat without asking questions." On at least one occasion, the missionary women took it upon themselves to cook. "As this is the day set part in Massachusetts for public thanksgiving," Levi Chamberlain wrote, "the sisters concluded that they would have a thanksgiving dinner & supper . . . [and] accordingly made some apple pies & a pudding, and prepared a chicken pie for supper, which was baked and brought on to the table in very fine stile." As the trip progressed, the food was decent if not altogether fresh, made from the missionary provisions that included, as Louisa Ely listed, "Beef, Pork, Hams, Butter, Cheese, Lard . . . preserves and dried fruit," along with flour for baking fresh bread and biscuits. The water the missionaries brought aboard soon became brackish, so they "brewed a barrel of beer once in three days for most of the time." Occasionally, someone would catch something from the ocean, perhaps black fish ("The flesh is very much like beef," Stockton observed, "and the liver like a hog's"), flying fish ("a delicious flavour, . . . equal to any fresh water fish I ever tasted"), shark ("flesh . . . very good when young"), or bonetta ("a very pleasant taste").[41]

But for Betsey Stockton, the company mattered as much as the cuisine. She and the other missionaries ate with the ship's officers at two tables, arranged to reflect the hierarchy of the officers and perhaps that of the missionaries themselves: "at the first, the captain and one of the mates, with nine of the missionaries . . . [at]

the second, two mates, three of the missionaries, the four natives and myself." If she had been relegated to the presumably "lesser" table, she didn't complain. She ate in the same space with the captain, which was more than common crewmen could say, and she got equal servings: "The provisions at both tables are alike," she noted, adding that "Mr. and Mrs. S. give me always a share with them. The last apple and orange were cut in three pieces, and divided between us." Stockton much appreciated the gesture: "The impression that such little things make on my mind will not easily be erased."[42]

Stockton's strong feelings for the Stewarts appear repeatedly throughout her journal—"I am becoming more and more attached to Mr. and Mrs. S," she wrote after eleven weeks at sea, and "I have learned to love them" four weeks later—but she had much less to say about the other missionaries. She typically referred to them in the collective, as "our family," occasionally singling out preachers who led Sabbath services. Of the "four natives," she mentioned only two by name, Stephen, "the Tahitean youth," and Cooperee, "a diverting fellow." Otherwise, she seemed to take the missionaries more or less for granted, as family members often do.[43]

Charles Stewart took more time to write about the "South Sea Islanders now on board with us," offering brief individual descriptions, apparently written in descending order of their interest to him and probable usefulness to the mission effort. Stephen Popohe, a native of the Society Islands, or Tahiti, started life as "an ignorant lad born & brought up in all the darkness & superstition of an idolatrous nation," but he had become a Christian convert at Cornwall. Stewart transcribed his conversion narrative in seven pages, adding his own estimation of Popohe as a "serious dignified & noble-looking man . . . of true refinement and is a very interesting character." The "next most interesting of the four youth" was William Krimoola (Kummooolah), an "intelligent & amiable young man" who "speaks our language more fluently than any of them" and "could be taken for a mulatto by anyone ignorant of his birth." Stewart all but dismissed the other two. He considered Richard Knoula (Kriouloo) "in most respects inferior" to the first two, and while he acknowledged the oldest member of the group, Cooperee ("about fifty"), to be "a good natured & kind creature" and a "real convert," he noted that he "is not in reality attached to the Mission." On the whole, though, Stewart found the four "encouraging specimens of the people to who we are hastening." Best of all, he concluded, "There is nothing savage in their nature."[44]

MISSIONARIES TO THE MARINERS

If the Pacific Islanders in the missionary family seemed safe enough, the young New England crewmen of the *Thames* seemed quite another matter. The missionaries interacted with them all the time, often trying to win them over spiritually. Doing so would be difficult, giving Betsey Stockton and her colleagues a foretaste of the challenges of conversion they would face in the islands.

In the early going, the best the missionaries could expect was a measure of religious toleration. Stockton took heart when some of the men came to services: "the sailors appear to treat the missionaries with respect." Charles Stewart likewise seemed reasonably pleased by the "respectful & interested attention" of some of the mariners. Levi Chamberlain agreed, appreciative that "the crew are so orderly & to so great a degree disposed to attend upon our religious exercises."[45]

But Chamberlain wanted to do more: "May our intercourse & acquaintance with the officers & crew of this Ship be the occasion of everlasting good to their souls." To promote that good, Chamberlain became assertive. He complained to the crewmen about attending to their own immediate needs on Sunday: "it is a practice for sea-men to wash and mend their clothes on the Sabbath," he noted, "though there is no necessity for it." When he reminded them about the Fourth Commandment—"Remember the Sabbath day, to keep it holy"—the sailors responded simply that "they have no other time to do it and that it is work that must be done." Chamberlain resolved to pray for the sailors, and his prayers seemed to be answered:

two Sundays later, he wrote with some satisfaction that "I believe there is now no washing done on the Sabbath."[46]

In the third week of the voyage, Chamberlain went a step further, going into the forecastle to solicit "several of the sailors proposing to them to join a bible class." Two weeks later, though, when he "went among the sailors in the steerage & forecastle in order to hear them answer their Bible questions," he came away in frustration: "There were none in the forecastle that had given attention to their questions." Like a teacher grinding through a dull and unresponsive class, "I read the Chapter from which they were to have been answered and gave them myself." Later forays into the forecastle yielded much the same result. One crewman essentially told Chamberlain to quit nagging him about reading his Bible: "I read it when I please but do not want any of your assistance," the sailor insisted, "I have told you before that I do not wish to have anything said to me about these things."[47] The crewmen likewise resisted hearing about the more severe forms of Christian doctrine, particularly eternal damnation. One raised "objections against several doctrines in the Bible," Chamberlain wrote, but the mariner refused to believe "that any would be eternally miserable." So it went with others. The ship's blacksmith "appears very stupid & seems to have some doubts as to the reality of endless punishment." Chamberlain was a bit more charitable to the third mate, who "is not entirely destitute of serious thoughts" and "acknowledged that he was not prepared for death." But Chamberlain later noted that the mate also pushed back about the price he might have to pay in eternity: "Does not think his sins are sufficiently numerous & atrocious to deserve endless punishment."[48] These mariners were no theologians, but they apparently shared a similar skepticism about the alleged afflictions of the afterlife. They may well have assumed that their seemingly endless isolation on the ocean was punishment enough.

Of all the crewmen on the *Thames*, one got the most missionary attention—Charles Ramsdell, a nineteen-year-old boat-steerer and harpooner. Charles Stewart wrote in his journal that Ramsdell "is very youthful in his looks & perhaps the most active & interesting of the Sailors." Stewart knew, in fact, that Ramsdell's background was much more than merely "interesting." Ramsdell had come to the *Thames* after an ill-fated voyage aboard the whale ship *Essex*, whose grisly history had already gained notoriety. The widely read *Narrative of the Most Extraordinary and Distressing Shipwreck of the Whale-Ship* Essex (1821), written by one of Ramsdell's shipmates, told the tale. Far out in the Pacific on November 20, 1820, the crewmen of the *Essex* lowered their whale boats to pursue a pod of sperm whales. Quite surprisingly, one of the whales attacked them, ramming the *Essex* with its huge head, then diving and coming back to ram again, finally sinking the ship and forcing the crewmen to take to the sea in three small whale boats. What followed was a sickening story of human suffering, starvation, death—and cannibalism. After drifting in the ocean for well over two months and eating the flesh of their shipmates as, one by one, they died, the last four survivors in Ramsdell's boat drew lots to see who would next be killed and eaten. A young cabin boy named Coffin drew death; it fell to Ramsdell to shoot him. And so Ramsdell survived.[49]

In the end, Ramsdell was rescued, went back to Nantucket, and then, perhaps amazingly, decided to go to sea again, on the *Thames*. One might only imagine the foreboding in Ramsdell's mind, but whaling was what he did, and life on the *Thames* could hardly be worse than it had turned out on the *Essex*. Given the many superstitions of sailors, one might also imagine the uneasiness of his fellow crew members, perhaps suspecting that Ramsdell could bring a burden of bad luck. But Ramsdell had the courage to come back for another voyage, and his new mates had to respect that. If nothing else, they also had to figure the odds would be pretty slim for one man to be on a ship stove in by a whale two times in a row.

Both Stewart and Levi Chamberlain focused special attention on Ramsdell, no doubt suspecting that his horrific experience on the *Essex* could make him a promising person for spiritual pursuit on the *Thames*, and that the conversion of this "most active & interesting of the Sailors" might be the key to reaching the rest of the crew. It would be difficult, though. Ramsdell didn't seem inclined to repent his sins. "O how hard is the human heart," Stewart wrote, "how blind the unconverted mind."[50] But the heart could be softened, the mind made to see.

Gradually, the missionaries seemed to get through to him. One night in late January, after the *Thames* had been at sea for just over two months, Stewart stood alone, he thought, on the darkened quarterdeck, when he felt something touch his arm. It was Ramsdell, who "had stolen from his station forward, to say that his spirit, like the troubled sea, could find no rest. . . . His words were few, but his look, while he trembled under his guilt . . . spoke volumes." Since the previous Sunday, Ramsdell had scarcely eaten or slept: "Everything, in his appearance, manifested sincerity and contrition." Ramsdell even began to counsel his shipmates about religious matters, explaining to one that the true path to salvation "is not *knocking off swearing, and drinking, and such like*; and, it is *not reading the Bible—nor praying—nor being good* . . . it is forsaking your sins, and looking for their pardon and the salvation of your soul." Stewart approved, writing that "A doctor of divinity might have given . . . a more technical and polished answer, but not one more simple or, probably, satisfactory." But although Ramsdell had become willing to forsake sin, he would not forsake his shipmates: "Religion, he thinks to be a good thing," Chamberlain reported, "but when urged to attend to it, says he finds in himself an unwillingness to renounce his companions, who are opposed to religion."[51]

Betsey Stockton likewise took note of the spiritual condition of the crewmen, but unlike the male missionaries, she had to constrain her conversion efforts. As the only single woman aboard the ship, she had to be especially careful about her personal relationships with the men; she certainly did not go down into the filthy forecastle for Bible study. Yet Stockton did see mixed signs of spiritual and behavioral change. "The Spirit of the Lord has, I trust, been striving with some of the sailors," she wrote in early February 1823, "though many are yet, I fear, in the gall of bitterness." In late March, she shared the general disappointment among the missionaries about the poor turnout for religious services: "There was not many of the sailors present. Satan is very much out of humour; he is either losing, or securing, some of the people on board." Still, she could take comfort in seeing a welcome change in the sailors' language when they took to their boats to go after whales: "Four months ago, these boats would not have been lowered without having our ears assailed with oaths," she wrote. "Now not a profane word is heard."[52] For Betsey Stockton, even modest improvements might be taken as signs of success.

In turn, the mariners had their own standards for determining the worth of the missionaries, and Stockton gained their respect with her fortitude. During a period of especially rough seas—"tossing and rolling," she wrote, "snow, hail, rain and one continued gale"—everyone suffered from the wet and the wind. Still, she made her way up to the deck one night, "when the ship was laying too [*sic*], under nothing but a close-reefed top-sail," and the men took note of her courage. "The sailors were always pleased to see me on deck in a storm, and tried more than once to frighten me; but when they found that they did not succeed, they ended with saying, 'well Betsey, you'll know how to pity poor sailors.'"[53] By sharing their suffering, Stockton proved herself worthy of their esteem.

Equally important, neither she nor any of the other journal-keepers on the *Thames* ever suggested that she had been subjected to sexual harassment or abuse. The closest she came to that, along with the six other women, was the salacious innuendo inherent in the traditional equator-crossing ceremony, a ritual hazing for all the sailors who had never crossed the line before. "In the evening, old Neptune visited us," Stockton wrote on January 4, "His appearance was the most ludicrous thing I ever saw in my life." The crew's initiates "were all put down in the forecastle, and afterwards brought up, one at a time, before his majesty, with their eyes covered." Each one was subjected to a slushy "shave" with a wooden "razor," then dunked in a tub of water, then splashed with a bucket of water in his face. But "Neptune" then "told the mission family, that as there were so many ladies on board, he had thought it expedient to bring his wife with him"—another sailor dressed as a woman—"but said he thought it not best for her to shake hands with them, as she had been handling so many of her dirty boys." As a sly concession to female sensibilities, Neptune said he would not "shave any one farther aft, among the ladies," if they would give him "some Spirits and Cakes." And thus Betsey Stockton recorded the crossing ceremony, with one final comment: "The manner in which they shave is very disgusting."[54]

DARK IN MIND

Two days after the Neptune ceremony, the *Thames* encountered an even more disgusting aspect of oceanic life—a slave ship. At 11 a.m. on January 6, 1823, a small brig appeared in the distance, soon coming close by so that, Charles Stewart wrote, "we knew she was waiting to speak us." As it happened, the captain of the ship was Portuguese and could not speak English, but one of his crewmen knew enough English to tell the *Thames* that his ship was bound for the west coast of Africa. "The moment her destination was known," Stewart continued, "a shade of sadness crossed the countenance of our company . . . for the horrors of a slave ship rose in our imagination . . . and filled our hearts with gloom. It seemed, as if the sighing of the captive & groaning of the oppressed, could be heard already from her hatchways." Stewart himself let out a "sigh over the depravity of man" that would continue such an unconscionable business: "Surely if anything on earth calls loudly for the righteous judgments of God, it is the prosecution of the slave trade."[55]

Betsey Stockton, the only once-enslaved person on the *Thames*, surely saw the slave ship. But her journal made no reference to the encounter: "Nothing new to-day," her entry began, "All going in good order." Stockton's silence seems surprising, certainly in comparison to Stewart's expressions of anguish, but it may have stemmed from her circumstances as a journal-keeper. Perhaps she avoided the issue in order not to create an awkward situation for Ashbel Green, her former slaveholder and now intended editor. Perhaps she assumed that Stewart would be a better, maybe more compelling, source for the account. Or perhaps the sighting of a slave ship elicited feelings of fright too painful for her to put into words.[56]

All was not in good order, however. Stockton's journal entry continued on a somber note: "I find my mind still dark; and do not feel quite happy."[57] The phrase "still dark" put her mental state into a longer-term context. Stockton had long before fallen into low spirits, and she had become engaged in a battle between hope and despair that would never be fully resolved during the voyage. In the early going, Stockton had to face her own fears. On the third day out, when "at daybreak shipped a sea," she committed herself to a divinely determined fate. "The day was spent in self-examination," she said, adding that "This, if ever, is the time to try my motives in leaving my native land." She had no desire "to perish so near my friends," but she "soon became composed, and resigned to whatever should be the will of my Heavenly Father." The process of self-examination would continue, doubts would repeatedly darken her spirits, and the composure of resigning herself to divine will would prove to be fleeting. Celebrating Christmas on the ship—"How unlike the last!"—served as a reminder of past years, turning her mind back to America—"could not forbear thinking of my native land." A few days later, on December 30, she wrote that she "enjoyed the Sabbath very much," but "still felt as if I was declining in the spiritual life. I attend a little to the study of the Bible, and find it pleasant. Yet I find a void within my breast that is painful."[58] Her spiritual situation may well have reflected pain of a physical sort. In mid-January, Levi Chamberlain wrote that "Betsey Stockton is quite unwell. She has spit some blood in consequence of straining her stomach a few days since."[59] Her physical ailments would heal in time, but the spiritual ones stayed with her.

Throughout the long journey, she was both included and isolated within the missionary family. Rather than bare her emotions, she put on a brave face ("for the sake of those around me I endeavor to appear cheerful"), sought to shore up her courage ("in the most dangerous situations, I have felt the easiest"), and acknowledged her need to confront both physical and spiritual challenges ("it is necessary, in order to keep me in my place, to have some doubts, some temptations, and some sickness to struggle with"). The struggle never ended, and by late March 1823, four months at sea, she still described herself as "wretched" and "dark in mind."[60]

But then, as the *Thames* neared its destination, her mood suddenly changed. One evening, she wrote, "the dark cloud was removed from my mind, and I felt as peaceful as the ocean with which I was surrounded." She stirred up her resolve, putting darkness and homesickness behind her: "I would not, I could not, I dare not, look with longing eyes toward my native land . . . my hand lies on the plow, and if my poor wretched heart does not deceive me, I would not take it off for all the wealth of America."[61] Betsey Stockton prepared herself for her task in the islands.

She also faced a much more immediate task—caring for Harriet Stewart as her pregnancy came closer to term. On the *Thames*, no one carried a bigger—and ever-bigger—physical burden than Mrs. Stewart, who was repeatedly sick, frequently soaked, and almost always uncertain about what would happen when, or perhaps if, she would deliver her child. As dangerous as childbearing could be in the best of circumstances, the squalid conditions of a shipboard childbirth would likely be worse. But when Harriet Stewart's time came, on the morning of April 11, 1823, the birth went surprisingly well. Betsey Stockton assisted as midwife, and soon "we had our little stranger in our arms, and his mother in a comfortable situation." Captain Clasby hoisted an American flag to ensure that the Stewart child would be as American as possible. But for Stockton, patriotic display mattered far less than personal intimacy. In addition to caring for Harriet Stewart, she now took responsibility caring for this "fine boy, which I consider as my charge," and he had an immediate effect on her: "From the first moment that I saw the little innocent, I felt emotions that I was unacquainted with before." The baby took her away from her worries—"The little fellow beguiles many of my lonely hours"—and she rarely paid attention to anything else. "Most of my time was spent below," she wrote, "and I heard nothing that was passing on deck. . . . I found employment enough to engross all my attention, and nothing occurred worth mentioning."[62]

But two weeks after the birth of the Stewarts' son, something occurred that Stockton found very much worth mentioning: "On the 24th, we saw and made Hawaii (Owhyee)."[63]

ISLANDS IN SIGHT

The *Thames* had been at sea for 154 days, and the last few had been ones of increasing anticipation. When the missionaries awoke on April 24, they fully expected to see the islands, but clouds obscured the horizon all morning, creating a tantalizing illusion of land in the distance. Finally, around three in the afternoon, the clouds lifted, and they first saw actual mountains, which might have been a joyful sight. Instead, arrival evoked spiritual ambivalence. "At the first sight of the snow-capped mountains," Stockton wrote, "I felt a strange sensation of joy and grief." Even the hymn the missionary family sang, "O'er the Gloomy Hills of Darkness," reflected the somber mood. "Literally gloomy hills of darkness," Levi Chamberlain mused as he looked ashore, and Louisa Ely echoed the feeling: "With peculiar emotions do I behold this dark region where its miserable inhabitants have so long been enveloped in darkness."[64]

Yet however dark they saw the region, however miserable they considered the inhabitants, the missionaries had come for a purpose, and the second stanza of the hymn they sang reminded them of their task:

> Let the Indian, let the Negro
> Let the rude Barbarian see,
> That divine and glorious conquest
> Once obtained on Calvary;
> Let the gospel
> Loud resound from pole to pole.[65]

To the Indian, the Negro, and the Barbarian they would now add the Hawaiian, soon to be the immediate focus of their "divine and glorious conquest."

Before they could go to the Hawaiians, though, the Hawaiians came to them. On April 25, "Two or three canoes, loaded with natives, came to the ship," Stockton reported. Thus began her encounter with the people she and her fellow missionaries had come to save. It did not go well. The missionaries directed their attention, if not their eyes, to one immediate feature: "their appearance was that of half man and half beast," Stockton wrote, "naked—except a narrow strip of *tapa* around their loins." Faced with this shocking sight, the other women "retired to the cabin, and burst into tears, and some of the gentlemen turned pale." Stockton herself found that "my own soul sickened within me," and she trembled at the prospect before her: "Are these, thought I, the beings with whom I must spend the remainder of my life!"[66]

Then, summoning her sense of mission, she reminded herself that "They are men and have souls." She quickly shifted to the work she had come all this way to do.[67]

4

A Missionary's Life Is Very Laborious

THE *THAMES* LAY AT ANCHOR just off O'ahu, rising and falling gently with the rolling of the ocean. In the early hours of Sunday, April 27, 1823, the missionaries were still aboard, looking out to the islands they would soon call home. "At 12 o'clock before morning Woahoo was in full view by moonlight," Levi Chamberlain wrote, and Charles Stewart could see the "wild and romantic outlines" of the mountains. As dawn began to break, Louisa Ely used the sunrise as a spiritual metaphor: "With the light of this holy morning we find ourselves in view of this spot toward which our eyes have been so long turned[,] the land of darkness where the light of the Sabbath is just beginning to dawn." Betsey Stockton also saw the situation in a new light. Getting over her initial shock at naked native bodies, she took a fresh approach to the people who paddled out to the *Thames*. With the four Pacific Islander members of the missionary family serving as interpreters, "We conversed with them freely . . . [and] gave them old clothes; and in return they gave us all the fish they had caught." The exchange of words and goods helped settle her: "This beginning of missionary labours seemed very encouraging; and in a short time our unpleasant feelings were dissipated."[1]

Two days later, the *Thames* entered the Honolulu harbor, towed by "twenty well manned whale boats," Stewart reported, "whose manoeuvres in passing the narrow channel were exceedingly novel." Once the ship had come closer, "within a stone's throw of the king's house and of the town," the missionaries could better discern other signs of a settled human presence on the shore—the harbor fort, a handful of huts, the two buildings of the missionary enclosure—and on the water, "quite a forest of masts in port . . . the 'star spangled banner' waving from the heads of most of them."[2]

Those masts and flags may have been a reassuring sight, but they also symbolized the larger and longer-term economic and political processes that would transform the lives of island inhabitants—and not always in a positive way. The members of the missionary family arrived in the early stages of that transformation, not yet fully able to understand their role in it. Other people soon would. "Not until I visited Honolulu," Herman Melville observed, "was I aware of the fact that the small remnant of the natives had been civilized into draught horses, and evangelized into beasts of burden . . . harnessed to the vehicles of their spiritual instructors like so many dumb brutes!" Mark Twain later echoed that sentiment, writing wryly but also seriously about how the missionary taught the native Hawaiian "what rapture it is to work all day long for fifty cents to buy food for next day with, as compared with fishing for a pastime and lolling in the shade through eternal summer, and eating of the bounty that nobody labored to provide but Nature." More recently, students of Hawaiian history have described the first waves of missionaries as early agents of a broader and deeper Christian imperialism.[3]

Betsey Stockton's work as a missionary and teacher in the islands contributed to the longer-term cultural transformation of Hawai'i, and it's necessary to recognize that. But it's equally necessary to recognize what that work meant for her personal transformation. Most important, she had her first opportunity to carry through on her commitment as a "a pious colored woman, qualified to teach a school," becoming the first among the missionaries to teach not just members of the island elite, but also the ordinary people, or *maka'āinana*. She would not spend the rest of her life teaching *maka'āinana* in Hawai'i, but she would spend the rest of her life as a teacher to Black people back in the United States. In that sense, her stay in the islands became a time not just for teaching, but for learning.

FIRST IMPRESSIONS

With the *Thames* safely moored, most of the missionary family disembarked and moved into the missionary enclosure. Betsey Stockton and the Stewarts waited for almost two more weeks, though, "owing to the state of Mrs. Stewart's health," Stockton explained, "who had been confined two weeks before we arrived," after giving birth. Charles Stewart judged it "most prudent for Harriet to defer removing to a *grass hut* as long as possible." The birth of the Stewarts' son had had a happily positive effect on Stockton's spirits: he "seems to have filled the vacuum in B.'s heart," Charles Stewart observed, "and beguiles her already of the moments which before left an opening for thoughts of sadness."[4]

Stockton and the Stewarts did have several occasions for ship-to-shore social contacts. On the Sunday of their arrival, Captain Clasby had Stewart and two other male missionaries rowed to shore, where Clasby quickly fell in with a group of whaling captains he knew, and the missionaries met some of the English and American missionaries already there. They all came together for morning worship, "with an audience of about 100 foreigners, about 60 of whom were American captains, and mates, and well dressed decent looking seamen." Stewart and the other missionaries received an invitation to visit the royal residence at Waikiki, where "we were very affectionately received and most cordially welcomed by the whole family." There was one notable exception—the king himself, Liholiho, the heir to the recently departed Kamehameha I. "We did not see Riho Riho," Stewart wrote, "and I am sorry to state the reason—he was *dead drunk*, in which state he had been four or five days."[5]

Stewart's initial reactions to Hawaiian royalty were decidedly mixed. A few days after his first visit to the royal residence, he again saw Liholiho, but the situation seemed the same: the king was "much indisposed, being just on the recovery from his drunken frolic . . .

reclining on a couch of black velvet, perfectly naked, except for a few yards of chintz thrown negligently around his waist." Stewart dismissed Liholiho as "stupid, and so much the worse for his debauch, as to be almost disgusting and brutish." Stewart's disgust softened some days later, though, when Liholiho visited the *Thames*, this time sober, well dressed in a blue suit. "He is a noble looking man," Stewart wrote, "perhaps the most so of any on the island. His manners are very easy, and his whole behavior polite and pleasing." Of the women around Liholiho, Stewart had an unwavering estimation of their dignity and decorum. The "queen, *Kamehamaru* [Kamāmalu]," struck Stewart as a "fine looking woman, very tall and large . . . her manners dignified and graceful, and her whole appearance that of a fashionable and *well bred* woman." Then "*Kaamanu* [Ka'ahumanu], the favourite wife of the late king," caught his eye: "To speak candidly, I do not think I ever saw any lady enter a room with more real majesty than she did. Her walk was stately, and look and manner really elegant."[6]

Betsey Stockton had her own opportunity to mingle among the island dignitaries. On the weekend of May 3–4, she accompanied Harriet Stewart to shore to superintend a dinner given by Captain Clasby for the American consul and the ship captains, and the following morning she attended an even more significant event, the baptism of baby Charles. "The chapel was thronged with the grandees of the kingdom, and the officers from the shipping," Stewart reported, and when the queen Kamāmalu saw the Stewart infant, she "immediately took the latter in her arms, and claimed him as her own."[7] Stockton and the queen had something in common.

COMING ASHORE

Soon the *Thames* would depart, and Stockton and the Stewarts would have to leave their quarters. The day before the ship sailed, Charles Stewart preached his first sermon in Hawai'i, "to a large audience, in which I was happy to recognize some of our friends from the *Thames*." Those crewmen had become "seriously impressed with the subject of religion on the voyage," but in the short time they had been in Honolulu, they had "disappeared under the influence of temptation and sin." The next day, they disappeared altogether, sailing away and leaving the missionaries with a painful sense of separation. "I could not help watching her 'lessening sail,'" Stewart wrote, "till she seemed but a speck on the horizon . . . gone most probably forever."[8]

And so the Stewarts and Betsey Stockton found themselves ashore, likewise "most probably forever." They also found themselves in less than commodious accommodations. The main house in the missionary enclosure—"which at home would be called small," Stockton observed—had been essentially prefabricated, with wood measured and cut in Massachusetts, then shipped around Cape Horn to Honolulu, and assembled on-site in 1821. It didn't have sleeping room for everyone, so most of the missionaries occupied small huts on the surrounding grounds. "We had assigned to us a little thatched house in one corner of the yard," Stockton wrote, "consisting of one small room, with a door, and two windows—the door too small to admit a person walking in without stooping, and the windows only large enough for one person to look out at a time." The missionaries came together for meals in the main house. As aboard the *Thames*, Stockton took note of the social arrangements: "The family all eat at the same table, and the ladies attend to the work by turns." Stockton took her turn, and she found value in the time she spent serving the others: "Had I been idle, I should not in all probability have been so happy in my situation as I was."[9]

Stockton kept to the enclosure most of the time, but she ventured away on a few occasions to fetch milk from another compound about two miles away—the home of Anthony Allen, one of the most significant Americans in Hawai'i, and certainly the most notable African American. Allen had first come to Hawai'i as a mariner in 1810 or 1811, and the following year he returned to settle on O'ahu. Up to that point, though, his life had been anything but settled, a "story of wanderings & adventures," as he told it, that took him around the world, eventually to the Pacific and remarkable success. Allen was struck to meet Betsey Stockton in Hawai'i—he "had never before seen a coloured female" in his time in the islands, she said—and she must have been equally struck by the story of how he came to be there.[10]

Anthony Allen had been born into slavery in Schenectady, New York, probably in 1774 or 1775. In May, 1800, he escaped and made his way to Boston, where, like many freedom-seeking Black men, he shipped out as a seaman. Over the next few years, he sailed to the Caribbean, across the Atlantic to France, to the Pacific Northwest, Indonesia, India, and China. After he came to rest, happily and successfully, in Hawai'i, his experience as a cook and steward got him a position working for King Kamehameha I. He also became close to a native high priest, Hewahewa, who gave him six acres of land on O'ahu, "having on it a few cocoanut trees & three small houses or native huts." From that initial holding, Allen expanded his operations, and by the early 1820s, Charles Stewart reported, he had become "quite a respectable man, and has a very neat and comfortable establishment for this country. His enclosure contains near a dozen good mud houses—one for a sitting and sleeping room, one for eating, a store house, kitchen, milk room, blacksmith's shop, &c. &c. and is a favourite resort of the more respectable of the seamen who visit Honoruru. At times his place is quite a hospital, the sick from the ships being generally sent to be boarded and nursed by him." To meet additional needs of visiting seamen and local residents, Allen also had a bowling alley and a grog shop.[11]

Betsey Stockton presumably knew something about Anthony Allen well before she left the United States. As early as the summer of 1821, American newspapers carried accounts of Allen's prosperous circumstances, and perhaps most notably his generosity to the first batch of ABCFM missionaries. Sybil Bingham, the wife of Hiram Bingham, the leader of the initial arrivals, offered a promising profile: "When we arrived at Mr. A's territories," she wrote, "we found him at his gate waiting to give us a polite and cordial reception." She took note of the structures in his enclosure, but she seemed especially impressed with the food available, "a garden of squashes, and in one part a fold containing a cow, several sheep, and three hundred goats." Allen laid a sumptuous spread before the missionaries: "The table was set in the American style: the first course was what we call pot or sea pie," followed by "boiled pig and fowls, cold meat and tarrow-cakes; then baked pig, afterwards pudding, ending with wine and melons." As Mrs. Bingham looked back, she stated the obvious: "This was not missionary fare."[12]

The introduction to Mrs. Bingham's description directed readers to the larger point that underlay the missionary venture: "It shows that the inhabitants of those islands, possessing a productive soil and one of the finest climates on the globe, only need the benefits of civilization and the consolation of religion, to make them independent and happy."[13]

There could be an alternative understanding of Anthony Allen's story. He had become "independent and happy" only after he had escaped the "civilization" that enslaved him, which often relied on the "consolation of religion" to justify human bondage. He suffered hardship and abuse, even the specter of re-enslavement, during his days as a seaman on white-owned ships, but when he arrived in the Sandwich Islands, he did so as a free man with his own hard-earned stake: "I came ashore with my wages which amounted to about 150 doll." He entered a favorable environment, not just in the quality of the soil and the climate, but in the relative racial equality of island society. With the help of the high priest of a very different religious tradition, Anthony Allen found Hawai'i to be his true land of liberty, and he made the most of it: "In 1813 I began to build me small thatched houses."[14] A decade later, when Betsey Stockton encountered him, he provided living proof that a once-enslaved American could become a Hawaiian success story. Perhaps she, in a different way, could too.

MOVING TO LAHAINA

As much as Betsey Stockton enjoyed Anthony Allen, she soon had to leave for a new assignment, the creation of a missionary station on

FIGURE 4.1. View of Lahaina, Maui, from Charles S. Stewart, *Private Journal of a Voyage to the Pacific Ocean, and Residence at the Sandwich Islands, in the Years 1822, 1823, 1824 and 1825* (New York, 1828).

Maui. She and the Stewarts and fellow missionary William Richards departed O'ahu on May 28, 1823, on Liholiho's Massachusetts-built ship, *Cleopatra's Barge*, which the king's mother, Queen Keōpūolani, had arranged for them; three days later, they caught sight of the settlement at Lahaina. "We had not seen a tree that looked green and beautiful since we left home, until we came here," Betsey Stockton wrote, and her companions almost rhapsodized about the view. "The settlement appeared far more beautiful than any place we have yet seen on the islands . . . covered with luxuriant groves, not only of the cocoa-nut . . . but also of the bread-fruit, and of the *ko* [kou], one of the handsomest of ornamental trees. The banana and tapa tree, and the sugar cane, seemed most abundant and flourishing, and extended almost to the beach, on which a fine surf constantly rolls." After six months on a whaling ship and four weeks "on the dreary plain of Honoruru," Lahaina looked like paradise found.[15]

But Lahaina was not a pristine, unpopulated spot. The missionaries estimated that the settlement contained about 400 dwellings, with some 2,500 to 5,000 people living there. One of those residents was Edmund R. Butler, an American who had arrived in the islands in 1813 and, by 1819, had established a good-sized enclosure on Lahaina, with "luxuriant grounds" where "the murmurs of the mountain streams which encircle his yard, and the coolness and verdure of every thing around" welcomed the missionaries. Butler gave them food and shelter and, as Betsey Stockton gratefully explained, "did every thing in his power to make us comfortable." Hawaiian royalty gave them even more important support. Queen Keōpūolani granted them a prime spot of land on the beach for constructing their residence and a church, along with three plots of land for raising fruits and vegetables. Perhaps most encouraging of all, she worshipped with them.[16]

After less than a month in Hawai'i, Charles Stewart had begun to have a very good feeling about the future. "We have been received with open arms by the government and people," and he took special pleasure that the royalty and chiefs seemed intent on throwing off their old religion—"abolishing all visible practices, which had their birth in the ignorance of former days"—and embracing the new one he and his fellow missionaries were bringing them. As the leaders went, Stewart assumed, so would go the people, and so would go their culture: "the *ancient* customs of this people . . . probably will soon be lost forever."[17]

In fact, that process had already begun well before any of the missionaries arrived.

HAWAI'I'S TIME OF TRANSFORMATION

It's unclear when the first Europeans came to Hawai'i, but the arrival of Great Britain's Captain James Cook in 1778 (and his death there in 1779) put the islands decidedly on the map, and certainly on the navigational charts of mariners plying the Pacific. From the mid-1780s onward, the Sandwich Islands, as Cook called them, became an increasingly common stopping place for ships flying a wide variety of flags—British, French, Russian, Dutch, Portuguese, Spanish, and American—to take on fresh water and supplies. They took on Hawaiian people too, women to provide sex while in port, men to supplement the crew for the longer voyage. They brought trade goods, but also an invisible import, disease—tuberculosis, leprosy, mumps, smallpox, and syphilis, among others. As is almost always the case when new pathogens enter formerly isolated places, the death rate among native people proved devastating, the population decline astounding. Estimates for the Hawaiian population before the arrival of Europeans range widely, but a half-million seems reasonable for the mid-eighteenth century; by 1850, the population would decline by up to 90 percent. In the early part of the nineteenth century, the trajectory of death had already become apparent. One American observed that "the introduction of vile diseases by ships touching the islands" has been so rampant that "not even Christianity has been able to stay this infection, whose deadly taint is infused so widely throughout the nation."[18]

What had also become widely infused, though, was the potential for power and profit, largely from sandalwood trees, which grew wild in the uplands. Hawaiians had little use for sandalwood, but people in China did, grinding it into incense for ceremonial use. A low-value commodity grown in one place and sent as a high-value trade good to another made for a surefire business: by the first decades of the nineteenth century, sandalwood gave Hawai'i a central place in the China trade.[19] The question was who would benefit most.

In Hawai'i, the answer was clear: Kamehameha I, who had lately become the single most powerful person in the islands. In the 1790s, he had reached beyond his own realm on the island of Hawai'i to unite four island chiefdoms—Hawai'i, Maui, O'ahu, and Kaua'i—into one, through either military conquest or diplomatic accommodation. He came to be called "King of the Sandwich Islands" in the American press, and he impressed Euro-Americans with his combination of military prowess ("Bonaparte or Peter the Great conjoined in one") and spiritual power (*mana*). Some foreigners figured it would be better to deal with one strong leader rather than with several lesser ones, and they provided him with weapons, ammunition, and other resources to consolidate his authority. As early as 1792, the British captain George Vancouver gave Kamehameha a ship, and by just over a decade later, Kamehameha had bought or built twenty ships, some of them substantial. He outfitted one of them for direct sandalwood trade with China, but he had more success in his relationship with a Boston-based firm, J. and T. H. Perkins, to whom he granted a monopoly on sandalwood exports. Kamehameha had a monopoly of his own on the sandalwood supply, putting a restriction (*kapu*) on which trees could be harvested when, and by which of the lesser chiefs (*ali'i*). By the second decade of the nineteenth century, Kamehameha had not only overpowered his island enemies but had curried favor with foreign friends, expanding his standing as *the* central figure in Hawaiian society.[20] And then, in May 1819, he died.

Kamehameha's death was as dramatic as an earthquake, creating a sudden shift in the cultural landscape. His position as king (*mo'i*) devolved to one his sons, Liholiho, now Kamehameha II, who was in his early twenties, still too young (and often too inebriated) to command the *mana* of his father. Instead, two older adults, Kamehameha's most prominent widow (out of twenty), Ka'ahumanu, and his most trusted counselor, Kālaimoku (called William Pitt) assumed control and navigated Hawai'i through a turbulent period of political, economic, and religious change. In their own ways, these two leaders used their authority to honor Kamehameha's legacy, but also to put his kingdom on a new path to stable relations with the many foreigners—including missionaries—who showed up on their shores.[21]

Kālaimoku took Kamehameha's spot at the center of the sandalwood trade just as the business was booming. Agents representing European and American merchants engaged in a very competitive process of offering attractive trade goods to Hawaiian *ali'i* in exchange for more and more sandalwood, driving both consumer demand and indebtedness. In turn, the *ali'i* drove their common laborers (*maka'āinana*) in the difficult and often dangerous work of cutting the trees and hauling them down from the mountains to load onto the merchant ships. But the *ali'i* were not mere dupes of consumerism. They knew what they wanted in trade goods, and they knew shoddy merchandise when they saw it. Under Kālaimoku's guidance, they banded together to deal with the merchants, insisting on getting the right goods and resisting going too far into individual debt. The sandalwood trade could be a frustrating business on both sides, but while agents and *aliʻi* had their complaints about each other, they also needed each other.[22]

What the merchants didn't need was any intrusion by missionaries, who began to arrive in 1820, right after the death of Kamehameha and just at the beginning of the upsurge of sandalwood exports. American merchants suspected missionaries of warning the *aliʻi* about devious dealings in trade relations, and they resented their intervention. One agent called the missionaries "blood suckers," Protestant parasites who lived an easy, luxurious life while making life difficult for hardworking businessmen like himself.[23]

American missionaries received a more generous welcome from Kaʻahumanu, Kamehameha's formidable widow. She combined an imposing personal presence with a keen political sense to make herself coruler, or *kuhina nui*, as the power behind—or beside—Liholiho's throne. It was she who announced that Liholiho would be Kamehameha II, the successor to his father. It was she who pushed him to break one of the most significant cultural customs in Hawaiian life, *ʻai kapu*, the long-standing rules regarding the preparation and eating of food, which kept men and women apart at meals and, more broadly, defined gender relationships. When Liholiho agreed, after some initial resistance, to eat a meal with Keōpūolani, another of Kamehameha's many wives, he defied not only custom, but the gods. Liholiho's break with tradition spread quickly throughout the islands, leading to the widespread destruction of idols and temples and undoing the authority of the priests (*kāhuna*). In a short time, a remarkable religious and political transformation swept the islands, and the cultural landscape of Hawaiʻi was suddenly in flux, with old customs discarded and new ones not yet fully in place.[24]

And that was the landscape the first ABCFM missionaries entered in 1820. None of the recent change was of their doing, but it prepared the ground for their work. They in turn prepared the ground for the ABCFM reinforcements who came three years later: Betsey Stockton, Charles Stewart, and their fellow missionaries.

ROYALTY AND RELIGION

The missionary station at Lahaina appeared to get off to a charmed start. On June 29, 1823, Betsey Stockton described an open-air worship service that "would have done an American's heart good to have witnessed," with Liholiho himself in attendance along with two of his queens and his entourage of lesser officials. When Liholiho had come ashore a few days earlier, Stockton could see that he was on one of his alcohol-fueled "frolics." She tried to be kind. "In his manners he is quite a gentleman," she reported, and took heart in his learning: "He reads and writes well." Still, "We regret very much that he is given to drink." On the morning of the Sabbath service, though, Liholiho seemed to be in better shape. He and some of his "principal persons" joined the missionaries in sitting on a sofa and several chairs set up on a mat under a big tree on the beach, while "kanakas, or lower class of people, sat on the ground in rows." As a refreshing ocean breeze blew in, one of the ministers, William Richards, delivered a sermon that seemed less sunny than the setting: "It is appointed unto all men once to die, and after death the judgment." As the interpreter, Honoru, passed the words on to the native people in attendance, "the audience all appeared very solemn." After the service, though, the mood lightened, and Liholiho's "favourite queen," Kamāmalu, asked Betsey Stockton to sit on the sofa with her, and they tried to talk as best they could, "although I could say but few words which she could understand."[25] Still, the Sabbath encounter symbolized a beginning of both conversation and conversion, and Betsey Stockton's place on the sofa next to the queen represented the emerging relationship between the missionary reinforcements and Hawaiian royalty.

Charles Stewart certainly understood the importance of that relationship, and he wrote a detailed description of "the relation of various characters, offices, &c, &c." He made a distinction between the small number of high chiefs, "with whom all the power and influence in the nation rests," and the more numerous "*small* or petty chiefs," who derived considerable wealth from land and the sandalwood trade, but who remained "inferior to the above in rank and consequence, as an English baronet is, to a royal duke, or noble earl or marquis." Having established this basic pecking order of the Hawaiian "*peerage*," as he put it, Stewart underscored his estimation of their shared superiority in island society. "Indeed they seem in size and stature to be almost a distinct race," he wrote, "all very large, and generally very corpulent," easily "distinguished by their walk, look, manner, &c." with a "consciousness of natural superiority and the pride of adventitious distinction, imbibed and nourished from their earliest infancy."[26]

Stewart paid special attention to the three people he deemed most superior of all. He rightly perceived the power dynamic between Ka'ahumanu and Kālaimoku, the designated guardians of Liholiho, who "have unlimited influence throughout the islands," and "perhaps happily for the king and nation, keep a good balance of power." He likewise took note of Keōpūolani, another wife of Kamehameha and mother of Liholiho, who was "the last lineal descendant of the ancient line of kings, and boasts the unmingled blood of royalty immemorial," making her "the highest chief in the nation" and having "no equal."[27]

Keōpūolani had no equal in another regard. On September 16, 1823, less than four months after the reinforcement missionaries moved to Lahaina, she died—but died a Christian convert, baptized at the last moment. Stewart understood the importance of her passing in the larger missionary effort, and he and William Richards coauthored an extended description of her last days for publication in the United States. "Of Keopuolani's kindness we cannot speak too highly," they wrote, noting the welcome she provided to the newly arrived missionaries. But they focused most on the development of her spiritual condition, recalling how she "took a very decided stand against immorality," even though doing so occasioned opposition and derision from other chiefs, and how she "always listened with attention to the preaching of the Gospel [and] made frequent and very interesting inquiries respecting the future state, and the way of salvation through Jesus Christ." And when she died, she became a model convert, giving the missionaries a means of influencing other chiefs, "urging upon them the importance of living like Keopuolani, that they might die like her." What Ōpūkahaʻia had meant in the American context, Keōpūolani would mean in the Hawaiian—a celebrated figure whose death gave life to the missionary message. As Stewart and Richards put it, "notwithstanding the greatness of our loss, we still feel that a victory is won."[28]

Yet whatever Christian comfort the missionaries took from the redemptive circumstances of Keōpoūlani's death, they found very disturbing the reactions of ordinary people to her passing. As word of her dying spread in a "universal alarm," Stewart wrote, her subjects reverted to "former and immemorial customs . . . with all kinds of extravagance, violence and abomination." Stewart expressed shock at the "personal outrages; not only by tearing off their clothes entirely, but by knocking out their eyes and teeth, with clubs and stones, and pulling out their hair, and by burning and cutting their flesh—while drunkenness, riot, and every species of debauchery continued to be indulged in for days."[29]

Stewart's dismay at such expressions of grief only underscored his negative estimation of ordinary Hawaiians. In his first missive after his arrival, in May 1823, he described the *makaʻāinana* as "uncivilized heathen, who are living not only in all the simplicity, but in all the *vulgarity* of untutored nature." Stewart saw them as "indeed a wretched people, for they are not only subject to a total blindness of heart and mind, but to the most abject poverty and privation. . . . Their only birthright is *slavery*." He had come, of course, to convert them to the form of freedom he believed in, and he had to remind himself of his Christian commitment, even as he admitted its limits: "whilst I sincerely say that in them 'I see much that I love, and more that I admire,' I must in candour add, 'and much (if not all) that I *abhor*.'"[30] Thus he undertook his mission work with ethnocentric and status-based assumptions, impressed by the powerful few, but discouraged by, even disdainful of, ordinary folk.

Betsey Stockton shared some of that sentiment herself. She at first found the *makaʻāinana* "a very pleasant people," although a bit disappointing in their personal hygiene and culinary habits, "much dirtier than I expected to find them. They eat baked dogs, raw fish." By December 1823, things seemed somewhat less pleasant. She could say that she still liked the islands "*pretty well*," but "I do not admire them for their society," which consisted of "drunken foreigners," mostly from England and the United States, and "yelling natives," using a language that struck her as "the most rude, and shall I say heathenish, that I ever heard."[31] Yet it was the language she would have to learn to use herself to do her duty as a missionary, and in time, she did.

EARLY LABORS ON LAHAINA

In her first letter to Ashbel Green after her arrival in Hawaiʻi, Stockton wrote that "A missionary's life is very laborious." Her labors, in fact, would keep her from writing more often. She initially apologized to Green for sending just a small portion of her journal, which she had to hurry to get onto an outgoing ship: "It is all I have copied. I am ashamed of it." In time, she apparently curtailed her journal-keeping altogether. "What I shall say to you respecting my journal I know not," she later explained. "Perhaps I am guilty of neglect—and perhaps not. During the first six months after we came here, I was pretty much engaged with the domestick cares of our family and had but little time to write and but little matter to write about . . . and find but little that is fit to send you." She admitted that by not keeping up her writing, "I have disobeyed one of your parting commands," but she assumed that Green could follow the doings of the mission in the official ABCFM journal Charles Stewart kept, "which would be much more interesting than any thing I could say."[32] In any event, she had work to do.

Some of that work involved responding to another of Green's

requests, that the missionaries send back information "relative to natural history, languages and customs, in heathen lands." Charles Stewart wrote most extensively about languages and customs and such, but Betsey Stockton became the main collector of natural history specimens and cultural artifacts. "Handsome shells are not very abundant here," she told Green, but "coral we have in great quantities, and some of the specimens are very beautiful." Lizards were also abundant and colorful, and "They often fall on our table, and run over our beds . . . I am one of their avowed enemies, and murder them whenever I can." She also noted, somewhat resignedly, the "lice and fleas of superior quality and quantity; cockroaches and ants without number—and all these belong to our household." Leaving the insects aside, Stockton gathered what specimens she could and sent a trunkful to Green by a mate on a whale ship, "a coloured man, who promised to present them to you himself if nothing prevented." When the trunk arrived safely, Green happily explored its contents, "shells, lava, coral, and a ring, apparently made of the tooth of an animal . . . and various other manufactures of the natives . . . several pieces of Tapa, or native cloth, variously and very handsomely coloured."[33] Betsey Stockton had done her duty in the name of science.

But specimen collecting was only a short-term sideline to her primary charge from the ABCFM, "to teach a school, and to take charge of domestick concerns." Working at those domestic concerns with the Stewarts took up much of Stockton's time, but the line between labor and love had become blurred, even nonexistent. That became particularly true of Harriet, with whom Stockton was forming a deep friendship. While almost all the missionaries, including Stockton herself, would suffer from sickness from time to time, Harriet Stewart's health problems would become especially serious, and Stockton repeatedly served as her nurse. She praised Harriet's courage and emotional balance—"She is neither elated in prosperity, nor depressed in adversity"—and declared that Charles Stewart was lucky to have a wife like her, "the best gift heaven could bestow on every missionary." Their infant son had been a gift too, and he became Stockton's to share: "little Charles I dote upon." The friendship Betsey Stockton forged with the Stewarts became a central commitment that endured throughout her adult life. "To me they have always been tender and kind," she wrote at the end of 1823, "and although I am far from all my other earthly friends, yet nothing would tempt me to leave them." In a sense, she never would.[34]

"I HAVE NOW A FINE SCHOOL"

Neither would she ever leave her commitment to teaching. She got her start at the end of June 1823, when "one of the king's boys came to the house, desiring to be instructed in English." Charles Stewart thought it wise that she get to work immediately, and so, Stockton wrote, "I collected a proper number and commenced."[35]

At the outset she followed in the footsteps of earlier teachers. The initial batch of ABCFM missionaries, led by Hiram Bingham, had faced the immediate challenge of the language gap that separated them from the island people. Talking through translation was a start, and the three Hawaiian men who had come with the original missionary band were very valuable in that regard. But speaking would not be enough. Bingham and his fellow missionaries were people of print, and they brought with them not just their books and Bibles, but a secondhand printing press and a young man, Elisha Loomis, who was trained as a printer. Teaching Hawaiians to read would be their key communication goal, and the printing press would be their most prized possession.[36]

Literacy had long been one of the main foundations of the Protestant approach to conversion, the means whereby a person could directly encounter the authority of the written word—or written Word, as it were. Members of the clergy would invariably refer to a specific biblical text as a point of departure in their preaching, but they would also assume that their listeners could read (and re-read) the text on their own, the power of print reinforcing the message from the pulpit. Creating that connection between the spoken and written word became especially important to Protestant missionaries dealing with preliterate peoples, whether in the Pacific islands or elsewhere. Print offered a means of supplementing, if not completely subverting, oral-aural communication—a powerful tool of cultural transformation through religious reformation. The missionaries of the seventeenth-century American colonies had embraced a similar approach, creating an alphabet and translating the Bible into Native American tongues, and that provided a promising model.

On January 7, 1822, the first item to issue forth from the missionaries' printing press was a sheet with the Hawaiian alphabet, five vowels and seven consonants, "to assign to every character one certain sound, and thus represent with ease and exactness the true pronunciation of the Hawaiian language," Hiram Bingham explained. But the missionaries looked to a larger agenda: "We commenced printing the language in order to give them letters, libraries, and the living oracles in their own tongue, that the nation might read and understand the wonderful works of God." Other works soon followed, including a fifty-page book of Hawaiian-language hymns ("capable of being sung in the favorite and most approved tunes") and basic texts on spelling and arithmetic ("elementary lessons for learners"). Bingham took pleasure in the sudden demand for print: "From sixty to seventy pupils were at once furnished with copies of the first sheet, as they could not wait until the work was finished. They found the lessons easy. They not only soon mastered them, but were able to teach them to others. In a few months, there were no fewer than five hundred learners."[37]

Bingham also took note of just who the learners were—primarily people in the upper reaches of Hawaiian society—and the reason for reaching out to them first. "To have neglected the rulers, and taught the children of the plebeians . . . would have arrayed prejudice and opposition against us in high places, and thus defeated our cause, or greatly retarded our success." Above all, he explained, "Liholiho requested a hundred copies of the spelling-book in his language to be furnished to his friends and attendants . . . while he would not have the instruction of the people, in general, come in the way of cutting sandalwood to pay his debts." Island leaders did initially seek lessons in literacy primarily for themselves and their immediate circle, and not simply for the religious benefits intended by the missionaries. Spelling and arithmetic became valuable tools in the sandalwood trade, giving *ali'i* better leverage in dealing with devious foreign merchants. More generally, learning to read and write—*palapala*—reinforced the mutually beneficial connection between the missionaries and *ali'i*.[38]

The best indication of that two-way relationship came in April 1824, when no less prominent a person than Ka'ahumanu put herself forward as the first student to show her work at an examination of Lahaina learners; she "spelled the first word, and exhibited her slate with a few sentences written upon it in a good hand, and signed with her name." She also passed the most important test of all: "Kaahumanu, who, at the examination, appeared only as a pupil, now appeared as an authorized teacher and ruler of the people. As such, she recommended to them, to cast off all their *old and evil practices*, and go in the *new and right way*, attend diligently to instruction, and observe the law of God."[39] Thus the most powerful female figure in Hawai'i further enhanced her *mana* in the eyes of her people and, in the process, further enhanced her standing with her missionary teachers.

The embrace of Christian education had begun to create a greater opening for learning on Lahaina. Early in 1824, Charles Stewart and William Richards had begun to sense "new excitement in favor of the *palapala* . . . in the minds of the chiefs and their attendants." The *ali'i* had been working assiduously on their own studies, and "till within a few weeks, they have themselves claimed the exclusive benefit of our instruction." In addition, "Mrs. Richards, Mrs. Stewart, and Betsey Stockton . . . have daily taught" perhaps fifty students from various households. But suddenly things changed, as the *ali'i* wanted more. "The chiefs have lately, for the first time manifested a special desire . . . to have all their subjects enlightened by the *palapala*, and have accordingly made application for books to distribute among them." Such a shift may have seemed puzzling, but it was certainly positive, and the missionaries seized the moment: "we have never, till to-day, had a regular, systematic school," but now they had one in a "neat and spacious house" of one of the chiefs with "25 boys or young men . . . as scholars." Several months later, Ka'ahumanu made the change official, issuing a proclamation that reading and writing ought to be taught to everyone.[40]

Betsey Stockton's initial stint at teaching, in the summer of 1823, had begun with "one of the king's boys" and a small handful of other elites, but in September 1824, she wrote that "I have now a fine school of the *Makeainana*, or lower class of people, the first I believe that has ever been established." Charles Stewart echoed the term—"Betsey Stockton has a fine school among the farmers and their families, held every day at the church." Neither Stockton nor Stewart said anything specific about the curriculum or the mode of instruction, but Stewart did note that Stockton had about thirty students, and that she was "quite familiar with the native tongue," and thus able to engage them in their own language. The initial impetus for the school had apparently come from the *maka'āinana*, "at the request of a respectable number of these, including their wives and children," but its "spirited operation," stemmed from "the superintendence of Betsey Stockton, who from the first took charge of it."[41]

Why Betsey Stockton became the one—and apparently the only one—to take charge of such a school is unclear. It could have been an assignment, reflecting the assumption that a Black woman would be best suited to teaching people in the lower ranks. But Stockton betrayed no note of compulsion, much less resentment. It makes sense to assume that her role stemmed from her own choice, perhaps her own sense of mission. She had long contemplated "taking charge of a day school for coloured children," the youngest members of the lowest rung of American society. Her subsequent contract with the ABCFM had called for her "being employed as a teacher of a school, for which it is hoped that she will be found qualified."[42] Now in Hawai'i, she had become just that.

SICKNESS AND SADNESS

Betsey Stockton's school may have been fine, but just as she started her school for the *maka'āinana*, she seems to have fallen into a notably blue period. She had occasionally suffered from the illness, isolation, and spiritual doubt she had experienced on the *Thames*, but now she felt lower, and for a longer time. On September 15, just two days after the school opened, she wrote to Ashbel Green that "it is much more difficult to keep the spirit alive here than it was at home . . . struggling with the corruptions of our own hearts, and an overflowing torrent of guilt." Her work weighed heavily on her, body and soul, and she undertook her task with a sense of commitment more than optimism: "The heathen are to be converted, I know, and God has put me into the little band he has chosen as instruments. I feel therefore that on me he has conferred a great privilege, but with a woe annexed to it if I am unfaithful." Ashbel Green had recently urged her to keep up her spirits, but she couldn't do so: "My spirits often sink very low," she replied, "and that this is criminal I do not pretend to deny." She knew that the task she had taken on was "great and glorious" and certainly strenuous, demanding "all my faculties of body and mind in its performance." Still, she felt that well-meaning people in the States—including Green himself, no doubt—"cannot judge what are the heaviest trials a missionary is called to bear." It wasn't so much missing physical comforts that saddened her, but being so cut off from the social and spiritual connections of community. "You are fully aware that, however widely separated from you, still the home and friends of my youth hold their place in my heart, and that time and distance only tend to endear them the more to me." But here she was in Hawai'i, living among the *maka'āinana* and the missionaries, and there she expected to die. "The missionary's sorrows and the missionary's joys are mine," she wrote in clear-eyed conclusion. "The missionary's grave, and perhaps the missionary's heaven, will also be mine."[43]

The grim thoughts stayed with her. Just over three months later, on Christmas Day, 1824, she wrote to Levi Chamberlain, now stationed in Honolulu, that "my spirits have been more depressed than at any other period of my life." She could again say that "I have a fine school," noting that nine new students had joined it, adding that "I trust the Lord will bless it to their souls." Her own soul, however, had become full of "wretchedness and woe," the result, she said, of wandering "far from the only source of comfort and life," her religious commitment. "I thought of my remissness in duty, my want of faith and my constant inclination to sin, and the clouds gathered thick and black around me." Part of the darkness came from spiritual isolation, "the want of some Christian friend in whom I could confide." As close as she was with the Stewarts, Charles was often too busy and Harriet sometimes too sick to share the sort of spiritual intimacy she sought. Chamberlain was, like her, an unmarried missionary, and she considered him someone "in whom I could confide," and to whom "I have spoken more freely on the subject of religion than to any other person since I left Amer[ica]."[44]

Like Betsey Stockton, Charles Stewart was being worn down by life in Lahaina. In his official reports, he had to maintain an upbeat tone as much as possible, but in his private journal he could sometimes voice his darker feelings. A few months after getting settled on Lahaina, he wrote about the desolation of the missionary station, where "there is an oppressive sameness in morning, noon, and evening, day and night . . . a deathlike silence, and want of animation in all nature . . . that drowns the spirits and destroys all elasticity of body and mind." Such an enervating environment, he suspected, "would be unsupportable as a permanent abode to every civilized and intelligent being, but a missionary." His work kept him from feeling too lonely, "but the want of all society, except that of our own little family, predisposes us in an unusual degree to frequent recollections of *home*."[45]

Stockton and Stewart and the others eagerly awaited word from home, and when it did not arrive on a particular ship, they could be quite unhappy with the family and friends who had apparently failed them. In her first few months in Lahaina, Betsey Stockton wrote of the pain that came from waiting and hoping: "I often visited the beach to watch for sails," but the ships from America "brought me no letters." As she began to feel lonely and sorry for herself, she also became wary about wallowing in self-indulgence: "Oh may I be taught, to be submissive at all times." Charles Stewart did not pretend to be immune to such disappointment. "We could hardly believe our eyes," he complained to his sister, "when we looked over near *thirty* letters, without recognising one from any place we could call *home*, or from any one dear to us by the ties of *blood*. It cannot be because we are forgotten—*they* will not be *the first* to *neglect us*, and they *ought* not to be *the last to write*." All the missionaries needed, he reminded her, was "a memento of remembrance and affection" to remind them of home.[46]

As much as the missionaries awaited the arrival of ships for mail, they also looked forward to fresh company from the men on those ships, particularly the officers. Incoming captains offered not just news, but shipboard hospitality, with food, drink, and other reminders of a more convivial life. In the first week of April 1824, Stewart reported almost daily on the social scene of the ships anchored at Lahaina. "Capt. Paddack . . . insisted on entertaining us on board the *Hydaspes* to-day," he wrote. "The whole family, Mr. and Mrs. Richards, and William—Mrs. Stewart and Charlie, and Betsey and myself, accordingly, dined and took coffee with him, in company with other captains." They visited other ships on other days, and that sociability reminded the missionaries of what they had left behind. "At these seasons we feel almost transported again to the bosom of civilized society," Stewart wrote, "and the change . . . makes us almost forget that we are the exiles of a far distant land." Almost, but when a ship had to sail away, and "while watching the vessel as it has gradually sunk beneath the horizon, we have involuntarily burst into tears." The tears could become bitter as the missionaries turned back to their own situation and charges. Charles Stewart, "beholding nothing beyond our little enclosures, but the vulgarity and wretchedness of heathenism," asked himself the troubling rhetorical question, "Can creatures so miserable—so ignorant—so debased and so polluted, ever be transformed into beings of purity and light?" He stopped himself just in time with the right response: "Lord thou knowest!" But after less than a year and a half in the islands, he, like Betsey Stockton, sometimes seemed less than fully convinced of the answer.[47]

In addition to their isolation, the missionaries always faced the threat of sickness and death. In December 1823, Betsey Stockton had written that "the health of the family is not so good at present," and by September 1824, she changed the diagnosis only slightly, to "but *so, so*." She could report that "Little Charles" had overcome bouts of sickness and "grows finely" but was still very thin. Other missionary children had not been so fortunate: "Mr. Bishop and Mr. Goodrich have each buried a child on these heathen shores." A report back to the ABCFM noted that "most of the females of the mission suffer materially from debility," with fevers, "dropsical symptoms," and "symptoms of an impaired constitution." The cause of such ill health stemmed less from the warm environment, the report continued, than from the "*severity of their domestic labors and cares*" in supporting the men of the mission and the "*exposures and privations*" women faced in leaky dwellings where the rain came pouring in. For one woman it became too much. Mary Ellis, the wife of William Ellis of the London Missionary Society, had to leave Hawai'i in 1824 because she seemed likely to die otherwise.[48]

Harriet Stewart might be next. In early January 1825, when she was seven months along in her second pregnancy, Charles Stewart wrote that she "was suddenly seized with a fainting fit, which alarmed us for a short time." Young Charlie also fell ill, "seriously affected with symptoms of the croup." In mid-February, the whole family, including Betsey Stockton, left Lahaina for Honolulu, where Charles Stewart had agreed to help out Hiram Bingham. En route they all became seasick, and "Harriet was extremely ill, as were Charlie and Betsey." A few weeks later, on March 7, 1825, Stewart reported that "Harriet is a second time a mother." The good news took a worrisome turn less than twenty-fours later: Harriet "seemingly trod on the borders of the grave . . . seized with a spasmodic affection of the chest—which, though itself of transient duration, apparently left an unfavourable effect on her general health."[49] And so it went through the subsequent months, with recurring concerns about Harriet's declining condition: "I found her, as I thought, evidently worse; she complained of a death-like coldness of her extremities—her pulse were few and feeble, and her eye ghastly and unnatural," Stewart recorded in April. "The last shades of a gloomy month have gathered around me," he wrote in May, "within the last few days an unfavourable change has taken place." By June, Harriet had shown some signs of improvement but still remained weak: "She cannot walk a step alone, but with my assistance, is enabled to take a little exercise, though without gaining much apparent strength by it."[50]

THE *BLONDE*, THE *FAWN*, AND A VOYAGE HOME

Meanwhile, the specter of death fell more broadly over the islands. In March 1825, a whale ship brought word of the passing of Liholiho and his queen, Kamāmalu. The royal couple had voyaged to England the previous year, but after arriving in London in the summer of 1824, both soon came down with the measles and died.[51] The news was both sad and disturbing. "The death of the reigning prince," Elisha Loomis noted, "has generally, if not always, heretofore been followed by a civil war . . . the opportunity for plundering the unfortunate." The work of the missionaries, however, seemed now to lessen the threat: "Great numbers of the people are now engaged in learning to read and there never was a time when the Mission stood so high in their esteem as now." In May, the bodies of the royal couple came back to Hawaiʻi, carried on board a forty-six-gun British frigate, the *Blonde*, commanded by George Anson Lord Byron, cousin of the famous poet. Lord Byron brought them home in two ponderous coffins, "of lead, mahogany, and oak, covered with crimson velvet, and richly studded with gilt nails and ornaments, and weighing together about 2200 lb." As the ship sat in the Honolulu harbor, the chiefs and people assembled at the wharf engaged in an outpouring of grief, "a loud wailing," Loomis wrote, "while the air was rent by their cries." Now, unlike the more extreme-seeming behaviors following the death of Keōpūolani less than two years before, the scene remained comparatively restrained. Byron provided a dignified display of respect at the funeral, with the officers and uniformed marines and the ship's band joining the missionaries and Ka'ahumanu and other members of the Hawaiian royalty in a procession toward a proper Christian burial. At the end of the ceremony, Charles Stewart reported, "part of our funeral hymn was sung . . . aided by the band with happy effect; and a prayer in the native language closed the solemn service."[52]

Byron provided an important service of a different sort for the Stewarts. He agreed to take them from Honolulu, on the assumption that a change of venue would be good for Harriet's health. On June 5, Byron had his men row Charles and Harriet out to the *Blonde*, and then they sailed for Hilo, on the island of Hawai'i, over two hundred miles away. Harriet was still very vulnerable, and the prospect of death still hung over her. Charles Stewart wrote that "the possibility of her not living to return to Oahu, made the separation from her children a severe trial," but she could take some comfort that the children would "receive every kind and affectionate attentions from our faithful friend Betsy, and from the ladies of the station."[53]

Moving from island to island didn't help, though. The *Blonde*'s surgeon determined that Harriet Stewart "ought to be removed to a colder climate, if her strength should be such as to enable her to undertake the voyage," and the missionary doctor, Abraham Blatchley concurred. By the time the *Blonde* sailed away in July, Harriet was still too weak to travel, but another ship and another captain soon came to her rescue. The *Fawn*, a British whaling vessel under Captain Charles Dale, arrived in Honolulu in late September, and Dale, demonstrating "distinguished kindness and liberality," offered the Stewarts free passage to London, with good accommodations and the care of the *Fawn*'s physician en route. The opportunity seemed almost too good to be true.[54]

The timing, however, seemed too bad. During the summer of 1825, the missionary community had become an enlarged target for both merchants and mariners, and Charles Stewart would be leaving right at the time his colleagues were coming under attack, first verbal, and then physical. Ever since ABCFM missionaries had stepped ashore, in 1820, merchants had been hostile to their influence, suspecting that the missionaries' labors would divert *maka'āinana* from their own in providing sandalwood. In June, 1825, the agent of a New England trading firm complained that "At present business is dull and very little prospect of getting wood at present. The chief attention is too much taken up, [with] the missionaries . . . their preaching, praying and schooling." The sex trade also seemed threatened by the missionaries. For years, Hawai'i had been a much-anticipated stopping point for mariners, a place to find not just fresh water and other supplies, but also alcohol and, most welcome of all, women willing to exchange sex for money and other favors. Where missionaries had been shocked to see half-clad women paddling out to their ship, sailors took such a sight almost as a right—and one they would eventually defend with violence.[55]

The assault on the sex trade stemmed from the emerging alliance between the missionaries and many of the *ali'i* Christian converts, who saw the benefit of promoting Protestant moral reform among their people, not to mention putting to an end the unruly behavior of drunken and sex-hungry sailors. In mid-1825, sometime between April and October, the *ali'i* placed a restriction, *kapu*, on the practice of Hawaiian women visiting the ships. Sailors became irate and turned their anger not so much on the island leaders, who had imposed the *kapu*, but against the missionaries, who were assumed to have pushed for it.[56]

One of the most dramatic attacks came at Lahaina during the first two weeks of October, when men from the English whaleship *Daniel IV*, not finding the easy access to sex they expected, confronted William and Clarissa Richards at the mission station, threatening to destroy the house and harm the couple. William protested that he had no hand in enacting the *kapu*, and Clarissa begged compassion from the enraged sailors; still, the couple declared themselves prepared to die for their beliefs. As it happened, local *ali'i* organized an armed guard to protect the Richardses, and thus cowed, the frustrated mariners returned to their ship. Charles Stewart, who had been in Honolulu, rushed to Lahaina for one last emotional meeting with the missionaries and the *ali'i*, and "in the course of an hour, after I had bid a hasty adieu to the chiefs and such of the people best known to me, we sorrowfully interchanged, perhaps, our last embraces in the world."[57]

And with that, it was time to go. Captain Dale and the *Fawn* were preparing to depart Honolulu, and even though Stewart's missionary colleagues said they hated to see him go, they knew that Harriet's life most likely depended on it: "Mr. S. will therefore embark immediately with his family, on board the *Fawn*, and sail for America by way of England, to try the effect of a voyage and colder climate on the health and constitution of his amiable, and truly excellent, but deeply afflicted, wife." They added: "Betsey Stockton returns with him, of course, as attached to his family, having proved herself a faithful assistant."[58]

Over the course of three years, Betsey Stockton had become much more than a "faithful assistant" to the Stewarts. She had become an essential member of the family, a mixed-race woman tied to a white couple first by their common commitment to religion, education, and mission, and not less by the shared experience of sickness. They came to Hawai'i expecting to die there, but the prospect of death came upon them sooner than they had imagined—too soon, as it happened. They now had young children to consider, and all three considered the children theirs. Betsey Stockton had helped bring babies Charles and Harriet into the world, she doted on them, nursed and cared for them, and she did the same for their mother as well.

They sailed away on the *Fawn* on October 17, 1825, and arrived in London in April 1826. They stayed there for a couple of months, where Charles renewed his connection with William Ellis of the London Missionary Society and Betsey Stockton continued to care for Harriet and the children.[59] In June, the Stewarts departed on the London-based ship *Richmond*, heading ultimately for Cooperstown,

New York, where they would live near Harriet's kin. The Cooperstown newspaper, the *Watch-Tower*, had kept tabs on the Stewarts, reprinting part of Charles Stewart's journal, reporting on Harriet's sickness, and finally anticipating their return.[60] They reached New York City on August 4, where the customs manifest listed them together—Charles Stewart, "Clergyman," aged thirty; Harriet Stewart, "Lady," twenty-six; the two toddlers, Charles, three, and Harriet, one; and Betsey Stockton, "Nurse," thirty-one.[61] Her age was probably wrong, and her title barely encompassed all she had done and seen since leaving the United States in November 1822.

In her journal for that time, she had begun her "history of things known only to those who have bid the American shores a long adieu," but now that she was back on American shores, she could hardly bid adieu to her round-the-world travels and her time in the islands. She had experienced physical and spiritual distress, even depression, which would occasionally recur. She had also experienced a remarkable personal transformation. Her missionary labor in Hawai'i had lasted a little over two years, not as long as she had expected, but long enough to matter, both to herself and to the Hawaiian people she encountered. Still in her midtwenties, she came back to America with a much clearer sense of calling, an awareness of what she had done—and what she could do.

5

Philadelphia's First "Coloured Infant School"

IN THE WINTER IN 1828, Betsey Stockton had to make one of her biggest decisions—to stay with the Stewarts in Cooperstown or take a teaching job in Philadelphia. For the first time, as a free unmarried woman around thirty years old, she could contemplate going off on her own, following the calling she had felt since her early twenties. But she also felt the Stewarts were family, people she had lived with and come to love in the same time. Leaving wouldn't be easy.

The Philadelphia offer came in a letter from one Amelia Davidson, secretary of the "Committee for the establishment of a coloured Infants' school in this city," a new educational program for children between the ages of two and five (rather like today's Head Start program), inviting Stockton to become the first "principal of that institution." The committee knew about her from Ashbel Green, living in Philadelphia as editor of the *Christian Advocate*, who had apparently suggested her for the job and said she would be likely to accept it.[1] Green's recommendation alone wasn't all the committee had to consider. Thanks to the publication of Betsey Stockton's journal in his paper, her identity as a pioneering teacher preceded her.

The committee knew more about Stockton than they did about what it would mean to be "principal of that institution," because the institution didn't exist yet. Fund-raising for it had gone more slowly than hoped, and "the committee do not think it prudent to open the school" until they had raised more money. In the meantime, Davidson assured Stockton that the committee "wish you to consider yourself engaged to be their teacher, and be prepared to come as soon as they shall have procured a schoolroom and funds sufficient . . . to commence, of which information will be given you in due time."[2]

And in due time, Davidson did write again, on April 1, telling Stockton that the committee had found a suitable schoolroom, and they had raised enough money so that it could be "fitted up, and all other preparatory arrangements made, in a few weeks." They could also offer Stockton an annual salary of $200, adding the tentative incentive that "should the school increase and find favour with the public, they will have no objection to raising the salary." The committee hoped to open the new school by the first of May, and they urged Stockton to "be here a week or ten days before that time, in order to . . . obtain a complete knowledge of the mode of instruction." To that end, they also wanted her to stop over in New York for a day or two, to see how an infant school already operating there worked.[3] Suddenly, time was short.

DEPARTURE

April became a blur. Stockton had only a few weeks to decide to accept the position and salary, pack her belongings, and share her farewells with Charles and Harriet Stewart and their children. She had been living in very close contact with them for over five years—in the cramped quarters of several ships, in missionary huts in Hawai'i, and finally in their Cooperstown home. The closeness was not just physical, but emotional. Charles Stewart occasionally left town to promote the missionary cause in one city or another, while Betsey and Harriet shared the intimate space of the household, always caring for the children and often for each other. Betsey had helped Harriet back from the brink of death several times already, and Harriet reversed the roles when need be. "Betsey is still with me, and quite well at present," she wrote in March 1827, but "her health during the winter has been poor." Then, in the following winter, Harriet again needed help when she had her third child, Martha, on February 5, 1828. Over the next couple of months, as Betsey Stockton contemplated her commitment to the family and her own future, there would be much talk and more than a few tears in the household—not all of them coming from the baby.[4]

Still, whatever sense of love and obligation she felt for the Stewarts—which was unending, really—she had to be impressed with the job offer. For the first time, she could have her own income and her own position, no longer working in someone else's household as a servant, nurse, or "assistant missionary," teaching *maka'āinana* in the islands. She could now be the lead (perhaps only) teacher in a new and innovative educational program for Black children in Philadelphia, the second-largest city in the United States. In Cooperstown, Betsey Stockton was not the only Black person: around eighty African Americans lived in the vicinity, comprising less than 1 percent of the population.[5] But she knew from her childhood that in Philadelphia the Black population numbered in the thousands and supported their own community institutions.

Becoming head of the "coloured Infants' school" would take her into unknown territory as a teacher, but it would also bring her back to a world she knew—and would come to know even more. On one level, the school represented an enlightened-seeming social experiment with one ostensible purpose, to provide early education to Black children. But even in its own infancy, the infant school movement would reveal deeper racial issues rooted in Philadelphia's past, with conflicting visions of the place of African American education—and of African Americans themselves—in a city where the veneer of educational innovation provided only a thin cover for the uglier underside of a racially conflicted society.

Betsey Stockton probably had few illusions, and she certainly had an opportunity. With no way of fully realizing all that she was getting into, she accepted the job and set out for Philadelphia.

The trip would be far from easy, an enervating series of segments, over ninety miles from Cooperstown to Albany by stagecoach, then down the Hudson River by steamboat to New York. After staying over a day or two, as requested, she could get to Philadelphia via stagecoach, another ninety-plus-mile trip that would take her through Princeton again. The Philadelphia infant school committee had provided fifteen dollars to cover her costs, but since the steamboat fare alone was eight dollars, she probably lost money on the trip.[6]

Comfort and cost were hardly the main issues. Black people traveling on any public conveyance in the North could expect to be subjected to segregation, humiliation, and harassment, usually delivered with racial epithets. Theodore Wright, the first African American graduate of the Princeton Theological Seminary, recounted numerous examples of Black people being denied decent accommodation on Hudson River steamships in the 1820s, sometimes resulting in sickness and death. One of the cases he mentioned specifically concerned "Miss Betsey Stockton, a coloured lady . . . an intelligent and philanthropic woman, who had crossed the ocean to aid in enlightening and converting the heathen." The Hudson trip probably came when she was heading to Cooperstown in August 1826—Wright referred to Stockton's being with a "white gentleman," no doubt Charles Stewart. Yet Stockton "was not permitted a place beneath the deck to lay her head on a damp night. By this exposure, her health was injured and her life endangered."[7]

GASKILL STREET

Whatever challenges she experienced en route, she got to Philadelphia on April 21, 1828, and she would open the doors to her school just ten days later, on May 1. In that span, she had much to do. It's quite likely that she took up residence with Ashbel Green, at least at the outset, because he was a familiar ally. He lived at 150 Pine Street, just off Second Street, not far from the old neighborhood she had known some twenty years earlier, and only a couple of blocks from her new school, at 60 Gaskill Street.[8] The walk would take about ten minutes, but it would take her into a part of the city where the growing concentration of African Americans had begun to define a community. Her school would soon be at the heart of it, a magnet for the area's Black families.

Gaskill Street didn't amount to much on the map, just a very narrow, three-block stretch that went essentially nowhere, running east to west from Second to Fifth Streets, sandwiched between Lombard and Cedar, at the south edge of the city. Yet Gaskill reflected the changing character of the larger neighborhood. During the first decade of the nineteenth century, Gaskill had been mostly white, with only three Black households in 1811. Over the next few years, though, the street became a racially mixed enclave of residents who followed a host of callings, mostly as tradespeople—sawyers, shoemakers, shopkeepers, and the like. By 1816, twenty-four Black households had moved onto the block where the new infant school would be situated. By 1828, Gaskill Street had become increasingly, although not exclusively, African American.[9]

The growth of the Black community around Gaskill Street was part of a larger demographic trend in Philadelphia. Between 1800 and 1830, the African American population more than doubled, from just under 6,500 to over 14,500, hovering between 9 and 10 percent of the city's total population. The pioneering African American social scientist W. E. B. Du Bois later described early nineteenth-century Philadelphia as "the natural gateway between the North and the South," through which came an influx of Black people, free and enslaved alike, from post-Revolutionary Saint-Domingue, the upper South, and parts of the North, particularly neighboring New Jersey. Philadelphia was by no means an altogether welcoming place, but it did offer a large enough critical mass for free Blacks to find a community—or, if need be, for freedom seekers to find a refuge. By the 1820s, the Black population had shifted substantially to the southern end of the city, where the most prominent African American churches—Richard Allen's Bethel AME and Absalom Jones's St. Thomas African Episcopal—provided the neighborhood anchors that supported the creation of additional churches and other community institutions, including schools.[10]

In the 1820s, Gaskill Street already had one school, the Public

Female Coloured School, which was soon joined by two new ones. The first was the Friends-supported Adelphi School, "designed exclusively for the instruction of coloured boys," in 1822. In short order, though, the number of students, "of whom about 80 usually attend the school," quickly overcrowded the space, so that by 1825, Adelphi moved to a new location. Then, in 1828, the infant school committee had found a suitable schoolroom, "large and airy and very well calculated for the purpose," in the same block, perhaps even in the same building. Thus Betsey Stockton's school extended the African American educational presence on Gaskill Street.[11]

Her position also placed her near the top of African American wage earners in the neighborhood—although the top was not at all high. To be sure, a few prominent Black men, such as hairdresser and perfumer Joseph Cassey and sailmaker James Forten—both of whom lived not far from Stockton's school—had become comparatively prosperous, and they stood at the apex of Philadelphia's African American elite. Various sorts of artisans did well enough to be comfortable, but even they represented only a small minority of Black male workers. Most working men labored for about a dollar a day, for however many days they could find work. Wages for Black women were worse, the occupations few—domestic servants, seamstresses, washerwomen—the work uncertain. In March 1829, a committee established by the Philadelphia town meeting to look into women's work issued a grim report, noting that "the wages paid to seamstresses who work in their own apartments, to spoolers, to spinners, to folders of printed books, and in many cases to those who take in washing, are utterly inadequate to their support, even if fully employed." Women who had to care not just for children, but also for their disabled, dissolute, or otherwise unemployable husbands faced more constrained circumstances, while women "unencumbered with families, and with steady employment, cannot average more than a dollar and a quarter per week." The qualifier "with steady employment" proved to be the catch: women were "often unemployed, sometimes for a whole week together, and very frequently one or two days in each week."[12] The report did not distinguish between the situations of white women and Black women, but given the realities of racial inequality, Black women almost certainly suffered from lower and less certain wages.

On the scale of things, Betsey Stockton did much better—for a woman, at any rate. Her starting salary of $200 per year put her within the range of male laborers who worked a full year, and since she was "unencumbered," she had no need to support anyone else. Better still, after only a month on the job, she received a considerable raise, to $250 per year. The committee wrote that "Betsey Stockton has not disappointed the expectations. . . . Considering her capability and the trying nature of her duties, your committee have thought proper to increase her salary." (Stockton's assistant teacher, nineteen-year-old Rebecca Cobb, who had attended the Female Coloured School on Gaskill, had an initial salary of $100 per year, but did not get a raise.) By comparison, the principal of the first white infant school, Ephraim Bacon, started at an annual salary of $500.[13] As always, race and gender made the difference.

"TWENTY-FIVE LADIES"

Race and gender made the difference, in fact, in the fundamental assumptions that governed the creation of Philadelphia's infant schools. In May 1827, the newly formed Infant School Society drew up a written constitution and designated a Board of Managers, consisting of "twenty-five ladies . . . to whom the business of the society was intrusted." Those female managers, all of them white, would provide the day-to-day oversight and take the lead in seeking donor support.[14]

They did a remarkably good job at fund-raising, tapping into their social and familial networks to drum up hundreds of donors. In 1828, they recorded 360 annual subscribers at two dollars per year and 40 life subscribers at twenty dollars, and in the following year, the numbers grew slightly, to 381 and 45, respectively. The 1829 report also listed every donor by name, offering a striking insight into the gender profile of infant school support. The life subscribers divided about evenly, with 23 men and 22 women, but the lesser gifts came overwhelmingly from women—331, or almost 87 percent of the total—48 of them apparently unmarried. The names of the city's social elite—Mrs. Andrew Bayard, Mrs. Nicholas Biddle, Mrs. William Strickland, Mrs. Roberts Vaux, to name a few—stood out, and the bigger picture of female philanthropy seemed impressive. At a time when women, whether married or single, had precious little control over familial financial resources, even a modest contribution could be a significant gift.[15]

The success of the first round of fund-raising, which had initially led to the creation of two infant schools for white children, encouraged the Board of Managers to expand the effort and to reach across racial lines, in hopes of addressing "the degraded state of a great part of the coloured population of our city." Yet this supposed concern went only so far, and their benevolence remained well within the bounds of white society's prevailing racism. The Infant School Society made it explicitly clear that the new institution would be not only racially segregated, but financially segregated as well: this school's funds "were to be kept wholly apart from those collected, or hereafter to be collected, for white children."[16]

The degree of such separate but unequal support became evident. Compared to the four hundred subscribers to the two white schools, the Black school had only twenty-one—two life subscribers and nineteen annual subscribers, "five of whom are persons of colour." The society had also created an additional lower level of subscribers for the Black school, at a dollar a year each, which brought in fifty-nine more donors, fifty-two of them African American.[17] The following year saw an increase to four life subscribers, all of them prominent and progressive white people, and twenty-seven annual subscribers, a few of whom came from families prominent in the African American community—Cassey, Douglass, and Forten. In all, the money collected for the Black infant school came to $658, well below the $1,906 raised for the white schools. But working-class Blacks also continued to make significant in-kind contributions, including labor—"Carpenters' and other work, (gratuitous,) by coloured persons." Most important of all, they put their children into

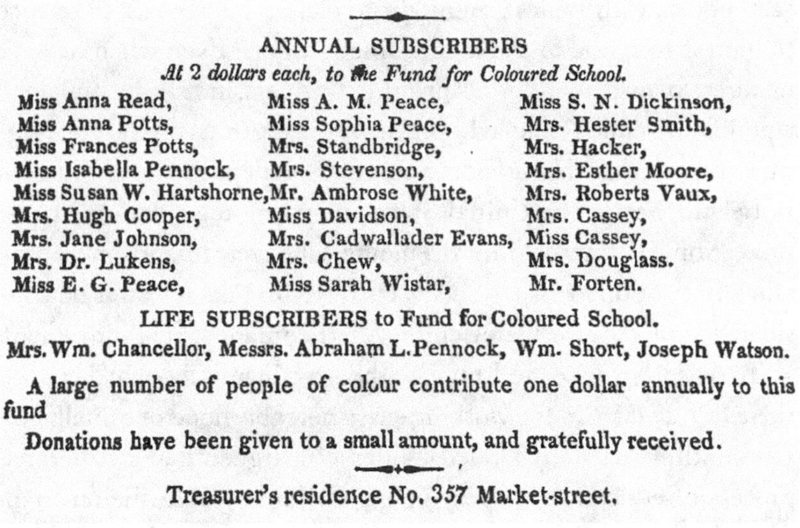

ANNUAL SUBSCRIBERS

At 2 dollars each, to the Fund for Coloured School.

Miss Anna Read,	Miss A. M. Peace,	Miss S. N. Dickinson,
Miss Anna Potts,	Miss Sophia Peace,	Mrs. Hester Smith,
Miss Frances Potts,	Mrs. Standbridge,	Mrs. Hacker,
Miss Isabella Pennock,	Mrs. Stevenson,	Mrs. Esther Moore,
Miss Susan W. Hartshorne,	Mr. Ambrose White,	Mrs. Roberts Vaux,
Mrs. Hugh Cooper,	Miss Davidson,	Mrs. Cassey,
Mrs. Jane Johnson,	Mrs. Cadwallader Evans,	Miss Cassey,
Mrs. Dr. Lukens,	Mrs. Chew,	Mrs. Douglass.
Miss E. G. Peace,	Miss Sarah Wistar,	Mr. Forten.

LIFE SUBSCRIBERS to Fund for Coloured School.

Mrs. Wm. Chancellor, Messrs. Abraham L. Pennock, Wm. Short, Joseph Watson.

A large number of people of colour contribute one dollar annually to this fund

Donations have been given to a small amount, and gratefully received.

Treasurer's residence No. 357 Market-street.

FIGURE 5.1. List of donors to the Fund for Coloured School, *The Second Annual Report of the Infant School Society of Philadelphia* (Philadelphia, 1829).

the school. "People of colour contribute to its support," the society noted with considerable understatement, "and some of the parents manifest an interest in the institution."[18]

Why they did so, however, did not fully reflect the underlying assumptions of the school's creation. In philosophy as in fund-raising, Philadelphia's movement for infant schools manifested a racial divide. The "twenty-five ladies" may have been middle- and upper-class white women, but the most important figure behind Philadelphia's Infant School Society was a white man, Mathew Carey (1760–1839), chair of the all-male Board of Advisors. By the time he became an energetic promoter of the infant school movement, he had also been a promoter of racial policies that put him at odds with Philadelphia's Black community—including those who put their money and their children into Betsey Stockton's "Coloured School."

MATHEW CAREY'S INFANT SCHOOL AGENDA

By the 1820s, Mathew Carey had long been a prominent publisher in Philadelphia, where between 1785 and 1821, he put out over a thousand books, with topics ranging from classical languages to science to humor to music to travel to women's rights. Even when he gave up direct management of his printing business, in 1824, he remained a prolific polemicist and avid philanthropist. An Irish-Catholic immigrant, he threw his support behind the independence movement in Ireland, and in the United States, he promoted a national bank, protectionism, internal improvements, labor reform, prison reform, and a host of other issues.[19] Always ready to take up what he considered a good cause, Carey embraced the infant school movement.

To do so, he looked to London. The first infant school had opened there in July 1820, in the working-class neighborhood of Spitalfields. Its founding teacher, Samuel Wilderspin, argued that a structured process of education for very young children would shelter them from the daily dangers of the street, bend their moral character in the right direction, and ultimately steer them away from a life of crime. Better they be in the safe, clean, and controlled environment of the infant school. The children could then spend the day learning, while their parents, Wilderspin hoped, could spend the day engaging in or looking for employment.[20]

What made Wilderspin's approach exceptional was the way children spent their days. Wilderspin took inspiration from the pedagogy put forth by the Swiss educational reformer Johann Heinrich Pestalozzi (1746–1827), who rejected the common practice of learning by rote memorization in a rigid, disciplined environment. Instead, Pestalozzi advocated a more individualized, child-centered, hands-on approach that would allow students to explore and learn from their own experience. Wilderspin thus created an ambitious curriculum that began each day with prayer and hymn, then moved on to the alphabet, spelling, and basic reading; arithmetic, including multiplication and division; measurement, including weight, time, and money; and geography and natural history—all this for children under the age of six. To keep students interested, Wilderspin promoted sensory experiences—singing the alphabet, talking about pictures, touching raised letters, building with wooden blocks, manipulating balls on a numerical frame for arithmetic, and so forth—but even so, he understood that a daily diet of schoolwork alone would "stupefy" his students. His plan also provided for periods of physical activity: "little children are naturally lively, and if they are not suffered to move, but kept constantly in one position, they not only become disgusted with their lessons, but likewise with the school." And so the children moved, both indoors and out, sometimes playing on a swing, sometimes circling a tree, sometimes marching in order.[21] By such means, so too was the brain put in motion, as it were. Wilderspin didn't have access to the findings of modern neuroscience, which now tells us that ages two to five mark a critical period in intellectual development, but he had hit on an innovative, even revolutionary approach to educating little children.

Other social reformers took note, and the infant school movement soon spread widely through England and Wales and then to the United States. Wilderspin's school provided a standard model in several northern cities—Boston, Hartford, Albany, and New York.[22] But with the emergence of Mathew Carey as the movement's most emphatic champion, Philadelphia soon became the infant school center of the United States.

Carey didn't have much to say about Wilderspin's pedagogical innovations, but he was quick to pick up the message about the social importance of early childhood intervention. Children, he observed, became susceptible to good or evil influences even earlier than most people supposed: "the crimes which disgrace human nature flow from circumstances, apparently of little importance, which take place at two, three, four, or five years of age." Among the lower classes, so the argument went, parents had little time or training to give their children proper guidance, consumed as they were (or should be) with trying to make a living. The infant school, Carey concluded, would protect children from "the contamination of an education in the streets," give them a solid moral education, and in the process inculcate "habits of docility and order, which cannot be too highly appreciated in their effects on future life." What could be wrong with that? Carey asked: "What person of liberal mind, can be indifferent to the success of such a beneficent undertaking?"[23]

Carey started small but dreamed big. He hoped a few infant schools could provide the model for a more comprehensive plan, eventually as many as twenty for the city, and if they succeeded, "the legislature at its next session, will incorporate it into the system of public schools, and thus render it as it ought to be, a public charge."[24] The notion of public education, however, was still a relatively new one. Only in 1818 had the Pennsylvania legislature passed a law supporting "the education of children at public expense, within the City and County of Philadelphia." The city moved quickly to establish six schools by the end of that year, with a total enrollment of 1,507 boys and 1,338 girls—all of them white. It was not until four years later that the board created the first public school for Black children, which opened to over two hundred students. Although there had apparently been "some doubts as to the propriety and even as to the legality of this step," a few years later the board started a second school for Black students, and the demand in the Black community would push the number higher in the next few years.[25] Still, all the students in the city's public schools, white and Black, were five years of age and up, and public support for educating younger children had not yet come into the city's vision.

Carey thus knew the necessary funding for infant schools would have to come from private sources, and he promoted a widespread philanthropic effort that would be a bargain in beneficence. "The poorest labourer in the community could afford to become a subscriber," Carey insisted, "as the subscription . . . only amounts to four cents per week!" Better still, Carey hoped to gain larger contributions from the "wealthy classes of society," who, he hoped, "will duly consider that self-interest . . . should induce them to afford this institution a liberal patronage." If nothing else, Carey urged potential donors to look to the bottom line: "For every dollar expended on Infant Schools, fifty will probably be saved to the community in the diminution of petty larcenies, and the support of paupers and convicts."[26] The message seemed to work.

MATHEW CAREY'S RACIAL AGENDA

But behind Mathew Carey's seemingly enlightened support for early childhood education lay a dim view of those people, parents and children alike, who happened to be Black. Carey had a long record of contradictory positions on issues of race. He could utter the near-obligatory words about the evils of slavery, but he would easily accommodate his positions to its perpetuation. He would also question the place of free Blacks in American society and call for their colonization to Africa. By the late 1820s, Carey could loudly promote an infant school for African American children while still disparaging the ability of Black people to achieve intellectual equality with whites. He was by no means the only white person to hold such positions, but as Philadelphia's leading publisher and polemicist, he had the platform to promote them.

Carey had written about race for years. In 1793, he published a widely read account of the yellow fever epidemic sweeping Philadelphia, in which he commended several of the city's Black clergymen who helped "to procure nurses for the sick, and to assist in burying the dead." Yet Carey immediately turned on what he called "some of the vilest of the blacks," alleging that many of those serving as nurses did so at an extortionate rate, taking "two, three, four, and even five dollars a night for attendance, which would have been well paid by a single dollar." He went a step further, charging that some "were even detected in plundering the houses of the sick." He quickly admitted that it "would be wrong to cast a censure on the whole for this sort of conduct," but the rhetoric was a transparent patch job.[27]

Two of the prominent Black clergymen Carey named in his account, Richard Allen and Absalom Jones, published their own pamphlet about the epidemic, taking Carey to task for his racist aspersions. Allen and Jones also offered a barbed criticism of Carey's own profit from the calamity as a publisher, observing that "he has made more money by the sale of his 'scraps' than a dozen of the greatest extortioners among the black nurses." It made little difference should Carey soften his attacks on Blacks: "any alteration he may hereafter make . . . cannot have the desired effect, or atone for the past."[28] The damage had been done.

There remained a much larger matter that deserved atonement—slavery—and Carey accepted it in the present and projected it into the future. In the wake of the War of 1812 and the Panic of 1819, Carey developed a vision of a reunited and reenergized United States that relied on slavery as an essential linchpin of a national political economy. If the economic interests of the nation required slavery to be maintained—and even, by 1820, expanded into Missouri—to ensure the survival of the "empire of liberty," then the "the freedom and comfort of the African race" would have to be set aside: "if they are to be bought at the expense of the peace and happiness of the country, the price is too great."[29]

On the other hand, Carey fixed on another price he considered well worth paying—the cost of colonizing the majority of the "African race" to Africa. He had initially considered colonization an "utterly impracticable" waste of money, "one of the wildest schemes that ever arrayed in its support a number of enlightened men." By the late 1820s, however, he had become one of those men, "converted" (to use his own term) to the promotion of colonization as a means of maintaining racial equilibrium—and racial control.[30]

Carey's attraction to colonization reflected his reckoning of the numbers, both economic and demographic. In late November 1827—the year he wrote two promotional pamphlets in favor of infant schools—Carey published two other essays against emancipation. To be sure, he opened with what seemed a self-serving self-evident truth, "That slavery in every form is an evil." But it was also a source of racial anxiety for white people. The size of the United States' enslaved population—"probably 1,750,000 souls," he estimated—seemed "wholly unprepared by previous habits for freedom, or for providing for their own support," so immediate emancipation would hardly be in their interest. "What an awful delusion!" Carey cried. To delusion, Carey added danger. He summoned the most fear-inducing image he could muster, of widespread uprising and "the horrible scenes of St. Domingo." It could happen here, he warned:

enslaved people in the American South could become "sullen, discontented, unhappy, and refractory"—and eventually rebellious, "laying the whole of the southern States in blood and ashes."[31]

Turning his eye to the North, Carey pointed out that the process of gradual abolition had been so slow and cumbersome, and that emancipation in the North had not led to equality, even decency, of condition, so what was the significant difference? "Is the situation of the free negroes, so very enviable compared with that of the slaves, as to render it advisable to incur the risque of convulsion for the emancipation of the latter?" Better to keep the enslaved Blacks in slavery, and as for the free Blacks, "the system proper to be pursued . . . would be to promote their colonization to Africa."[32]

Without that, Carey feared for the future. Citing an estimate that the annual increase of the Black population, both enslaved and free, was about fifty-two thousand, Carey calculated that it would cost about a million dollars a year to "keep them to their present numbers, by an export equal to the increase." The numbers of Black people made the number of dollars seem almost inconsequential, Carey concluded. Congress should certainly pay for colonization; if need be, he suggested, a constitutional amendment could assure that "an adequate portion of the superfluous public revenue might be devoted to this grand project." In the meantime, though, he expressed disappointment that private fund-raising for this "grand project" had not gone very far, even in Philadelphia: "It is to be lamented that the late collections in the different churches of this city . . . amounted to no more than $369."[33]

If Mathew Carey had hoped that any of Philadelphia's African American congregations would contribute to colonization, he woefully misread the situation. Black Philadelphians had long since soundly rejected colonization. When the American Colonization Society first came into existence, in 1816, some African American leaders in Philadelphia briefly supported the plan, thinking that colonization might help bring about the demise of slavery in the South and a provide a means of escaping racial hostility in the North. By the 1820s, some still saw hope in Haiti. But as it became increasingly clear that the ultimate goal of colonization would be to force the transport of free people to Africa, Philadelphia's Black community—first ordinary people, then the leaders—became increasingly united in opposition, and so they remained for decades.[34] By the late 1820s, Carey would have found no agreeable audience among African Americans.

At the same time Carey also began publishing essays in support of infant schools. What was he thinking? How did a hundred or so Black toddlers fit into his broader vision of racial issues? How could Carey be a proponent for both a multimillion-dollar transatlantic program for African colonization and a small-gift fund-raising effort of a few hundred dollars for one African American infant school? If there were no hope, as Carey asserted, that free Black people could ever achieve equality, that "no merit, no services, no talents can ever elevate them to a level with whites," why bother to educate the youngest ones? If the only solution to race relations in the United States meant shipping free Blacks to Liberia, why cultivate young minds in Philadelphia? Carey never made the connection explicit, but it seems plausible that he saw infant education as a form of preparation for colonization.[35]

A SCHOOL FOR THE BLACK COMMUNITY

Mathew Carey was only one infant school donor, of course, and the motives of other donors don't appear on the records. Some white supporters may have given out of a sense of social conscience, some may have shared Carey's concern for social control of the poor, and some may have echoed his call for colonization. But African American donors no doubt had their own motives. They didn't promote the infant school for the purpose of making Black children deferential and docile, much less making them good candidates for colonization. Instead, the school could be a means of educating and, equally important, protecting children, particularly in Philadelphia's hostile racial climate.

Philadelphia's Black people knew how much that hostility applied to them as adults. African American parents also faced a more dangerous threat directed at their offspring. As the largest northern city near the Mason-Dixon Line, Philadelphia became the prime source for an especially insidious form of the internal slave trade. Kidnappers routinely roamed the streets, looking to snatch Black children away into slavery in the South, where the demand for enslaved labor remained high, particularly after the outlawing of the international slave trade in 1808. Parents cautioned the young and vulnerable to be wary. Toddlers might not typically be the immediate target of kidnappers, but no one could know that for sure.[36]

Surrounded by menace, Black people could see the new infant school as a form of defense, a well-supervised safe haven for their children. It could also be a social space for the parents themselves, a place to meet during the drop-off and pickup periods, to share stories about work and home, and simply to support each other as parents. If it offered nothing more than that, the infant school would have served a useful purpose.

Betsey Stockton's school was much more than that—not just a day-care facility, much less a warehouse for poor children. It provided a supportive social structure for children under the direction of two African American women. Moreover, like the infant schools for white children, the "Coloured School" offered a surprisingly challenging and innovative curriculum with a foreign pedigree. No one in the city had seen anything like it.

On the other hand, no one knew exactly how it would work either—including Betsey Stockton. When she arrived in Philadelphia, the room at 60 Gaskill Street had been finished and furnished by members of the African American community, "almost all the articles required except lumber, having been obtained as donations, and all the work having been done gratuitously by colored persons." John B. Rosswurm, the editor of New York's first African American newspaper, *Freedom's Journal*, had donated a set of ten engravings of animals, "accompanied by explanatory sheets," which would be not just classroom decorations, but part of the curriculum. The society had also drawn up a set of rules for parents and children, stipulating that children have a certificate "of his or her freedom from whooping cough, measles, or any other contagious disease," and be brought to school "clean washed, with their hair cut short, and their clothes well-mended" at eight thirty in the morning, adding penalties for tardiness or excessive absenteeism.[37]

The schoolroom and the rules provided only a basic structure, and what Betsey Stockton would actually do in the school remained another matter. She had briefly visited the infant school for white children in New York, which was barely a crash course in the particulars of infant school curriculum. Once in Philadelphia, it's quite likely she observed the white infant school on Chester Street, which had been open for about a year under the guidance of Ephraim Bacon.

By 1828, Bacon had become Philadelphia's resident expert, publishing *A Manual of the System of Instruction Pursued at the Infant School, Chester Street, Philadelphia* and promoting many of the methods developed by Samuel Wilderspin. Learning would take place in an orderly, square classroom where a variety of engaging activities would keep little children quite busy during the day—and the adults equally so. A teacher and assistant teacher could work with students in small groups, "so that every child shall be taught one lesson in the forenoon and one in the afternoon, in the classroom." The plan called for special equipment that reflected the hands-on approach to learning through physical manipulation—"Alphabetical board or transposition frame, with 500 large letters pasted on blocks, to slide into the frame," "Large Numerical Frame, with balls," "1000 (wooden bricks) blocks . . . for the children to make block houses and walls," and musical instruments, such as tambourines and handbells. A basic lesson in the alphabet, for instance, would involve thirteen cards with letters on each side, upper case and lower case. "The cards are exhibited on the end of a walking stick," he explained, "elevated far above the teacher's head, and the children call out A a, and the card is turned over, and they say B b in concert. The time required to teach this lesson not to exceed five minutes." Bacon's design also required resources for religious and secular subjects, including "Texts of Scripture . . .

Spelling and Reading Books . . . Pictures of Scriptural Subjects and Natural History," and apparently a brief catechism on colonization:

> Q. Can the same mode of natural intuitive development be introduced into Liberia for the children of the Africans?
>
> A. Certainly; as I should conceive that these children are as capable of intellectual development as Americans.[38]

Lesson plans don't always reflect the reality of life in the classroom, however, and it's difficult to know how closely Betsey Stockton adopted Bacon's approach. Given the disparities in fund-raising for the white and Black infant schools, it's likely she didn't have at her disposal all the cards and blocks and musical instruments Bacon's curriculum called for. Given the background of her student body and their parents, it's also likely she didn't extol the intellectual benefits of colonization. Perhaps she and Rebecca Cobb somehow managed to provide small-group instruction, but that could be a challenge with several dozen students between two and five years old, all of them requiring occasional attention to their behavioral and biological needs. Crying, arguing, and other forms of misbehaving could be disruptive, and children who came to school hungry, unhappy, or unwell could test the best efforts of their teachers.

But Stockton and Cobb apparently avoided chaos. The best view of their efforts comes from members of the Infant School Society's oversight committee, who looked in on a regular basis and took note of overall progress. On the day the school opened, the visiting white women observed that the children were "generally clean and neat in their appearance, and the exercises were conducted with more order than could reasonably have been expected." That rather backhanded compliment gave way to greater enthusiasm within a few weeks, when the school's enrollment had increased from an initial forty-six to sixty-six: "It was not to be expected that in the short space of one month any material change could be effected in the manners and habits of children, ignorant and uneducated," the visiting committee reported. But the students had become "more cleanly in their persons, more regular in their attendance, and more attentive to their exercises." Moreover, "interesting accounts have been received of the attachment of some to the school and their teacher." Betsey Stockton herself merited particular commendation: "Active, energetic and intelligent, she appears well calculated for the situation in which she is placed."[39]

Perhaps the true measure of Stockton's worth came when she was temporarily unable to work. In July 1828, after the school had been open for just over two months, the visiting committee observed that "in consequence of the indisposition of Betsey Stockton, the improvement of the pupils has not been as rapid during the last month as was anticipated." Some of the committee members tried to fill the gap "by attending alternately, and instructing the children," but they suffered a fate common to substitute teachers everywhere: "their exertions effected but little." While Stockton was out sick, Rebecca Cobb also had to take time off for a death in the family, and at that point the women of the visiting committee gave up, thinking it "most expedient to dismiss the School, until the teachers should be able to resume their duties." When Stockton and Cobb eventually came back, the visiting committee offered repeated positive observations, month after month, from the fall of 1828 through the spring of 1829—"the school continues interesting," "the coloured school is very encouraging," "the school continues to flourish"—and noting a steady increase in students, to over a hundred.[40]

Then, on May 4, 1829, the Infant School Society's records noted one very significant absence: "Committee report that Betsey Stockton has left them for a few months to establish schools in the wilds of Canada."[41] After a year on the job, she had left the city and, once again, the United States.

THE WILDS OF CANADA

Betsey Stockton's reputation as a teacher had apparently grown during her tenure at the Gaskill Street school, and so had the reputation of infant schools. In April 1829, William Case, a Methodist missionary from Upper Canada, called on Ashbel Green "to converse about Betsey Stockton going with him to teach an infant school among the Indians." Case had come to Philadelphia on a fund-raising tour, also stopping in New York to speak to the Missionary Society of the Methodist Episcopal Church, about the missionary efforts among the Mohawk, Cayuga, and Tuscarora peoples. Using the standard missionary measure of success, Case claimed that before the missionaries arrived, the Indigenous people "were drunkards to a man," but in a short time they had been converted to Christianity, and "now they desire the knowledge of God conveyed to their children; and in accordance with their wishes so many schools have been established."[42] Given Stockton's experience as a missionary teacher and an infant school teacher, she could serve as a short-term educational adviser to start a demonstration school for the youngest of those children. It wasn't hard to see why Case recruited her.

The question, though, is why she chose to go. Perhaps the daily demands of teaching dozens of young children under the age of six exhausted her, and she needed a break. Perhaps the reality of the racism behind the benevolent facade of Philadelphia's philanthropy likewise wore her down, and she needed to get away. Perhaps she saw an opportunity to enhance her professional profile, and the challenge of starting a new infant school seemed impossible to resist. Or perhaps she hoped working in another missionary setting might provide a stepping-stone back to Hawai'i: she would later tell a Canadian acquaintance that she "cherishes a hope of ending her days in the Sandwich Islands." In any event, she went, and on June 2, 1829, she started work at a small encampment on Grape Island.[43]

Grape Island was about as far away from Philadelphia as she could expect to get, culturally if not geographically. Only eleven acres, it lay in the Bay of Quinte on the north side of Lake Ontario, across from Rochester, New York, and immediately south of Belleville. The Methodists had leased it from the Mississauga Ojibwa, who had suffered the loss of both land and population in the years after the American Revolution. Even though the Ojibwa had fought on the side of the British in both the Revolution and the War of 1812, the British government had allowed white settlers to move into Upper Canada, overwhelming them. By the 1820s, the Ojibwa population had fallen to a few thousand, and many had begun to convert to Christianity under the influence of energetic Methodist missionaries. The Grape Island mission opened in 1826, under the leadership of William Case and a Mississauga convert named Kahkewaquonaby (also known by his English name, Peter Jones), with about 150 people living in a cluster of tents. By the spring of 1827, the mission residents had built a few wooden buildings, including a handful of houses, a chapel, a couple of workshops, and a school.[44]

The school would be central to the mission. No less than other Protestants, Methodist missionaries considered literacy the key first step to conversion, the means whereby Indigenous people could learn to read the Bible, embrace the habits of Christian behavior, and perhaps become missionaries themselves. Conversion and education went hand in hand, underscoring the need for building schools and finding teachers. In May 1828, when William Case returned from his fund-raising trip, he was happy to report that most of "the societies and schools are still prospering and progressing in religion and learning." He was particularly pleased with the Grape Island mission's success at education: "The school contains nearly sixty children, ten of whom are reading in easy lessons. Some are writing, and many of the girls are knitting." Betsey Stockton would also arrive soon, and she would bring a new dimension to the education of Indigenous people, particularly the youngest of them.[45]

The record of her time in Canada is sparse, just a few scraps from Methodist missionary sources. "Paid travelling expenses etc. to Miss Stockton," one noted, "who was employed to introduce the Pestalozzian system of instruction in the school at Grape Island." The appeal of the "Pestalozzian system" in the Indigenous context stemmed from its accessible approach to the first principles of English language and literacy. One missionary noted that the use of visual images (alphabet cards and pictures of animals, for instance) and physical objects (wooden blocks and a counting frame with colored balls) seemed "particularly suited to the tastes and dispositions of Indian children." It seemed also well suited to the dispositions of Methodist missionaries, who saw the early education of children as a means of reaching their parents, thus reinforcing family inclusion within the fold. Within two months, the fruits of Stockton's work were apparent—"She came for the purpose of setting up an Infant School, which has succeeded admirably"—and other teachers across the region would build on her success well into the 1830s.[46]

Betsey Stockton wouldn't be around to see that process unfold, however. By July 1829, she had done what she came to Canada to do, and she returned to Philadelphia.

FINAL DAYS IN PHILADELPHIA

In Philadelphia, Betsey Stockton went right back to work in the infant school on Gaskill Street. In September 1829, the overseeing committee issued as series of glowing reports: "The school is in good order, and great improvement observable in several branches," "school in good order—children fond of their teachers," "very encouraging," and "intelligence manifested by the children is marked with surprise by strangers." Enrollment was robust, with around 140 children registered and eighty to a hundred attending on a given day. (Attendance tended to fluctuate, according to the children's health and their family's situation.) On the whole, the Infant School Society declared Stockton's school to be "in a flourishing state, encouraging the hearts of those who feel an interest in the welfare of this long-suffering people."[47]

But then Betsey Stockton experienced suffering of her own. Her dear friend Harriet Stewart, whose health had long been a matter of concern, died in Cooperstown on September 6, 1830, leaving her three children motherless. They had also been effectively fatherless for well over a year: in February 1829, Charles Stewart had gone again to sea, this time as navy chaplain on a voyage to the Pacific. When he got back to New York in June 1830, one of the first things he heard was that his wife, "the object of my attachment . . . was then lying in the interior of the state, at the point of death." He arrived in Cooperstown soon enough to see her, even to hope "that she might still be rescued from the grave, and restored to health, to her family, and to society." But, he wrote sadly, "it proved illusive."[48]

To Betsey Stockton, Harriet Stewart's death proved conclusive: she decided to return to Cooperstown and to the Stewart family, of which she considered herself a member. She had left them in the spring of 1828 for the sake of opportunity, but she came back to them just over two years later with a sense of obligation—and love.

On October 4, the infant school committee recorded that "Betsey Stockton has resigned her charge owing to private duties. Her place is not yet permanently supplied." In a sense, it wouldn't be. After Stockton left, so did some of the parents and children. While regular attendance had hovered around eighty with Stockton as principal teacher, the committee reported fifty-two children in November 1830, then, in January, 1831, "a very small number in attendance," despite "some effort to increase the school by visiting among the coloured people." A month later, things were about the same, with "a small attendance about sixty being the average—other circumstances of the school satisfactory."[49] But "satisfactory" seemed a disappointing drop-off from "good order," "flourishing," and "very encouraging." Betsey Stockton had been the founding teacher, she had given it first life, and some of that life went with her when she left.

Her own life, however, would soon go in a new direction, even if back to old locations—Cooperstown for a few years, then Princeton. Betsey Stockton had been around the world, but she would spend the second half of her life within the small compass of Princeton, where conflict simmered between two communities, Black and white, with a college in between. Princeton may have been a modest-sized town, but it confronted Black people, including Betsey Stockton, with momentous challenges.

6
From Ashes to Assertion

IN 1835, THE INDEPENDENCE DAY celebration in Princeton went on a little too long. Late in the afternoon of July 6, someone shot one last skyrocket in the vicinity of the Presbyterian church, and the rocket's red glare traced a trajectory right onto the roof. Sparks set the shingles on fire, and within minutes the whole building became engulfed in flame. The ensuing alarm interrupted five o'clock prayers at the college, causing both students and professors to run toward the burning church. They couldn't do much, and neither could the town's firefighters, since their engines didn't have enough water pressure to reach the roof. Instead, Princeton's townspeople, Black and white alike, just watched helplessly as the fire burned steadily through the building, consuming everything inside, until "nothing [was] left of it but the naked brick walls."[1]

News of the fire soon spread across the country, with notices in the nation's press, ranging from Portland, Maine, to Lynchburg, Virginia, and as far west as Cincinnati. Princeton Presbyterian was *the* church of the town. Princeton had three other religious institutions at the time—a long-standing Quaker meeting, an Episcopal church, and a recently formed Black AME congregation. But none of them had the membership or the prominence of Princeton Presbyterian, with almost four hundred active members and a sanctuary that served both the community and the college, "in which the College Commencements have been held time out of mind." Since 1766, when the church was founded, all of Princeton's presidents had worshipped there, as had most of the students. So had scores of African American people—including Betsey Stockton.[2]

By this time, she had been back in town for about two years. After Harriet Stewart had died in 1830, Charles Stewart took a leave of absence from his duties as navy chaplain for a little over two years, but in 1833 he went to sea again. At that point, Betsey Stockton took Stewart's three children to Princeton, for several reasons. First, she had a very valuable personal connection there in James Sproat Green, the youngest of Ashbel Green's sons, the one closest to her in age, who had reputedly helped in her childhood self-education. By the 1830s, he had become a well-established lawyer, a trustee of the college, and the US district attorney for New Jersey. Second, Princeton had good schools. Ten-year-old Charles Seaforth enrolled in the Edgehill School, already a bastion of rigorous classical education for boys. His sisters, eight-year-old Harriet and five-year-old Martha, presumably went to one of the several female academies in town. Finally, Betsey Stockton had her own ties to Princeton. Even though she had been away since 1822, she still knew both the community and the church, and she renewed her connection to Princeton Presbyterian.[3]

All that would change in 1835. Charles Samuel Stewart came home from his naval voyage at the end of 1834, began a four-year tour of shore duty in New York City, remarried, and brought the children back to live with him in a new household.[4] Betsey Stockton stayed in Princeton, now an independent adult with no immediate family of her own; the Black community would be her main source of social identity for the rest of her life. The destruction of the Presbyterian church—*her* church—became the critical first step in defining her future in Princeton. The fire cast a harsh, bright light on the separate paths soon to be taken by Princeton's Presbyterians, white and Black, making them emblematic of the growing social distance between the races in the town as a whole. Princeton's racial divisions, which had existed for years, would become only wider and deeper in the quarter century leading up to the Civil War—the period when Betsey Stockton became a central figure in the town's Black community.

SELLING PEWS, SEPARATING PEOPLE

With the Presbyterian church in ruins, white and Black parishioners needed somewhere to worship, and they moved in different directions—and with very different intentions. The white members settled into another distinctly Presbyterian space, the chapel at the Princeton Theological Seminary. They immediately set out raising money for rebuilding a "new and handsome church edifice" on the old site, just adjacent to the college on Nassau Street. By November 1836, construction had progressed to the point that they could hold services, using temporary seats. A year later, the sixty-by-eighty-foot brick building—with an all-metal, and presumably fireproof, roof—was finished.[5] The new church had a new look inside as well: an all-white congregation. As the Reverend James W. Alexander, a Princeton professor and member of the church, explained, "the negroes worshipped apart, in a little place of their own."

In a sense, they had always worshipped apart. Previously, Black Presbyterians could be full, communion-taking members—as was Betsey Stockton—equal in the eyes of God, but separate inside the house of worship, where they still had to sit in the second-floor galleries. The church had designated a sexton to "take care that the Black people sit in their proper place and if any of them misbehave to report who they are . . . with the name of their misbehavior." Now, the white members of the Presbyterian church sought to remove Blacks even from that "proper place." As James Alexander explained, "the majority of the pew-holders wish them to remain as a separate congregation." Alexander figured that if the eighty or ninety Black members were to come back, "they will take up about half the gallery"—if, indeed, the new building would have the same sort of racially segregated seating as the old one.[6]

One of Alexander's fellow leaders, Albert B. Dod, made sure it would not. An elder in the church, a professor of mathematics, and a slaveholder in his own household, Dod oversaw the reseating process, organizing the auction for pews on the main floor and designating the gallery for white children's Sunday school classes. He was also a member of a committee appointed to confer with the Black members about forming a separate church of their own, on a permanent basis. The conversation did not go at all well. After two uneasy meetings, Dod reported that the committee "had done their duty but had not obtained their object." Black people wanted to be back in the main church. James Alexander took a dim, even dismissive view of their resistance: "I think the blacks very unwise in insisting on such a privilege now."[7]

In fact, it was white people who were insisting on their own privilege. They were the ones who had begun to worship apart, who had begun to push for a separate Black congregation, who had persisted in that effort in the face of Black reluctance, even resistance. In the ashes of the fire, they found an all-white opportunity.

Their growing insistence on separating Black members seems especially striking in light of a similar move only three years before. In 1832, twenty-three white members of Princeton Presbyterian petitioned the session about "forming & organizing a Second Presbyterian Church in this Borough." The reason initially had to do with unhappiness with the pastor, the Reverend George Woodhull, and some of his theological positions, but the proponents also cast their request in terms of pew pressure. The problem, apparently, was that "our church is now too small to accommodate all who wish to obtain pews, & that there are probably at this moment many persons & indeed whole families who absent themselves from the house of God solely for the reason that they cannot be accommodated without intruding on their neighbors." That seemed to be news to most of the members of the session, who pointed out that the church did have available pews, and that it would also provide "ample accommodation in the gallery for such as cannot obtain seats below." The gallery, of course, was where the Black people sat, and not what the white petitioners wanted.

Still, the session questioned the very notion of the request, "whether you could reasonably expect that they would as officers of the church approve & recommend a division of the congregation?"[8]

But three years later, the session promoted division when the opportunity arose to exclude Black members. "I am clear that in a church of Jesus Christ, there is neither black nor white," James Alexander admitted, "and that we have no right to consider the accident of colour in any degree." By the 1830s, nothing seemed accidental about the implications of race. Princeton's white Presbyterians reacted fearfully to the 1831 uprising led by Nat Turner, which terrified white people not just throughout the South, but in the North as well. In 1837, Alexander pointed to the racial profile of Princeton, which was "said to have a larger proportion of blacks in our population, than any town in the free States." He wasn't far off: Princeton's African Americans would number over six hundred in 1840, almost 21 percent of the population. Alexander had no need to fear a slave rebellion of Nat Turner proportions—at the time, there were only twelve people still held in slavery in Princeton—but the presence of so many free Blacks could unsettle white people, including a southerner like Alexander.[9]

And so the white Presbyterians pressed for separation. In August 1839, the session named John Lowrey, a ruling elder in the church and significant political figure in town, to assume "special supervision of the Coloured people of our Congregation" and negotiate about becoming a new congregation. Another leading member of the church, John Breckinridge, a professor at the Princeton Theological Seminary, led a fund-raising campaign for the construction of a separate church building, on Witherspoon Street. The two churches would be only a few blocks apart, but they represented very different parts of town.[10]

TWO STREETS, TWO CHURCHES

In July 1836, a local newspaper, the *Princeton Whig*, published a boosterish report on "Princeton Prospects," which seemed to be quite bright. The essay celebrated the "remarkably good health" of the town, noting that the "best evidence of which may be seen in the number of strangers from the cities and the southern States, who annually spend the summer with us" in the "capacious accommodations of our Hotels and Boarding Houses." Visitors who came to Princeton for leisure might also be impressed with an underlying bustle of a construction boom, with "private edifices that are going up in town," along with new buildings on the campus and on Nassau Street, including a "handsome building, for a Banking House" and "large Brick Presbyterian Church . . . on the site of the one burnt a year ago."[11] And thus the paper baited the hook for "men of capital in the Cities, to invest a few thousand dollars in this Borough and its vicinity, in Real Estate."

But lest those men buy up all the bargains, several Princetonians also jumped into the real estate market, most notably in the environs of Witherspoon Street. Witherspoon Street starts—or ends—at Nassau Street, directly in front of the college, and since the early eighteenth century, it had been one of Princeton's main thoroughfares. Princeton Presbyterian itself stood on Nassau Street, but thanks to an 1804 bequest from church elder Thomas Wiggins, the parsonage was on Witherspoon. The burying ground had been there even longer, first established by the college in the 1760s and then conveyed to the care of the church in 1783. Like the church itself, the Presbyterian cemetery had a separate section for Black bodies, designated in 1807 and set off a short distance from the graves of the whites.[12]

Black people also had a living presence on Witherspoon. At least as far back as the turn of the nineteenth century, whites had referred to it as "African Alley" or "Guinea Lane." That racial identification became even stronger in the 1830s, when a handful of white investors bought land on the west side of Witherspoon, directly across from the cemetery, and divided it for development. Three new streets—Jackson, Green, and Quarry—were laid out perpendicular to Witherspoon, and the area soon became the residential center of Princeton's Black community, a status that would endure for well

FIGURE 6.1. First Presbyterian Church, Princeton, NJ, Collection of the Historical Society of Princeton.

over a century.[13] Given this rapid expansion, the district seemed a likely place for building a new Presbyterian church, which soon rose at the corner of Witherspoon and Quarry.

On April 13, 1840, James Alexander, who had been serving as supply pastor for the Black Presbyterians, wrote that "We dedicated our new African meeting-house." It was not as grand as the new ionic-columned brick church for white Presbyterians on Nassau Street, but a simple wooden structure that could accommodate a good-sized congregation. On one level, the building was a gift to the Black Presbyterians, but on another it signified a guarantee that they would not come back to the main church—a hard bargain, but one they could not easily refuse. Within a few months, John Lowrey, apparently speaking "in behalf of the Coloured People," came before the Presbyterian elders to request "a separate Communion in their own Church." At that point, the racial separation of Princeton Presbyterian seemed to be complete.[14]

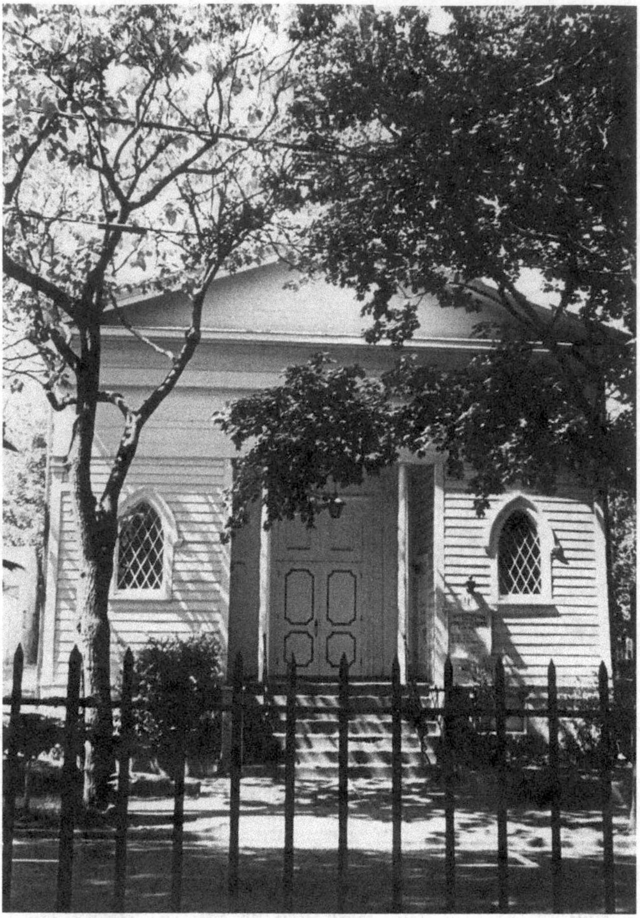

FIGURE 6.2. First Presbyterian Church of Colour of Princeton (renamed Witherspoon Street Presbyterian Church, 1848), Collection of the Historical Society of Princeton.

But not quite. The white elders still continued to count Black Presbyterians on the membership rolls, and they reserved the right to examine them for membership, certify them for baptism, and, above all, subject them to discipline. Black people were brought before the session to face accusations of impropriety—intoxication, disorderly behavior, and above all, various forms of sexual behavior. When word reached the session that "two coloured members of the church have been guilty of the crime of Adultery and have each had a child," the all-white, all-male body of elders summoned both women. One of them appeared, the other did not, but the penalty was the same for each: "suspended from the privileges of the church until she give satisfactory evidence of repentance." The same fate awaited a man who "confessed that he had had criminal intercourse" with a woman in town, but he "manifested no repentance" and refused to appear before the session. A married couple was called for "unchristian and violent conduct towards each other . . . [and] manifest unwillingness to be reconciled and to live together as husband and wife." They had apparently already been required to meet with "a committee of the Coloured members of the church appointed to supervise the conduct of their brethren," but they treated that committee "with contempt." When the man and woman eventually "confessed their faults [and] professed repentance," they received "solemn admonition from the moderator" and were then "permitted to enjoy the privileges of the church." On the whole, Black people called before the Presbyterian session responded with varying degrees of repentance and resistance, sometimes humbling themselves before the white elders, but sometimes refusing to appear at all. If they were not welcome in worship, some African American Presbyterians felt no need to bow down to the session's authority.[15]

The members of the session adopted a similarly ambivalent position toward the Black congregants. On a couple of occasions in 1845, they held their meetings "in the Session Room of the African Church," but that seemed a mild gesture of respect, at best. They took a more meaningful step that spring when they "Resolved that Two hundred blank certificates of dismission be printed." By then it was becoming clear that the blanks would soon be filled by the names of Black Presbyterians.[16]

And then they were, less than a year later. On March 10, 1846, "The Coloured members of this church were dismissed to the number of ninety to form a church under the name of the First Presbyterian Church of Colour of Princeton." This dismissal did not stem from the desires of the Black Presbyterians. They had not asked to become a separate church, but had been steadily driven in that direction for a decade. They were not a breakaway congregation, but a push-away one.[17]

Once established, however, they made their church a strong and supportive institution for Princeton's Black community. The racial tensions that underlay life in Princeton had shown they needed one.

TURMOIL IN TOWN

In September 1835—just two months after Princeton Presbyterian burned to the ground—a white abolitionist came to town for a secret meeting, apparently to promote subscriptions to William Lloyd Garrison's newspaper, the *Liberator*. Students at the college got wind of his arrival, and according to a contemporary account, "about 60 in number went down to a negro man's house," where the man was meeting with people in the Black community. While most of the boys waited outside, two barged in and seized him, but the man refused to budge, saying he "had the law on his side & that he would make use of it." The two students countered that they "had Lynchs law which was sufficient for them," and they dragged him outside, threatened him with tar and feathers, and burned his subscription papers. Then they ran him out of town, parading him past the seminary and telling him to run for his life.[18] The *Princeton Whig* took an indulgent view of the Princeton boys' behavior, reporting: "We rejoice for the credit of our borough that nothing more serious was attempted, this being the first ebullition of public feeling on this subject."[19] It would not be the last.

In October of the following year, a southern student attempted similar treatment of Theodore Wright, the first Black graduate of the Princeton Theological Seminary. When Wright came to town to attend a talk at the seminary, someone stood up in the audience and yelled a racial epithet at him. "I had not the least idea that I was the victim," Wright wrote, "until seized by the collar by a young man, who kicked me two or three times in the most ruthless manner." It became a shameful and embarrassing story for the seminary, but the

Princeton Whig did not carry it; Wright's account of the incident appeared in the *Liberator*.[20]

By far the most newsworthy incident of this sort in Princeton came in 1843, with the arrest and trial of James Collins, an enslaved man from Maryland who had found refuge in town. He had escaped in 1839, when the owner of the plantation where he was enslaved gave him five dollars to run an errand. Seizing the opportunity, Collins took off northward, traveling by foot, steamboat, and train, eventually making his way to Princeton, where his money ran out. He added a new last name, Johnson, managed to find work as a custodian for the college, and was living peacefully until a student from Maryland recognized him and alerted the authorities. Feeling bound by the provisions of the Fugitive Slave Act of 1793, Princeton officials put Johnson on trial, an event that attracted attention throughout the North.[21]

Johnson's lawyers figured that a jury of Princeton citizens would never convict a well-known campus figure and return him to slavery, but they figured wrong. Even though the jury foreman was an influential and seemingly sympathetic Quaker, the jurors ordered Johnson back to Maryland. There are different versions of what happened next. One of the lawyers for the prosecution, John Hageman, later praised the people of Princeton for peacefully upholding the rule of law, "without a riot or arrest for disorder." Other contemporary accounts, however, noted more evidence of unrest: "The negro . . . put in a wagon to be taken off . . . jumped out, and some attempt was made to rescue him, which was unsuccessful. In the fracas that ensued some of the students at Princeton college from the south took part, and dirks and knives were drawn."[22] The Maryland slaveholder published a note of thanks for "the kindness of those of the citizens and students whose prompt interposition . . . so efficiently sustained the supremacy of the laws." The use of the term "interposition" reflected the language of southern resistance being employed by John C. Calhoun and other pro-slavery politicians; in those emotionally charged times, it could hardly have been an unconscious choice.[23]

A more significant interposition came from Theodosia Prevost, a woman with an impressive Princeton ancestry, with family connections to John Witherspoon, Samuel Stanhope Smith, and Aaron Burr Jr. She also had enough of her own money—she was unmarried and had a family inheritance—to pay the slaveholder $500 for James Johnson's freedom. Why she did so remains a mystery—she came from a slaveholding family and had never been an active abolitionist—but the result was clear. Johnson became a free man, agreed to repay Theodosia Prevost over time, and lived the rest of his life in Princeton as a popular, although often patronized, fixture on the campus.[24]

For a brief period in 1843, the James Collins Johnson case put Princeton in the nation's spotlight, or at least those beams that shone in the North. Some observers questioned Princeton's complicity in accepting, if not supporting, human bondage. "Princeton is in New Jersey, a free state," a Maine newspaper pointed out. "Have the free states, where juries are called upon to decide whether the souls and bodies of men belong to themselves, nothing to do with slavery?" The *Philadelphia Gazette* concluded that "We cannot but think that nothing more proves the horrible oppression to which the poor blacks are to be subjected, by their unfortunate birthright, than so shocking a case as this."[25]

Anyone who imagined, however, that such a shocking case might have led to a rethinking of race relations in Princeton would have been sadly mistaken. White hostility toward Black people persisted.

In 1846, for instance, racial incidents revealed the continuing tensions, particularly regarding Black women. In late June, a Black man confronted students for harassing a young Black woman walking near them, and in the altercation that ensued, one of the students had been injured and "led off bruised & bleeding to his Room." Two days later, a group of fourteen of his fellows, all from the South, sought revenge. They found the Black man working at a nearby farm, and despite some resistance on the scene, succeeded in bringing him back to town for legal proceedings, determined, if need be, "to try the Victim before the worshipful Court of Judge Lynch." The situation then escalated into another fight, this time between the southern students and an opposing group of students and a prominent professor, John Maclean Jr., who had come to the Black man's defense. The southerners prevailed, and, as one of their sympathizers reported, the man was "taken out & whipped within an inch of his life."[26] A few months later, an out-of-town newspaper pointed to another "recent case of daring cruelty, in which a colored man, on his way to church, was knocked down at the side of his own wife . . . because he had dared to protect her from the insults of a band of colorphobic rowdies."[27]

When the mayor, John T. Robinson, raised the specter of local disorder to the Borough Council, he took as his target not the violence of college boys, but the menace to morality he saw in women, especially "colored girls strolling about all parts of the town at all hours of the night" and allegedly stirring up student lust. Princeton already had an ordinance, passed in 1813, "to prevent nocturnal Riots and disorderly and tumultuous meetings of Negro and Mulatto slaves or servants within the Borough of Princeton." Now the nocturnal movement of young Black women seemed to exacerbate white people's fears and fantasies about the collective behavior of Black people, which became especially pronounced when projected into the darkness of night, then enhanced by lurid suspicions of Black sexuality. The *Princeton Whig* echoed the mayor's concerns, saying that "Princeton for a long time has been infested with a number of loose characters, chiefly colored women," and noting with apparent satisfaction that "Five women and one man got summary leave of absence from the town."[28]

Princeton's Black people always had to be attuned of the "colorphobic" tendencies of the white residents, whether the rowdy boys in the street, the men elected to local government, or even the members of the session of the Presbyterian church.

FOUNDING THE FIRST PRESBYTERIAN CHURCH OF COLOUR

When Princeton's Presbyterian church recorded the names of the ninety-two Black people dismissed in March 1846, Betsey Stockton's was the first. It's not clear how and why it came to be there. The list was not arranged alphabetically, nor did it divide by gender, family identity, or social status. The placement might have been happenstance, but it might have symbolized her prominence among Black Presbyterians. She had joined the church thirty years before and was now counted as a long-standing member of the church community, someone with institutional memory and integrity. Or perhaps her position simply reflected her frustration with the decade of steady segregatory pressure, and she just wanted to be done with it. In any event, there was her name at the top of the list, where anyone could see it.

But no one could see deep into her heart. In the midst of the town's racial turmoil, Betsey Stockton experienced her own emotional turmoil. Even though she had become a visible figure in the church and community, she lived alone—and that could sometimes leave her lonely. In October 1845, she wrote to Charles Samuel Stewart a grim-seeming letter lamenting her "bitter anguish and silent grief of one who knows that they have not on earth one single friend to whome [*sic*] they could disclose the deep sorrows of their hearts." Poor health had again darkened her mood, and even though she hoped to "try to do all the good I can to those around me," she worried that she had somehow failed "those who have been burdened with me." She accepted her own burden: "it is good for me to be afflicted"—even if the affliction should end in death. "Already the grave is strip[p]ed of much of its gloom to me—and should this be my last winter it will be a happy release." In January 1846, she again wrote Stewart, saying that she was "still quite sick" and asking that if some "old ragged stair carpet" in his household had not been given away, "I should be very thankful for it, the cold floor injures me now and prevents my getting better." The loneliness, the sickness, and the spiritual doubts all echoed emotional and physical discomforts she had felt before, and she turned to Charles Stewart as someone who knew that. But in the end she tried to be upbeat, with a closing (but perhaps unconvincing) note that Stewart not "be troubled about me, I know all will be right."[29]

Two months later, adding her name to the list of people dismissed could have been a step in making things right. Her church would develop an identity not just as a place of religious refuge, but a source of community resistance. As a founding member, she became committed to an institution that would define her place in Princeton for the next two decades.

Betsey Stockton and her fellow Black Presbyterians had just begun to have Black pastors—Elymas Payson Rogers (1845–48) and Charles W. Gardner (1848–52)—after several years of white interim (or stated supply) pastors. Regrettably, there is no surviving record of what they actually preached, but it had to be quite different from what their parishioners had heard from white preachers. Both Rogers and Gardner came from abolitionist backgrounds, and they played a critical role in the early history of the church.[30]

Elymas Rogers was younger than Betsey Stockton, but he had shared some of her life experience. Born in 1815 in Madison, Connecticut, into not slavery but poverty, he was sent by his parents to live in another household from ages nine to fifteen. By his late teens, he had begun to study for the ministry. In 1834, he attended Gerrit Smith's new school for young Black men in Peterboro, New York, and then in 1836, with Smith's recommendation, he moved on to the Oneida Institute in Whitesboro, New York, the interracial center of antislavery education. To support his own education, Rogers taught school for Black children, and when he graduated from Oneida, in 1841, he became the principal of a public school for African Americans in Trenton, New Jersey. Still pursuing his goal of becoming a clergyman, he became licensed by the New Brunswick Presbytery in February 1844, and in the following fall, moved to Princeton to preach at what the Presbyterian General Assembly listed as "Princeton (col'd) cong." He stayed there through 1847, perhaps into 1848, and then took a position at the Plane Street Church in Newark.[31] But in his brief time in Princeton, he broke the color barrier of the pastorate, and for that he holds a place in the community's history.

In 1848, the church changed its name to the Witherspoon Street

Presbyterian Church, and late that year or early next, it also got a new pastor, Charles W. Gardner. Betsey Stockton probably knew him from Philadelphia in the late 1820s, through Ashbel Green. Gardner had been pastor of Philadelphia's First African Presbyterian Church—the church established in 1807 by John Gloucester, with some assistance from Green—serving first in 1827–30, then again from 1836 to 1848. Green had remained an ally of the church for years, occasionally preaching guest sermons or sharing the service with Gardner: in February 1830, for instance, he "administered the communion in the First African Church, [and] Mr. Gardiner, the preacher there, made the first long prayer and I performed the rest of the service." Green also became enough of a supporter of Gardner to include him in his final bequest, specifying that "the best Suit of my wearing apparel, with two shirts & my hat should be given to the minister of the First African Presbyterian Church after my decease." Green died in May 1848, and perhaps Gardner occasionally wore some of those clothes when he preached at Witherspoon Street.[32]

But as much as Gardner might have respected Ashbel Green in return, he took a much more forceful stance on racial issues. In Philadelphia, Gardner had been an increasingly visible member of the antislavery and anticolonization movements, serving as chaplain to the National Negro Convention, delegate to the Anti-Slavery Society of Pennsylvania, and member of the Vigilant Committee of Philadelphia. In 1837–38, he coauthored a treatise against the impending attempt to disenfranchise Black people in Pennsylvania, *Memorial to the Honorable, the Delegates of the People of Pennsylvania in Convention at Philadelphia Assembled.* The white members of the convention considered the document's defense of equal rights and political representation far too radical and refused to have it printed. In fact, the memorial made a moderate appeal, emphasizing the importance of Black self-improvement and underscoring the value of education as a source of social uplift: with "the establishing of schools, and Sabbath Schools . . . the colored people are a rising, a rapidly rising people." In his own church, Gardner apparently put to practice what he preached. His successor at First African, the Reverend William T. Catto, wrote that Gardner had made education a cultural cornerstone of the congregation: "I assume that no church of color in Philadelphia, and I omit not one, could compare with the church at this time . . . for the number of young intellectuals that were members of it."[33] That was the profile Charles Gardner brought to Princeton, a commitment to education buttressed by a belief in abolition and a condemnation of colonization.

Gardner had also been a leader in the Philadelphia Vigilant Committee, an organization devoted to the support and protection of fugitive freedom seekers, working to "adopt more liberal & systematic measures to aid them in their efforts to escape." Gardner had no doubt followed the 1843 case of James Collins Johnson. When Gardner served as pastor to the Witherspoon Street Church, Johnson was still in town—and probably in the congregation. In December 1852, Johnson married Catherine McCray, Betsey Stockton's fellow teacher in the Sunday school, and he presumably joined her as member of the church. If Charles Gardner ever wanted to see the face of a former fugitive living in freedom, he had only to turn his eyes to the pew where the Johnsons sat.[34]

Charles Gardner's tenure at the Witherspoon Street Church would be troubled and ultimately terminated by conflict with white people associated with the church, but for the Black members, he must have seemed a welcome and powerful presence in the pulpit. Years after he left, he would be remembered in the Black community as "a man of high mental attainments . . . a profound thinker and leading ecclesiastical . . . [whose] preaching was eloquent, impressive, and effective."[35]

BLACK PRIDE IN PRINCETON

In the years Witherspoon Street Presbyterian Church had been solidifying its identity as an antislavery congregation, another Black church, Mt. Pisgah AME, had done the same. Founded in 1832, Mt. Pisgah sat just up the block on Witherspoon Street. It is possible—but almost impossible to document—that both churches may have been sites of resistance in the Underground Railroad. The most detailed nineteenth-century history, Wilbur Henry Siebert's *The Underground Railroad from Slavery to Freedom* (1898), included Princeton on the map as a transition spot "where horses were changed and the journey continued." Given the secrecy of the Underground Railroad's operation at the time and the exaggeration of the number of stations in later years, Princeton's place warrants historical caution. Still, if Princeton were at least a stopover, it's certain that Black people played a role, and quite likely that their churches provided refuge.[36]

Black people in town were also becoming part of a larger movement that made an open display of racial pride, combining moral discipline with an antislavery stance. On September 1, 1846, the *Princeton Whig* reported that "A Colored People's Temperance Convention was held at Princeton," and over the next few years that movement would give the Black community connections to a national cause and, in the process, have local repercussions.[37]

Temperance had long been an important focus of moral reform, and Black people had taken up the antialcohol cause with as much fervor as whites. In 1830, the Reverend Theodore Wright and the Reverend Samuel Cornish, both outspoken abolitionist pastors in New York City, joined together to form a Temperance Society among people of color, with about forty members at the beginning, "embracing various ages from 9 to 60 years." Within a few years, the numbers nationwide had grown dramatically, and so had the connection between the temperance and antislavery movements. In 1848, the *Liberator* described "A Brilliant Scene—Temperance among the Colored People in Philadelphia," a mass meeting organized by the Daughters of Temperance, who boasted some six hundred members. Featured speakers included prominent abolitionists, such as the fiery and energetic Henry Highland Garnet, "who for an hour and a half portrayed the terrible evils of alcohol," and Martin Delany, "who made a brief and able speech." Together, the efforts of the Daughters of Temperance and the parallel Sons of Temperance proved that "people of color are doing good service in this great reformation."[38]

In turn, the temperance movement gave Black people both a voice and a vehicle for demonstrating strict standards, especially in an era when white critics routinely derided them for loose morals and lazy behavior. Temperance events offered an opportunity to display racial respectability, all while enjoying a collective celebration. In August 1849, the *Trenton State Gazette* reported on a gathering of African American temperance organizations from around the area—including Princeton—in which "several hundred well dressed and well behaved colored persons had congregated together to participate in a moral and intellectual festival." Dressed in colorful regalia and accompanied by two brass bands, the crowd marched to Trenton's "African church" for a ceremony, then "paraded through several of our streets, headed by bands of music and carrying banners beautifully designed and executed." The white writer did not follow the procession "out to the grove selected for the addresses" or stay around for the rest of the festivities, but he did "presume that every thing went off satisfactorily to the parties most interested."[39]

Some white people, however, took a much less appreciative view of the temperance activities of Black people. In 1850, Frederick Douglass's newspaper, the *North Star*, carried a description of the national meeting of the Sons of Temperance, which had grown to some three hundred thousand members and claimed to be "as perfect and efficient an organization for the promotion of total abstinence as was ever presented to the American public, or the world." The meeting, held in Boston, opened with an impressive procession of four to five thousand participants, both white and Black, including several sections of the youth brigade, the Cadets of Temperance. "We noticed with pleasure among the Cadets, a section of colored boys," the *North Star* reported, "as neat and prim as any in the ranks, and appeared perfectly delighted." But during the speech-making that followed, a leader in the Sons of Temperance told newspaper writers that one of the delegates from the South "desires that the reporters will not mention the fact that *colored* boys walked in the procession, for fear it might *injure the reputation of the Order*." Other white delegates apparently felt the same: "We learn that several gentleman of tender nerves, on seeing the happy little colored fellows in the procession, quietly slipped their collars off, and left the ranks." The *North Star*'s account concluded with a sigh of resignation: "There is no accounting for taste in some folks."[40]

But the Sons of Temperance did take account of the political pressures emerging in 1850, both in their organization and in the nation as a whole. The white leadership at the Boston meeting determined, by a vote of seventy-six to six, "that it is improper and illegal to admit colored men into the general union." Some observers in the North found the sudden exclusion of African Americans to be a shocking "subserviency to the dictation of the South that is truly saddening." It added only the latest insult to a host of injuries: "Our colored brethren have been driven from the ballot-box, and contumeliously expelled from the railway car and church pew, and now here are men seeking to aggravate those crimes and insults by ostracizing them from the people's moral unions."[41] Still, the Sons of Temperance sought to remain a national organization by bending to the will of its southern members and, in the process, became an all-white organization.

That expulsion of Black members underscored the context when, on September 5, 1850, Princeton was "enlivened by a procession of the colored Sons of Temperance," as one resident wrote. "They marched through the streets with drums beating and banners flying to the western end of town, where they received the societies from Trenton and other places." The celebratory display did not just emphasize the evils of alcohol; it also embodied an act of racial solidarity, a sign of pride and defiance to spite the national organization. It also took place in light of a larger national political issue, the Compromise of 1850, a collection of bills about the future of slavery. The part of the package most immediately menacing to Black people, a more draconian Fugitive Slave Law, made slaveowners' property rights even more a matter of public policy than before, creating financial incentives for the capture and return of alleged runaways and, in the process, putting the burden on Black people to prove their free status. The Princeton event was not just a parade, but a protest.

The downside to the day came from "the efforts of a gang of white rowdies to create a disturbance," one of whom fired a pistol, "the ball from which grazed the cap of a young man who stood near." A Princeton student from Georgia wrote his parents about the Black people's parade: "They marched through the streets . . . with all the pomp and circumstance imaginable. Orations were delivered, I understand, by several of the order; and the whole procession, followed by women and children, proceeded a mile or two out of town to indulge themselves in a picnic." He neglected to note the pistol shot, but he did conclude that this public demonstration by free people of color "was a strange sight to those of us who were from the slave states."[42]

It might also have been a strange sight to many people in Princeton. By 1850, New Jersey still accommodated slavery, with 256 people held in bondage, six of them in towns surrounding Princeton. Princeton itself had no enslaved people, but it did have a comparatively large population of free Blacks, numbering 552, down somewhat from 1840, but still the fourth largest in the state, and the second largest by proportion, at 18.2 percent.[43] By 1850, Black people in Princeton had by no means overcome the white community's racial hostility, but they had developed their own institutions that would promote mutual identity, support, and even resistance.

A PRESENCE IN PRINCETON

And where was Betsey Stockton in all this? In a town the size of Princeton, she couldn't miss anything, and she was most likely in the midst of everything. From the 1830s to the 1850s, Princeton's Black community had become big enough to matter, but still small enough to be familiar. Everybody knew Betsey Stockton, and she knew them. Even though she lived mostly alone and sometimes suffered from feelings of emotional isolation, she also lived a life of involvement in her church and her community.[44]

But she also felt the sting of death, especially with the loss of two people important to her, coming in close succession in 1848. In late February, her fellow church member Peter Scudder died, a blow to both Stockton and the Black community. Scudder had operated what he called a public garden on Nassau Street, where he invited the public to "refresh themselves with Ice Creams, Mead & Beverage." Scudder had worked shining shoes and cleaning rooms for the students at the college, and his deferential manner caused many people to call him "Peter Polite." The local newspaper observed that he was "known to all . . . for his remarkable suavity of manners." But beneath the conciliatory surface lay a savvy business sense, particularly in real estate, and he became a successful and respected economic player. Betsey Stockton knew him better, however, as a founder of the First Presbyterian Church of Colour.[45]

Then Ashbel Green died, in Philadelphia, at the age of eighty-five. A train bore his body to Princeton, where the funeral service brought together a who's who of prominent Presbyterians in the region, a "large number of eminent divines and civilians, and alumni of the College of New Jersey . . . and all the professors of the College and of the Theological Seminary." (Charles Samuel Stewart was among them.) The women in attendance were presumably among the "numerous others . . . whose names we did not gather."[46] Betsey Stockton must certainly have been one of those. She had known Ashbel Green all her life, during which he had caused her pain, given her support, and for better or worse, had had a profound effect on her. Now, he had come back to Princeton, and his burial ceremony took place right across from her church and neighborhood. She had only to walk across Witherspoon Street to pay her respects.

Betsey Stockton had earned respect of her own on the other side of the street, in the Black community that had grown up around Witherspoon since the 1830s. She lived there, worshipped there, and most important, taught there. In a college town that had made its reputation on educating young white men, Betsey Stockton made hers on educating Black people, both in the church and in Princeton's one public school for Black children. In the shadow of the college, she made the Witherspoon neighborhood her own campus, its uplift her calling.

7

Betsey Stockton's Princeton Education

PRINCETON'S SUPERINTENDENT OF schools, George W. Schenck, started a new page in the Common School Register, writing "Dist. No. 6" across the top. Below that, he penned an entry for August 1, 1847, that began with discouragement: "Owing to a want of united effort it has been difficult if not impossible to maintain a large district school in this district suited to the wants of all classes." District 6 was the main part of town, Princeton Borough, which had three church-supported schools—one Episcopal, two Presbyterian—but not much in the way of public education. "The only district school," Schenck noted, "is for colored children under the care of Betsey Stockton (formerly a Missionary to the Sandwich Islands)." The schoolhouse itself seemed decent, a "rectangular neat & convenient" wood-frame building, but Schenck took an especially appreciative note of what went on inside. Betsey Stockton was an experienced teacher—her missionary reputation preceded her—and she had an enrollment of forty-five students of various ages, with about thirty attending on a daily average. On the whole, Schenck deemed Stockton to be "an excellent teacher" who ran "an excellent school." He came back again in October ("Visited the school & found it doing well"), then December ("Visited Betsey Stockton's school—school prosperous"), and January ("Visited the colored school still under the care of Betsey Stockton & found it as usual admirably well conducted"). Schenck's "as usual" made everything seem deceptively simple.[1]

But there was nothing usual about education for Black children. In the ten years Stockton had been in charge of her school, she had precious few models to follow, certainly not in New Jersey. In Newark, about forty miles north of Princeton, the town council had allocated a few hundred dollars a year for an "African School" in 1829, and by 1837, the city had two schools for Black children, one for boys and one for girls. New York's *Colored American* reported that when Newark's mayor visited the Colored Female School, he "alluded to the great fact that God has made of one blood, all nations, and reminded us that the elevation of our race depends upon the instruction of our daughters." The *Colored American* declared that the same applied to the sons, so that "our young men can rank in intelligence with their paler faced brethren." It was one thing to be able to "read, write, and cypher, with a mere smattering of geography and grammar," but Black people needed to strive for more: "The time has come in which Education should occupy a larger place in the minds of Colored Americans, than it has heretofore done. . . . All that mind and philosophy can procure for our children, should be industriously sought after."[2]

Those encouraging words ran up against a disconcerting reality, however. Schools for Black children were still very rare in the North, and sometimes the target of racism. Since 1833, the experience of Prudence Crandall, a white teacher in Canterbury, Connecticut, had served as a chilling warning to anyone who favored educating Black children, even in the North. When Crandall admitted one Black student into her otherwise all-white girls' school, the white parents became outraged, taking away their daughters and turning their venom on Crandall. When Crandall then turned her school into an academy for Black females only, the town and the state had her arrested, briefly jailed, and put on trial. When Crandall still refused to yield, people in Canterbury took extralegal action, attacking both her school building and her students. Crandall's case turned out to be drawn-out and divisive, but it sent a clear message to anyone contemplating a "colored school" in a largely white community: teaching Black children could be a risky business, even a dangerous one.[3] Betsey Stockton no doubt knew the story.

As it happened, white people at Princeton didn't respond to Stockton's school with open violence, but with quiet acceptance, even indifference. She wasn't trying to integrate a white school, after all, but to maintain a separate school for Black children—and a public school at that. The very idea of public education, much less public education for Black people, had yet to be widely embraced in Princeton. The town had almost no end of educational opportunities for families that could afford them, with new private and parochial schools appearing year after year. People of lesser means, both white and Black, faced only limited options, not to mention very limited support. Superintendent Schenck's reference to the "want of united effort" in sustaining public schools seemed almost an understatement. The effort to provide public education in Princeton moved fitfully through the 1830s to the 1850s; in most years, well under half of the school-aged children in town attended public school. Betsey Stockton's "school for colored children" remained a minority institution within a larger educational environment that sustained social and racial inequality. Most white people seemed not to notice, much less care.

THE POLITICS OF PUBLIC EDUCATION

In early 1837, a booster writing in the *Princeton Whig* seemed supremely satisfied with the town's situation. He extolled the many benefits of Princeton, claiming it to be "one of the handsomest towns, one of the healthiest, and one of the pleasantest in the state." Part of what made it that way was the kind of industrial development it didn't have—"no extensive factories and mill ponds to boast of . . . no spinning jennies and water wheels to keep the town in an interminable buzz, buzz, buzz." Instead, the main industry was education: the town "has long been known to the literary world, as a seat of learning and science," with "seminaries of learning unsurpassed . . .

Colleges, Academies, and Schools, male and female." The combination of Princeton's bucolic setting and abundance of education made it "a pleasant residence, to retire from the bustle of the city, where one may educate his children, and have them under parental care."[4]

No one would have to look far to see what the writer meant. The pages of the *Whig* repeatedly carried advertisements for Princeton's private schools and academies, with tuition prices included. A notice for Miss Billings's School for Young Ladies promised to provide, for three to five dollars per quarter, "all the higher branches of an English education, with the Latin language" and, beyond those academic challenges, "Plain and ornamental needlework will receive attention if desired." Miss Hoye's School likewise offered "All useful and ornamental branches required for the completion of female education" for about the same rate, with add-on costs for music, drawing and painting, and waxwork. For upper-class parents, five or six dollars a quarter might be affordable; it was about the equivalent of a week's wages for a common laborer, two weeks for a farmhand, or the cost of a hundred pounds of wheat flour. The combination of "useful and ornamental" education would be a bargain, setting the foundation of a girl's future standing in society.[5]

Schools for boys offered more and cost more. The Princeton Academy promised that "All branches necessary for entering into College or into business will be taught, and particular attention will be paid to the habits and morals of the pupils." The price per quarter ran eight dollars for "Languages and Mathematics," five for "Arithmetic, Writing, Geography, and English Grammar," and three for "Reading, Spelling, and Mental Arithmetic." Mr. Alvord's School provided much the same curriculum at about the same cost, with the business-savvy addition of "Book keeping *by double-entry*" for three-fifty. For those families who could afford it, this seemed a small price to pay compared to college itself. In 1836, a year at the College of New Jersey—tuition, room and board—cost $150 to $184, even though "there has been within a few years a considerable deduction in the charges."[6]

The leading boys' school in town was the Edgehill School, where

Charles Samuel Stewart sent ten-year-old Charles Seaforth Stewart, in 1833. It had been founded in 1829 by a former member of the College of New Jersey faculty, and throughout the 1830s, it was the school in town with the closest ties to the college. It was also by far the most expensive, charging $300 a year, essentially twice the cost of attending the college. For that, the students got room and board and a rigorous college-preparatory education: "While it is distinctly understood," the Edgehill School principals announced, "that the Greek and Latin languages, and the Mathematics, form the basis of the intellectual education received at this Seminary," students would also engage in many other areas of inquiry, from modern languages to history and geography to "Penmanship, Book-keeping, Drawing . . . and the Elements of Astronomy and Natural History." What they would not study, however, would be works of fiction and other "improper books," for which "their desks are often inspected, to see that none of an objectionable character are secretly introduced." It would be all but impossible for anything to be secretly introduced, since the rules required that the boys, no more than fifty in number and all under the age of twelve, live "under the care and control of the Principals and their Assistant, at all hours: eating with them at the same table; sleeping under the same roof; and in all respects constituting one family." The school did not admit day students, and the students in residence would "be entirely secluded from intercourse with other boys" in town.[7] The Edgehill School made private education exceedingly private.

Such was the educational environment in Princeton in 1837, when Betsey Stockton began teaching in the town. Stockton's school emphasized not "all branches necessary for entering into College or into business" but the basics—alphabet for a handful of the younger students, spelling and reading for most, and, for a few of the older students, geography and arithmetic ("not beyond simple divis.").[8] But the school's curriculum was not as critical as its continuity: it was not just the only public school for Black children, but at times the only public school at all.

It's unclear, in fact, exactly how "public" a school was—that is, how much financial support came from taxpayers. New Jersey had been slow to promote funding for education, with most state and local officials clinging to the notion that education for the children of ordinary people ought to be the province of poor relief and private charities. (In Princeton, a Female Benevolent Society had formed in 1817 to provide schooling for poor white children.) Only in 1829 did the state legislature pass a more comprehensive approach to public education, offering funds to support local common schools. But that money, which was hardly enough to begin with, all too often wound up being "appropriated to other uses" while no one took responsibility for overseeing it. Moreover, an 1831 revision of the law defined "common school" so loosely that private academies and parochial schools became eligible to share in the funding, thus spreading the allocation even thinner. Throughout the 1830s, a few writers making the case for common schools decried the situation, one of them complaining that the "present school-law of New Jersey is generally acknowledged to be useless; by many it is believed to be even worse than that." While New York and Pennsylvania had been "making rapid advances" in public education, "New Jersey is far below several of her sister states . . . [and] has either remained stationary or, more probably, been actually retrograding."[9]

Perhaps surprisingly, some of the most outspoken support for common schools came from a handful of advocates in Princeton. In 1834, a group of prominent men in town established the New Jersey Lyceum, a forum for promoting public education, and one of their members, E. C. Wines, started a publication, the *Monthly Journal of Education*, as a sympathetic print platform. They passed resolutions and pressured the state legislature to spend more money on both schools and teacher training.[10]

One of the most sustained voices came from a writer using the nom de plume "Philanthropos," who contributed a series of essays in the *Princeton Whig*. Philanthropos proceeded from what he considered a seemingly self-evident truth: "That the conditions of our schools is lamentable needs no demonstration." Throughout the United States, he asserted, "there is only about one out of five who can read, write, and cast accounts systematically." (In a footnote, the *Whig* editor admitted that there was no real evidence for that claim, but "we have been long satisfied that an exceeding deficiency exists in the knowledge of the lowest branches of education throughout this state.") The issue went well beyond skills alone, though, and came to rest at the very foundation of a free society, with a warning that "unless we sow the germs of intelligence in the early minds of our children our benignant liberties must soon vanish before the shrine of despotism." Uneducated people could themselves become a justification for that despotism, because "the tighter the chains must be to curb their fierce passions and unreasonable prejudices."[11]

But the larger problem lay in economic inequality. Too many parents, Philanthropos wrote, were "too much taken up by business of a pecuniary nature to bestow the requisite care on the education of their offspring." Thus the "children of the middling classes" would typically be left to be instructed by "a majority of ignorant, pedantic, and totally unqualified" teachers while their wealthier neighbors enjoyed better options: "The rich and opulent too often send their children to some higher school, in a town, than the poorer classes can afford, and the consequence is that a good school teacher cannot be secured in a district."[12] The difference between the educational prospects of the poor and the privileged thus reflected and reinforced a class divide.

Yet despite the dire warnings of Philanthropos and others, most white people in Princeton seemed to take little heed. The push for public education faltered. Over the next few years, several new private schools appeared on the scene, and the Episcopal and Presbyterian churches also established their own church-supported schools.[13] The 1840s became a time of trial for public education in Princeton—a test the town all but failed.

THE UNSTABLE "FOOTING OF PERFECT EQUALITY"

In October 1841, Princeton opened a new common school for white children, set in a "commanding, yet retired" location, "removed from the bustle of the village, and yet sufficiently easy of access." With an upper room for boys and a lower one for girls, the new school was "provided with all the necessary furniture and apparatus," including a separate desk and chair for each student. The school also boasted separate playgrounds, one for boys and one for girls, "on different sides of the building, and enclosed by a high fence, so that there can be no possible communication between them." Although the trustees of the school could not countenance coeducation, they did announce that it would be "open to all, between the ages of five and sixteen, whose parents or guardians reside within the limits of the District"—and who would pay tuition of two dollars per quarter, "for which instruction will be given in all the ordinary branches of an English education."[14]

Charging tuition for public education apparently struck some people as odd, even unjust, further exacerbating educational and class divisions. One critic explained the all-but-obvious problem: "the poor are unable of themselves to pay for schooling, and consequently keep their children home, while in the meantime the rich receive the benefit." But the trustees of the new school insisted that "those who think it ought to be a charity school" did not fully understand the connection between tuition and equality. Tuition-free education, the argument went, would be "unreasonable and impracticable . . . [and] establish the most odious distinctions." By providing state funding for public schools, the New Jersey legislature had "acted upon the principle that what costs us nothing is not generally valued highly, and the parent should cooperate with the State, and contribute somewhat at least towards the education of his child." The cost of such cooperation "should be so low as to be within the reach of all, and yet so high as to require some little effort on the part of the parent." In the end, if every family made some sacrifice to pay tuition, "the children of the poor and the rich might enjoy the very same advantages, and meet together upon a footing of perfect equality."[15]

The illusion of "perfect equality" aside, pupils at Princeton's public school for whites soon had little opportunity to meet together on any sort of footing at all. The teacher hired to run the school in 1841, Oliver H. Willis, left town for better opportunities two years later because, as a local observer later put it, "the school fund was too small and the school system too imperfect" to succeed. For the next few years, it became all but impossible to keep a common school for white children open in the district. In September 1847, the town again established one, this time under the charge of a Mr. Stewart, "a young man well qualified for the situation," who had taught for six months elsewhere before coming to Princeton. After three months, the superintendent visited Stewart's school, which had twenty-three students enrolled, and pronounced it "increasing and well conducted." But six months after that, in June 1848, he noted, without explanation, "White school not in operation." Then, in 1849, the superintendent acquired a new teacher, William R. Murphy, and District 6 again had a white school open.[16]

Throughout these comings and goings and openings and closings, Betsey Stockton's school remained "admirably well conducted."

In 1851, a new Princeton superintendent, O. H. Bartine, tried to summarize the past and look ahead to the future, in a reasonably positive light. "You will be pleased to learn," he wrote in his annual report to the state, "that the cause of education seems to be growing more and more important in the estimation of the inhabitants of Princeton township." The voters had agreed to raise a tax "equal to one dollar for every child capable of attending school," which according to his figures, would be $613. The question, though, was where that money would come from and where it would go. Most of the children and most of the tax money, he noted, "are embraced within one district (number 6) . . . [which] embraces the greater part of the borough of Princeton," but only "a very small portion of the children in this district attend the public district school." By far the majority attended other private and parochial schools, "some for girls, some for boys, some . . . under the control of religious denominations."[17]

Parochial schools posed the real problem. Secular private schools didn't draw on tax dollars, but Princeton superintendents "had been in the habit of distributing the public money among these church schools proportionately with the public schools," a practice that seemed to be not only acceptable to the Princeton citizenry, but preferable. In 1850, Princeton allocated a total of $239.06 for schools in District 6, with $74.48 going to the public school for whites, $53.20 for the school for Blacks, and $111.38, or 46 percent, for the parochial schools operated by the Episcopal church, the Presbyterian church, and the Presbyterian Female Benevolent Society. Bartine confessed to being a bit perplexed by the practice, but being mindful of the people who put him in his position, he noted that parochial school parents "by reason of their number, as well as their influence, are entitled to a respectful consideration." He eventually (and for self-preservation, wisely) concluded that everybody had a right to school choice, and everybody would benefit: "The whole population will enter upon the cause of education . . . and thereby more money will be contributed, more children will be at school, and a more cordial support will be insured to the system of primary education throughout our state."[18]

That seemed like an equitable idea, but it didn't work. In 1855, Bartine observed that "the schools are not as flourishing as they ought to be, owing principally to the parochial schools, which absorb so much of the public money." He saw no solution: "Until there is a change in this respect, the public schools cannot prosper." And they couldn't. The following year, his successor reported that the public schools in District 6 "are at present certainly not what they ought to be. Owing to the limited appropriation for their support, they have been closed nearly half the year."[19]

Princeton was not by any means alone in that regard. In 1849, New Jersey governor Daniel Haines noted with alarm that barely half the state's school-age children were actually in school. The state had been moving to remedy that, first in 1844 by putting into its constitution a provision for a secure school fund, then, in 1846, by passing legislation to create a state school superintendent and offer greater incentives for cities and towns to establish more robust tax-supported school systems, with locally elected superintendents. By the early 1850s, school reform had become a prominent concern.[20]

Eventually, in 1857, Princeton got on board with the trend, instituting a township-wide board of education, electing a superintendent, and reorganizing the school districts. The voters also approved allocating a thousand dollars to purchase a lot on Nassau Street and five thousand for the construction of a building, seeking to create "a public school that shall not be inferior to any in the state." The school opened in January 1858, ushering in what a local historian later called "a new era in the public schools of Princeton."

The new era still had some of the old racial restrictions, however. Princeton set aside fifty dollars—less than 1 percent of the $6,000 budgeted for the new school for white students on Nassau Street—for repairing "the house for the accommodation of the school for colored children" on Witherspoon Street. The renovations would make it, superintendent H. M. Blodgett explained, "now both comfortable and convenient," a standard he apparently found acceptable, but certainly not best in state or even best in town.[21] The separate but unequal school structures for white and Black students gave physical form to the comparative disparities in public education.

Still, the "school for colored children" did have one marked advantage: it had long been "well conducted by a female teacher, (colored) and is thought to exert a healthful influence among the colored population."[22] After two decades, Betsey Stockton had gained at least that much recognition among the powers that be.

ANOTHER SCHOOL ON SUNDAY

Stockton had a second teaching position in Princeton, one that predated her work in the public school. In 1835, soon after she and the other Black congregants had been separated from the town's main Presbyterian church, they began a Sunday school. The driving force behind the effort was Anthony Simmons, like Stockton, a founding member of the Witherspoon Street Church and, like her, born into slavery. After gaining his freedom and coming to Princeton, he became a successful entrepreneur, operating a popular Nassau Street eatery, a catering business, and a bathhouse "for the accommodation of the Gentlemen of Princeton." While serving white people, he also became active in his support for Blacks. In 1833, he had applied to the Presbyterian session "for the privilege of using the upper part of the session house as a school room for coloured children"; a group of white women had earlier begun to use the lower part as a school for white children. He received permission to do so, but with the stipulation "that he cause to be repaired all damages done to said room, and that no disturbance be occasioned to the school below." Over the next three decades, he would become one of Betsey Stockton's main allies in promoting the education of Black children in Princeton. He would also become one of the town's antislavery mainstays. In 1835, he made a donation of five dollars to the American Anti-Slavery Society, and he remained identified with the movement for the rest of his life. By the time he died, in 1868, he was by far the wealthiest African American in Princeton, a donor to both the college and his church. In 1860, he modestly listed his occupation as "Confectionery," but that greatly understated the larger reach of his influence.[23]

Simmons spearheaded the Sunday school, but Betsey Stockton and the women of the church made it work. Of the six women who became the original teachers, Stockton was the only one who could be considered experienced—four of the other five later appeared in census records as "washer-ironer," the most common occupation for women of color in Princeton—but all of them had been founding members of the Witherspoon Street Church, lived close by, and labored consistently with the church's children. Women would remain the most consistent teachers, making the Sunday school an essential part of the church's mission. For the first thirteen years, as a brief historical sketch later explained, "it was altogether in the hands of the colored people."[24]

Those hands lost at least some of their grip in 1848, when students from the Princeton Theological Seminary became increasingly involved and changed the administrative structure. A succession of white male Sunday school superintendents—at least ten over the next decade—assumed authority over the operations, and other men from the seminary came in as teachers, eventually outnumbering the Black women.[25] What had originally been an in-house initiative in the control of an all-Black congregation soon became an accessory of the seminary, a teacher-training ground for some of its missionary-minded students and advocates of colonization.

There was nothing altogether new about Sunday schools, nor about the sometimes-conflicting notions of what they might best do for African American people. Like the religion from which they sprang, Sunday schools represented, in microcosm, the two sides of the coin of Christianity—liberation and subjugation. In a nation that failed to provide regular weekday schools for Black children, Sunday schools offered at least a few hours of education, and not just in religion but in literacy as well. In the two decades before the Witherspoon Street Church started its own school, a handful of northern churches, mostly in urban areas, offered Sunday instruction to Black children from families of both the free and enslaved.[26] While many white people were wary of any attempt to elevate the minds of Black people, some saw the utility in promoting obedience and order through "steady attendance at the Sanctuary" on the Sabbath: "No more is the voice of quarreling and accompanying profanity to be heard on that day along our streets; but . . . the delightful buzz of . . . scholars reading or learning to read the word of God."[27] Learning to read the word was a big step beyond simply listening to it, and learning to write it gave them another skill as well—taken together, two critical tools they could use in all aspects of their lives, on every day of the week.

In the particular case of the Witherspoon Sunday school, the most extensive inside view comes from Thomas R. Markham, a seminary student who served as superintendent in 1852–53. Markham came from Vicksburg, Mississippi, and he knew he faced a challenge as a white male newcomer in a Black female activity. "Lord, give me grace & strength," he prayed. Over the course of his first week he would meet with the female teachers and write that "My heart warms toward these people." But he also turned a critical eye toward their Sunday school: "Classes & lessons are confused & indeed the school is sadly in need of system & order."[28]

To help rectify that, Markham wrote out three pages of procedures, which began with "Order of Exercises," a step-by-step outline of a typical session. Beginning at 9 a.m., the whole school took part in the recitation of the Ten Commandments, followed by lessons and questions from the catechism, the distribution of books and other reading materials, and finally the collection. Then, at 10 a.m., "the bell is rung, when the number of scholars & teachers present, and the amount of the collection, are made known. The Teachers from the Seminary are then at liberty to withdraw." At that point, apparently, the female teachers would take charge for the remainder of the day's lesson, in which "Each class recites publicly, one or more questions in the Catechism," according to their levels of age and advancement.[29]

Instruction underscored the importance of literacy. When the students participated in the collection, they would know that their pennies were to be "appropriated to the purchases of libraries, for destitute Sabbath schools." They also learned that some of the reading material they received—the *Youth's Penny Gazette*, a publication of the American Sunday School Union—was not just for them alone, but "one paper to go to each family, represented in the School . . . [and] if enough are left, each scholar, in the adult classes, receives one."[30] In that sense, young children learned about the value of providing reading materials to people poorer than they were as well as of promoting literacy at home.

Markham held regular meetings with the female teachers, with the venue rotating from one home to another, but "On the last Saturday of each month, it is held at 'Aunt Betsy's' (Miss Betsy Stockton)." Even though he used a patronizing term common in the South, Markham recognized how much Stockton stood out. In September 1852, he noted that teaching colleagues elected her treasurer of the Sunday school (although she could report only $6.28 available). Later that fall, the school held an exhibition of speaking and singing performances by Stockton's students, which "surprised everyone," Markham reported, and "greatly surpassed my expectations." In keeping with the school's emphasis on literacy, the three best speakers received prizes of books—the Protestant standby *Pilgrim's Progress* for first place, and "Testaments & Psalms" for the other two—and afterward children and adults alike "proceeded to the School house where a handsome repast was spread with very creditable taste." Markham came away quite impressed: "The whole affair passed off pleasantly & harmoniously; in a way highly creditable to Aunt Betsy's efficiency as a teacher & the management & good taste of our female teachers."[31]

Markham had good sense in giving credit to those female teachers. He and other men from the seminary almost always outnumbered the women as teachers, and they generally took charge of the classes for older students, including some adults (the "Ladies Bible Class," "class of old Ladies," "class of girls," "the Bible Class of Young men," and the "class of boys"), leaving Betsey Stockton and other longtime female teachers with the youngest ("Infant class of girls," "Infant class of boys").[32] But Stockton had taught infants well before coming to Princeton, and she knew how important that first foundation in learning could be.

"AN EPOCH IN THE HISTORY OF THE SCHOOL"

In sharp contrast to the good words Markham had for Betsey Stockton and the other women, he wrote with nothing but scorn for the Black pastor, the Reverend Charles W. Gardner. In 1850, Gardner had become embroiled in a tense situation with Markham's immediate predecessor, Edwin T. Williams, a personal rift that also pointed to the larger political divisions on race and religion that had been developing for years. In writing about the affair in the Sunday school records, Markham underscored its seriousness: "This affair was an epoch in the history of the school."[33]

Sunday school disputes aren't usually an epoch in any sort of history, but this one took on a surprising significance, in Markham's

FIGURE 7.1. The Reverend Charles W. Gardner, Library Company of Philadelphia.

telling. It opens up a larger picture of the relationship between Witherspoon Street Church and the Princeton Theological Seminary. In this case, as in almost everything that involved religion and education in Princeton, the politics of race lay at its heart.

Markham cast the controversy in stark terms, of a good white Christian, "dearly loved by the people," undone by an evil Black one, "a most unruly and unfortunate specimen of Christian character." The alleged victim, Williams, had been a student at the College of New Jersey, class of 1850, and he became superintendent of the

Witherspoon Sunday school while still an undergraduate, in the spring of 1849, serving two years, until the spring of 1851, when he was a first-year student at the seminary. Williams had been "zealous and indefatigable" in his labors, Markham wrote, and his service had become the "culminating point of the school's success": "There were over 20 Teachers & more than 100 Scholars in regular attendance; the prayer meetings & monthly Concert were well attended even by the Smaller children; the contributions to the Missionary fund were liberal regular & a lively active spirit pervaded the School in every part of its arrangements." Williams apparently even planned to postpone his professional goals and spend an additional year at the seminary "rather than interrupt his cherished work" with the Sunday school.[34] In Markham's description, there seemed to be no end to the young man's diligence and devotion.

But then Williams seemed to have "interfered with the Pastor, & stepped in between him & his people." Exactly what that transgression was, Markham didn't say, but it was apparently enough to undermine Williams's relationship with Gardner and his future at the school. In Markham's Manichean telling, the evil stemmed from Gardner, who apparently resented Williams. "Their attachment to Bro. W, & the fact that he was a Southerner, aroused the jealousy, and gained him the ill will of their preacher, a colored man." Not only was Gardner Black, Markham continued, but he was a "negligent pastor & violent abolitionist . . . Devoid of spirituality, & immersed in secular pursuits." Gardner "gave no attention to his pastoral charge," Markham asserted, and left his people "neglected, & spiritually starved." Using "both open and underhand opposition," the pastor made it impossible for Williams to work at the church. Williams's mentor at the seminary, the longtime professor Archibald Alexander, advised him to give up his position, and "as this seemed the only prospect for peace, he resigned." This, Markham said, "was a heavy blow, to both him & the people." Williams continued to visit with some of the people at the Sunday school, but "The connection between Bro. W. & the people was sundered, & 3 years, of anticipated labor, brought suddenly to a close. . . . Still the separation was a season of severe suffering, & it was then out of human power, to see how good could be evolved from so much evil."[35] Markham noted in 1853: "Bro. W. is ready to sail this summer for Africa," where he would become a missionary in Monrovia, Liberia. A few months later, Markham would also depart, back to Vicksburg, Mississippi, where he would later become a chaplain in the army of the Confederate States of America.[36]

There is no way to corroborate Markham's account of the controversy, but there is an alternative way to read it—from the standpoint of Charles Gardner. Gardner might well have found Edwin Williams a worrisome presence, not simply as a southerner from Savannah, but as a student at the two educational institutions most associated with colonization, the College of New Jersey and the Princeton Theological Seminary. Williams's adviser, Archibald Alexander, was for decades one of the most prominent Presbyterian supporters of colonization. In Gardner's eyes, Williams may have been essentially a proxy for Alexander.

Just a few years earlier, in his 1846 *History of Colonization on the Western Coast of Africa*, Alexander had pointed proudly to the role the college and the seminary had played in creating the colonization movement in 1816: "The first public meeting which ever took place to consider the subject of African colonization in this country, was held in the Presbyterian church in the borough of Princeton," Alexander wrote. "The meeting was small, but in the number of attendants were most of the professors of the College and of the Theological Seminary. It was apparent that the interest of those to whom the scheme was made known was increased the longer they thought upon it." That church was also the site of the 1824 founding meeting of the New Jersey Colonization Society, and again, Alexander wrote with pride that "the entire faculty and about half of the Seminary's Board of Directors were present and volunteered to play key leadership roles for the coordination of the colonization efforts in New Jersey." Alexander and other white Presbyterians, in Princeton and elsewhere, may have seen colonization as a benign means of righting the wrong of slavery, and they may also have seen an equally benign purpose in training young men like Edwin Williams to go to Liberia to minister to the masses.[37]

But Charles Gardner, like the vast majority of Black people, clergy and laypeople alike, had long since rejected the colonization movement as a wrongheaded and fundamentally racist nonresponse to slavery, and he had no sympathy for the seminary that had so long been its source of support. If Gardner could have been accused, as Thomas Markham argued, of being "immersed in secular pursuits," he could have said the same thing about the Princeton Theological Seminary, as other members of the Black clergy did. In 1837, Samuel Cornish, the African American abolitionist newspaper publisher and Presbyterian pastor, had called Princeton Theological Seminary a school of "colonization abominations . . . proslavery influence and sinful prejudice against color." Three years later, Cornish and Theodore Sedgwick Wright wrote a lengthy tract titled *The Colonization Scheme Considered*, in which they argued that the "American church is not *opposed* to slavery and the slave-trade" and pointed out that in West Africa, colonization and slave-trading comfortably coexisted. Gardner, who had himself been part of a five-member committee of prominent Black Philadelphians to write a remonstrance against the American Colonization Society, came to Princeton with his own solid credentials as a critic of colonization.[38]

Gardner could see the larger political picture. It was not just a question of being wary of a seminary-trained missionary-to-be but also of feeling at odds with the influence the Princeton Theological Seminary exercised in his church. Moreover, the timing of the troubles, in 1850–51, could only have heightened Gardner's sense of the menace surrounding himself and his congregation. The Fugitive Slave Act that came with the passage of the Compromise of 1850 had immediately become the most terrifying aspect of the law for Black people.

No doubt frustrated and certainly aged—Gardner was approaching seventy at the time—he resigned his pastorate in 1852. He probably wouldn't have been surprised to learn afterward that, as the church record put it, "a gentleman from the Seminary, Bro. Eli C. Botsford, supplies the pulpit."[39]

BETSEY STOCKTON'S STABILITY

It had been a tumultuous couple of years in the Witherspoon Street Church. By late 1853, both Edwin Williams and Charles Gardner had left, as had Thomas Markham, the man who took so much trouble to chronicle the controversy. In their wake came a succession of white men from the seminary—pastors, Sunday school superintendents, and male teachers—creating enough turnover to give everyone good reason to wonder when things might settle down. The members of the congregation could take heart, however, in several longtime stalwarts, none more notable than Anthony Simmons and Betsey Stockton, both of whom had established the Sunday school as "altogether in the hands of the colored people." They still kept their hands in throughout the 1850s and into the early 1860s, helping to provide stability.

On several occasions, Betsey Stockton became a bridge between the Black congregation and the white men in authority. She could apparently engage them in terms of simple human decency. James H. Brookes, an impoverished Tennessean who served briefly as superintendent of the Witherspoon Sunday school, credited her with saving his life through her personal generosity. "But for the kind ministrations of a quaint old negro woman, 'Aunt Betsey,'" Brookes's nineteenth-century biographer wrote, "he used to say that he could hardly have lived through those few months in New Jersey." Stockton also developed a positive personal relationship with George Musgrove Giger (College of New Jersey, class of 1841, and longtime member of the faculty), who became interim pastor at Witherspoon in 1856. She gave him "a small token of Affection and gratitude from one of his humble Flocks"—a just-published copy of a book by Charles Samuel Stewart, *Brazil and La Plata: The Personal Record of a Cruise*. Her connection with Giger would prove to be useful in the world beyond the church: in 1860, he would become superintendent of the public schools in Princeton.[40]

In the meantime, her Sunday school teaching served to complement the work she did at her public school. She had been at both jobs since the mid-1830s, and she showed no intention of stopping either one, especially at a time when people needed peace and reassurance—and literacy. She also knew the importance of literacy to older people, and in 1859, she took the Sunday school in a new direction, providing education to adults. Clearly, she had identified a critical need: the 1860 US Census would identify 165 Black people in Princeton as "Persons over 20 years of age who cannot read & write."

To address this issue, she turned to the latest superintendent of the Sunday school, Lewis W. Mudge (College of New Jersey, class of 1862), to initiate the program. Mudge was only a sophomore, best known on campus for introducing baseball, but Stockton convinced him to help bring literacy to the Black community. "She was very deeply interested in the higher education of her people," Mudge later recalled, "and at her solicitation I started a night school for the young men and women." During his time as superintendent, 1859–65, Mudge took responsibility for running the adult school, recruiting some of his fellow students to teach, and noted that it "was very well attended." Mudge gave the greatest credit to the driving force behind it: "It is but giving due acknowledgement to say that the success of this night school was due in large measure to the preparation obtained under Aunt Betsey's tuition." She was "the most influential person in the colored community," he would write. "Among her own people she moved a queen and her word was law."[41]

She apparently had an equally impressive effect on Mudge and some of the other white men who encountered her at the Witherspoon Street Church. For over thirty years, Betsey Stockton had labored six days a week for the education of her community, for people of all ages, and the fruits of her efforts pervaded Princeton—the Witherspoon neighborhood, to be sure.

BOOKS AND BIBLES IN "NEGRO TOWN"

The significance of education in Princeton's Black community certainly impressed one observer, a white woman from the South named

Ann Maria Davison, who visited Princeton in May 1855. She knew something about the white side of town, but she didn't know much about the Black community, "about the manner of their living—in what way they supported themselves, and what were their characters generally." Those were big questions, and to answer them, she set out into the neighborhood white people called "Negro Town."[42]

Davison visited fourteen homes—not Betsey Stockton's, as it happened, but four occupied by women who taught alongside her in the Sunday school—and she took a good look at people's possessions, paying special attention to books and writing materials. In the first house, Davison asked for pencil and paper to record her notes, thinking she might not find any elsewhere, only to be reassured by the lady of the house, "I guess Madam you will not go into any of the houses of the colored people and not find pen and ink, or paper and pencil." And so it was: Davison found "Pencil Pen Ink and Paper" even in the poorest of homes, "Books on Centre table" in some of the more comfortable ones, sometimes a newspaper, and "always the Bible"—in sum, basic tools of literacy embedded in the Black community.[43]

Davison also took note of the community institutions that nurtured literacy and learning. "The colored people of Princeton have a church," Davison added, and "a Sunday school of over a hundred scholars." She also reported seeing "a group of some five or six colored children, as if just out of school, dressed well, deporting themselves as well as white children, with their school bags on their arms, seeming to contain a goodly number of books."[44]

Ann Maria Davison apparently never met Betsey Stockton, but she was writing about Stockton's church, Stockton's Sunday school, and Stockton's students. Stockton embodied an important point of human connection between the church and school—a founder of both, a teacher in both, a leader who helped make both into welcoming institutions for Black people, providing them with the intellectual tools they needed for existence, if not equality, in white society. As the main face of education in Princeton's Black community, Betsey Stockton had become an institution herself.

8

A Time of War, a Final Peace

ONE MID-JUNE AFTERNOON in 1860, Eli Stonaker came to the door of Betsey Stockton's house, carrying pencil and paper, poised to ask some personal questions. Stonaker had a new job as assistant US marshal for the federal census, and his instructions were to make "a personal visit to each dwelling-house, and to . . . approach every family and individual of whom you solicit information, with civil and conciliatory manners . . . as a means of obtaining the information desired with accuracy and dispatch." Accuracy mattered, and so did thoroughness. From June 8 through July 18, Stonaker would cover every house in Princeton, counting every head and taking every name, until he eventually recorded a total population of 3,723. (Getting to know the town so well apparently paid off: in 1868, Stonaker would be elected Princeton's mayor.) For his more immediate benefit as census-taker, he would be paid "two cents for each person enumerated."[1]

Two cents was all he would get for visiting Betsey Stockton: she was the sole resident of her house on Quarry Street, around the corner from her church and school. That had been the case for the almost three decades of her life in Princeton. She never married, an uncommon though not unknown situation for Black women in America, despite the gender conventions of their era. Some postponed or rejected marriage because of their commitment to engaging in religious or reform activities. Some did so because of their insistence on maintaining their own emotional or economic independence, not wanting to live under the authority of a husband. Some did so because of their sexual identity, an issue seldom addressed publicly.[2] All of these could have contributed to Betsey Stockton's situation, but there is nothing written by her or about her to indicate why she lived as she did.

Eli Stonaker didn't ask, but listed her as a household of one. For the sake of the census, "one person living separately and alone in a house, or a part of a house, and providing for him or herself" qualified as "family."[3]

The form Eli Stonaker had to fill out required basic information for every resident—age, sex, race, place of birth, and so forth—but he found in the Black community that the answers hinged on some measure of supposition. In Betsey Stockton's case, he listed her age as sixty, although, like many people born into slavery, she didn't know the exact date of her birth; around 1800 would have to do. Under the column for race—or "Color," as the census form had it—the instructions called for the census-taker to make an indication in the box provided: "in all cases where the person is white leave the space blank," making that essentially the default option; if "black without admixture insert the letter 'B'; if a mulatto, or of mixed blood, write 'M.'" The instructions were very clear that it was "very desirable to have these directions carefully observed." Exactly how Stonaker would follow such directions, though, remains unclear. Perhaps he would ask if a person had "mixed blood," or perhaps just guess. In any event, he put an "M" next to Betsey Stockton's name. In the end, he counted 126 people in Princeton as "Mulatto," 495 as "Black"—621 in all, over 16 percent of the population.[4]

PRINCETON'S BLACK COMMUNITY

Stonaker also asked people to give their occupation and the value of their property, both real and personal. His instructions said that

"Exact accuracy may not be arrived at, but all persons should be encouraged to give a near and prompt estimate for your information." When Stonaker inquired at Betsey Stockton's, she gave him a figure of $400 in personal property. Collectively, his census records provided a rough economic profile of the Black community after decades of local struggle and institution building—and on the eve of a national Civil War.[5]

The range for property and occupation was quite limited. Anthony Simmons—Betsey Stockton's abolitionist friend and fellow church founder and Sunday school teacher—stood alone at the top of the pyramid among Black people, with $10,000 of real estate and $1,600 of personal property. That put him well below the wealthiest white people in town—Susan D. Brown, listed as "Lady," with $100,000 in real estate and another $100,000 in personal property, or Charles Smith Olden, the Republican governor of New Jersey, at $70,000 in each category—but about on par with several white shopkeepers and a few professors. After Anthony Simmons, though, the picture changed dramatically: seven Black people owned real estate worth over $1,000, while only sixteen others could claim real estate valued between $500 and $1,000.

Like Simmons, the "Confectionary," a few people in the Black community had specific-seeming occupations: a couple of barbers, a grocer, a musician, a coachman, and the proprietor of a clothing store—James Johnson, the former fugitive who had settled in Princeton and sold used clothes and furniture to the college students. Everyone else fell into broader, more common categories. Almost thirty men were in food service—eleven cooks and eighteen waiters—and over forty women and men worked as servants, either at the college or in private homes. By far, the main occupation listed for Black men was "Laborer" or "Farm Laborer," with a total of sixty-two, and twenty Black women appeared on the list as "Washer & Ironer." Only one Black person in Princeton was counted with the title of "Teacher"—Betsey Stockton.[6]

Neither Betsey Stockton nor any other African American counted in the more significant national activity that came later that year, the election of 1860. Black people in Princeton certainly had their opinions about the momentous issues facing the nation, the state, and their own community, but they had no way to express them in the electoral process—nor did white women. The critical decisions lay solely in the hands of the white men who had the right to vote.[7] Everyone else would have to accept the results and deal with the consequences. And those consequences soon became clear, and not just for the nation but for Princeton in particular. The presidential election and its aftermath would highlight the social and racial divisions that had existed in the town for years, giving Princeton's Black people a new sort of visibility. Over the last five years of her life, Betsey Stockton would witness more dramatic changes in Princeton than she had seen in the previous sixty.

THE PRESIDENT PASSES THROUGH

A little after 11:00 a.m. on Thursday, February 28, 1861, a powerful locomotive—the smokestack painted red, white, and blue, with "1776" on the front and "Union" on each side—and two well-appointed cars chugged along the railroad tracks near Princeton, slowing but not coming to a stop. Braving the winter chill and snow flurries, a crowd of excited townspeople had been waiting for quite some time, and when the train came through, "cheer after cheer rang up in honor of the people's President." Abraham Lincoln and his wife were aboard, along with "a bevy of New York reporters." Earlier that morning, the Lincolns had crossed by ferry from New York City into Jersey City, where Lincoln spoke briefly to an assembly of people estimated at twenty thousand, then headed slowly southward down the track past shouting crowds in Newark (twenty-five thousand) and into Elizabeth (fifteen thousand), Rahway (seven thousand), New Brunswick (five thousand), Princeton ("a large concourse"), and finally Trenton, where they arrived at noon. There, the president-elect got off, met the mayor and some local dignitaries, climbed into a waiting carriage, and rode behind bands of musicians, a mounted company of horsemen, and two companies of local militia—120 men in all—to the State House. There Lincoln gave a short speech to New Jersey's governor and members of the state senate, then crossed over to the chamber of the state assembly to make another address, which the legislators cheered with "shouts of applause, prolonged for many minutes."[8]

Lincoln had no illusions about the apparent enthusiasm of the crowds along the track, much less the politicians at the State House. "The welcome you have given me is a patriotic one," he thanked them with sly humility, "for a majority of you did not agree with those who thought me the best man for the Presidency." New Jersey was the sole northern state that had not given him a majority in the election, with only 48.1 percent of the popular vote, and the only one to have split its electoral vote, 4–3, just barely in his favor. A few days after the election, the *New York Times* ran an acerbic headline, "New Jersey the Only Free State known to be Untrue to Freedom."[9]

The issue was more complicated than that, however. In the years leading up to the election, the notion of freedom had taken many forms in the minds of voters. Slavery had become the inescapable issue, although not many voters yet called for its complete abolition. Lincoln and the Republican Party took the strongest antislavery position in 1860, calling for slavery's containment in the South and a restriction of its expansion into the West—or even, as some people feared, into the North. The debate over slavery also heightened the emphasis on other issues, from sectionalism to popular sovereignty to states' rights to secession to economic collapse to nativism to, as always, racism. In New Jersey, shifting partisan alliances, not to mention the personal ambitions of individual politicians, added to the complexity. Many Republicans, trying to avoid being associated with the "radicalism" of Lincoln and the national party, began to identify themselves by another term, Opposition. Most of the New Jersey supporters of the three other presidential candidates—Stephen Douglas of Illinois, John C. Breckinridge of Kentucky, John Bell of Tennessee—came together in a shaky, late-breaking fusion ticket just over a week before the election, which resulted in

Douglas's getting the three electoral votes that didn't go to Lincoln. Small wonder, then, that Lincoln began his Trenton remarks as he did.[10]

Still, he had won, and now, as the "people's President," he had to lead the people as best he could—and lead them in war, it seemed, to restore the Union. A newspaper account relayed Lincoln's direct question to the assembled politicians: "If you think I am right you will stand by me, won't you? [Yes, yes!] This is all I ask. If I weather the ship through the storm during four years, you may get, at the end of that time, a better pilot." With that, he "closed amid immense cheering," went to have a quick lunch at a hotel, and then appeared on the balcony to say a few words to an enthusiastic throng of Trentonians. After that, Lincoln headed for Philadelphia and, eventually, Washington, DC, where in a few days he would give one of the most significant inaugural addresses in American history. "So much for Mr. Lincoln in New Jersey," the newspaper report concluded.[11]

And so much for Princeton, hardly worth a whistle-stop. Lincoln might have taken heart in the knowledge that the pro-Republican (and, since 1859, only) newspaper in town, the *Princeton Standard*, supported him. He would likewise have found encouragement in the crowd of people who came out to cheer him—men, women, and children, white and Black. But he also knew that most of them weren't eligible to vote, and he no doubt knew the numbers for those who were: only 44 percent of Princeton's voters had supported him, a rate lower than that of the state as a whole.[12]

Lincoln also knew Princeton's reputation, a conservative college town with long-standing ties to the South, which stemmed from the College of New Jersey. The students set the tone for the college, the college set the tone for the town, and for years, the tone had reflected the regular presence of southerners. "The North and South are generally pretty evenly represented," a student publication explained in the early 1850s. "But few students ever come to Princeton from farther north than New York," noting that "the Yankees giving the preference to their own Colleges." From the 1840s through the 1850s, that regional difference remained distinctive: the proportion of southern students at Harvard and Yale typically hovered at under 10 percent, while at Princeton the figure sometimes exceeded 50 percent. In 1860, Princeton counted some 115 undergraduates from the South, still almost 37 percent of the student body. Moreover, the southern influence had become embedded in campus culture. As a member of the class of 1845 later recalled, "Does any one wonder that this was called a Southern College—and that, to some extent, we had Southern influences and ways." A Louisiana-born member of the class of 1859, Henry Kirke White Muse, underscored that sentiment, writing to his father in his freshman year that those southern influences in a northern college essentially eradicated sectional differences and gave Princeton a national identity: "Let the Southerns come here," Muse said. "I believe that old Princeton College is THE College, not the college of the South, nor of the North, but the college of the Union." But by the time of Muse's graduation, the Union could hardly be taken for granted as a source of unity. As he wrote his father, "Politics is the engrossing topic here now, and we have every class: Southern Fire-eaters, ultra-Democrats, Black Republicans, Abolitionists, old line Whigs, etc." The diversity of viewpoints did not mean that all positions had equal numbers, much less equal voice: "The Black Republicans and Abolitionists," Muse assured his father, "are very few, and have sense enough to keep their principles to themselves."[13]

The politics of college students probably didn't matter much to other people in Princeton in more normal times, but with a critical election looming and some students eligible to vote, campus passions more easily spilled out into the town. When it came to the issues of slavery and race, students gave rowdy expression to opinions that otherwise lay more quietly suffused throughout the white community. That became dramatically evident on the evening of December 3, 1859, when a sizable crowd of students marched through the streets carrying banners denouncing leading abolitionists, most notably "John Brown, the horse thief, murderer and martyr." Brown had been hanged earlier that day in Virginia for his failed attack on the federal armory at Harpers Ferry, triggering the triumphant demonstration by antiabolitionist students. They also carried banners denouncing William Seward, the staunch antislavery senator from New York, and Henry Ward Beecher, the equally prominent abolitionist pastor, along with effigies of the two men, which they subsequently burned in front of the college. One of the students involved noted that the demonstrators were not all southerners, but "a large part of the crowd was composed of Northern men from New York, Pennsylvania and New Jersey." Thus the effigy-burning was not just "an outburst of Southern feeling; but the expression of disapprobation on the part of liberal students from all sections." Additional disapprobation also came, so the newspapers reported, from "a large crowd of spectators from the town," who cheered the speakers. Members of the college faculty tried to break up the protest, but they proved to be too few and too feckless, so "the powers that be were set at naught, and the work proceeded."[14]

Princeton had never been a safe place for antislavery sentiment, and the events of that evening brought together town and gown, northerners and southerners, in sufficient numbers to make that point even clearer. When the presidential election came less than a year later, many of those protesters, including some college students, showed up at the polls. Lincoln may have been lucky to get the percentage of the vote he did in Princeton.

But by the time he passed through Princeton in late February 1861, Lincoln was facing a much bigger conflict than a student street demonstration. In the four months since his election, seven states in the South had already seceded from the Union, and several other states seemed poised to join them in the Confederate States of America. While Lincoln had been making his way to the capital, a group of 131 influential political figures—including former senator Robert F. Stockton of Princeton and twelve College of New Jersey alumni—had been meeting for almost a month as a Washington Peace Commission, making one last effort at conciliation to forestall war. The commission proposed constitutional amendments that would not only preserve slavery in the South but allow it to extend to the West, directly undercutting Lincoln and the platform of the

Republican Party. The Peace Commission came to an end on February 27, the day before Lincoln's train came through New Jersey, and he had no intention of bowing to its pro-slavery proposals.[15]

But a few weeks later, on April 12, Lincoln saw any prospect for peace vanish in the smoke of the Confederacy's attack on Fort Sumter in Charleston, South Carolina. As he would put it so succinctly four years later, in his second inaugural address, "And the war came."

PRINCETON GOES TO WAR

The outbreak of war changed everything in Princeton, or so it seemed. The most immediate and visible change came to the college, where the benign embrace of southerners suddenly appeared suspect. After the Confederate attack on Fort Sumter, several pro-Union students climbed to the top of Nassau Hall to hoist an American flag, shout out some rooftop speeches, and fire a few old muskets as a show of support for the national government. This display was also an act of defiance toward the faculty, and particularly President John Maclean Jr., who had sought to remain officially on the fence in the run-up to the rebellion. An undergraduate later recalled that "Before the outbreak of hostilities the policy of the College was wisely that of neutrality. It favored the Peace Commission at Washington, and hoped that through mutual concessions war would be averted." Maclean openly admitted that he had not voted for anyone in the presidential election, although he did note that "My preference was for a Southern man." His sympathy for southern boys led him to order the flag taken down, so as not to offend anyone who might see it as an institutional political statement. But in the context of open conflict, Maclean's moderation had lost traction among northern students, and the flag went back up—and stayed there.[16]

The end of the 1860–61 academic year brought an end to any significant southern presence on campus. Acting "in consequence of the state of the country," the college adopted a generous policy of offering "honorable dismission" to over fifty students from seceding states. Before everyone departed, classmates from both North and

South engaged in emotional farewells, expressing their affection for each other and promising to see each other again—even if on the field of battle.[17] By the beginning of the fall semester, the College of New Jersey had become a different place, a northern college after all, and the remaining students were beginning to cast aside the polite deference formerly paid to pro-South sentiment.

At least one student and, more important, the college leadership learned that the hard way. In September 1861, a member of the class of 1863 from Brooklyn, New York, became so obnoxiously outspoken in his support of the Confederate cause that three pro-Union students pulled him from his bed at midnight, hustled him to the college water pump, and subjected him to a cold-water cleansing of his political views. The pumping became a well-publicized warning to others, leading a neighboring newspaper to suggest that "There are other persons in Princeton who might be subjected to the same process with advantage." The faculty suspended the three who did the deed, but most of their fellow students and a good number of townspeople rallied to their support, giving them a patriotic parade to the train station. The *Princeton Standard* reported on the "long procession, preceded by martial music, and exciting on the way to the depot the wildest enthusiasm. Animating cheers made the town ring and aroused the curiosity of the whole population." Facing animosity in both the campus and the community, President Maclean backed down, issuing a public letter stating that the faculty "will not permit the utterance of sentiments denunciatory of those who are engaged in efforts to maintain the integrity of the national government." The moral to the story, so the *Standard* concluded, was that the College of New Jersey could no longer claim to be neutral: "Our sons must not be dead to the struggle in which their fathers are now engaged."[18]

The local reaction to the events at the college provided a barometer of political sentiment. The townspeople who had turned out for the student burning of the abolitionist effigies in 1859 might well have been a different crowd from those who cheered the three "heroes" of the water pump incident in 1861. It was quite possible, of course, for someone to have supported both demonstrations, to be opposed to abolition and support the Union at the same time. At the outset of the war, politics in town remained very much in flux, and pro-South sentiment did not by any means vanish overnight. As John Hageman, the prominent local lawyer and chronicler of the community, later concluded, "there were a few families who were open and avowed secessionists," but on the whole "it became evident that Princeton would stand by the President in defence of the government." In the community as in the college, the most visible symbol of that stance became the American flag. It flew over the offices of the pro-Republican *Princeton Standard*, and according to Hageman, a procession of local people marched in quasi-military manner through the town, stopping at the houses of Princeton's most prominent political figures—including Senator John R. Thomson, Governor Charles S. Olden, and Commodore Robert F. Stockton—to make sure that they displayed the flag as a sign of support for the Union cause.[19]

The greatest sign of support came from enlisting to fight, and several hundred Princeton townsmen did so. In Princeton and elsewhere in New Jersey, local militia units and state-level regiments were limited to whites only, but Princeton repeatedly met the demand for recruits, even as the war dragged on into its second year and the initial enthusiasm for the fight began to dissipate. Princeton women did their part as well, supporting the combatants by sending them off with extra shirts, socks, and other necessities, and raising money to put together box after box of food, clothing, bedding, reading material, prayer books, and medical supplies. Although the men in the field remained a whites-only force for the time being, the support effort at home involved Black people as well, including those at Betsey Stockton's Witherspoon Street Church, who, as Hageman explained, "also sent hospital stores to the soldiers, and deserve to be remembered for their contributions in this department of loyal cooperation."[20]

BETSEY STOCKTON FACES THE FUTURE

In the midst of all the activity and anxiety brought on by war, Betsey Stockton began to prepare for the ultimate peace: death. On November 22, 1862, she made out her last will and testament. One of the most significant figures from her childhood, James Sproat Green—Ashbel Green's youngest son, who had helped her learn to read—had died in Princeton less than two weeks earlier, and his passing might well have prodded her to contemplate the limits to her own life. She was in her early sixties, an old woman by the standards of the era, and after years of recurring ill health, the time seemed right to get her affairs in order.[21]

A will is an important legal document about property, but it is also an intensely personal one about people. Betsey Stockton didn't have an immediate family of her own—husband, children, or grandchildren—the typical recipients of bequests. She didn't leave her property to her church or her school, nor did she scatter it about among various friends in her community. Instead, she left what little she had to three people with whom she had had strong and long-lasting ties, and her choices spoke directly to the nature of her relationships.

The first lived just around the corner: "I give & bequeath unto my niece Emeline Brazier all the clothing & wearing apparel I may own at the time of my death." In calling Brazier her "niece," Stockton most likely claimed fictive kinship with this younger woman, a nearby neighbor who needed all the help she could get. The 1860 census listed Brazier as a forty-three-year-old mulatto woman, literate but propertyless, working as a "Washer & Ironer." She had three dependents in her household, twenty-year-old Martha Brazier, fifteen-year-old David Brazier, and two-year old James Lane. Brazier had become a teacher in the Sunday school at Witherspoon Street Church in 1848, and in the early 1850s, she occasionally hosted teachers' meetings at her house. Stockton also knew Brazier's two older children as students in her District 6 school and in the Witherspoon Sunday school. Above all, she knew of Brazier's struggles as a single mother, and the challenges she faced making a living. Leaving her clothing to Emeline Brazier might not ease the woman's financial burdens, but it might underscore psychological support, inviting Brazier to clothe herself in Stockton's garments and, in the process, to see herself in Stockton's image. If nothing else, it was an act of generosity and respect from one neighborhood woman to another.[22]

The next bequest went to Betsey Stockton's oldest friend: "I give & bequeath unto the Reverend Charles S. Stewart U.S. Navy, the picture of the landing of the first missionaries at Otahite and also all my library, books, letters & other papers."[23] These were the prized possessions of a highly literate, even bookish woman, set aside for a man whose spiritual and intellectual values she had admired for years. Unfortunately, neither she nor Stewart left a list of the books or an inventory of her personal papers, so it's impossible to appreciate the full intellectual reach of her reading or writing. The picture she left to Stewart was an 1803 engraving of the first British missionaries in the Pacific and the people they encountered in Tahiti in 1797. Even though it didn't portray Stockton's own missionary experience, the engraving was an important symbol of that time in her life and of the lifelong connection she had forged with Stewart across divisions of gender, race, and class.[24]

Everything else went to his son, the boy born at sea: "All the residue, and remainder of my property both real and personal . . . I give devise and bequeath unto Captain Charles Seaforth Stewart U.S. Army, to him his heirs and assigns forever." Again, there is no list of the leftover property, but she counted on the younger Stewart to take care of the last details, naming him, along with his father, as coexecutor of her will. A decade after he had left the Edgewood School in Princeton, the younger Stewart attended the US Military Academy, graduating first in the class of 1846, joining the Corps of Engineers, and rising to the rank of captain by the time of the Civil War. During his service in the 1862 Peninsula campaign in Virginia, he became ill and had to take leave to recuperate. Betsey Stockton worried more about his health than his heroism, and she took him into her home for a couple of days, where "she cared for me and nursed me," he would write, "as she had done when I was a child."[25]

Finally, she had as witnesses to her will Ashbel Green Jr. and Robert S. Green, the two surviving sons of the Reverend Ashbel Green. Neither of them lived in Princeton—Ashbel Jr. was in New York, Robert in Elizabeth, New Jersey—but she had still maintained enough of a connection with them to include them in her final affairs and, in the process, to honor the memories of their late brother and father. Like the two Stewarts, the two Greens were not just respectable men to serve a formal legal function; they also served as living links to her youth as she faced the prospect of dying.[26]

Several months after making out her will, Betsey Stockton took one more step toward preserving her memory: she sat for a photograph, probably the only such likeness in her life. (She also had the image put onto a *carte de visite*, a still-new form of social connection and memory-sharing.) The exact date of the sitting is uncertain, but most likely sometime in the first half of 1863. She had her picture taken in the same studio as Charles Samuel Stewart, on the occasion of his receiving an honorary doctor of divinity degree from New York University that June.[27] Stockton did not dress in finery for the photograph: she wore a simple dress and a turban-like cap, looking the way she did on a normal day. Neither did she strike a dramatic pose: her expression seems stolid yet sad, with a weary-looking gaze into some distant space. She had seen a lot in her long life, and what she was seeing now, in the lowest point of the Civil War, could hardly have given her much hope for the immediate future.

PRINCETON'S INNER CIVIL WAR

The summer of '63 would bring Betsey Stockton more weariness, as her community became threatened—first the entire community of Princeton itself, and then the town's Black community, the people Stockton had nurtured and taught for thirty years. The war was coming alarmingly close, as Robert E. Lee's Confederate army made a menacing incursion into Pennsylvania. But the war also took

FIGURE 8.1. Betsey Stockton, ca. 1863, HMCS Family Photo Collection, Hawaiian Mission Houses Historic Site and Archives, Honolulu.

on a new purpose, as Abraham Lincoln had made ending slavery an explicit goal. As much as Stockton and other Black people in Princeton must have welcomed emancipation as a war aim, they still remained vulnerable to violence from white people—including some in their own town.

By mid-June, New Jersey was on edge. Governor Joel Parker issued a series of proclamations, warning that "a hostile army is now

FIGURE 8.2. Charles Samuel Stewart, ca. 1863, HMCS Family Photo Collection, Hawaiian Mission Houses Historic Site and Archives, Honolulu.

occupying and despoiling the towns of our sister State," and calling on New Jerseyans to respond to the threat with "unprecedented zeal" by organizing militia regiments to come to Pennsylvania's aid. But Parker also made it clear that New Jersey's zeal would have limits. "The troops will be received for service in the state of Pennsylvania, without being required to be mustered into the U.S. service." He urged New Jersey soldiers already in the field, some of whose enlistment commitments were about to be up, to extend their service long enough to deal with the immediate crisis—and no more. "You will not be required to go out of the State of Pennsylvania," he promised, "and will return as soon as the emergency will admit." In the midst of a war that had been raging for over two years, with the fate of the Union suddenly very seriously at stake, Parker cast his appeal as an ad hoc act of short-term support, from one neighboring state to another—but not to the nation as a whole, apparently, and certainly not to its president.[28]

Joel Parker (College of New Jersey, class of 1839) was a northern politician who might have been more comfortable as a states-rights spokesman for the South, a wartime governor who preferred making peace, a Democrat who detested the Republican president and his policies. Parker took office in January 1863, just after Lincoln's Emancipation Proclamation had taken effect, and he made no secret of his opposition, calling it an unconstitutional overreach of presidential power. In his inaugural address, he took care to note that he stood against secession and supported the war, but only as long as the focus remained primarily on restoring the Union, not ending slavery by force of arms. Emancipation would have to wait, Parker insisted, "to be solved hereafter by the people of the States where the institution of slavery already exists." In the interest of ending the war, he would be willing to make concessions to those states by restoring the Union to its *status quo ante*, with slavery still intact. Just as New Jersey had provided for gradual emancipation in the past, he felt, so could southern states in the future. In the meantime, he preferred pursuing the war effort on a state basis, relying on an all-white, all-volunteer militia over national draftees—and certainly over Black men, whom he considered "a distinct and inferior race." Parker might not have openly identified himself as a Copperhead—a Democrat who nominally supported the war effort but also called for accommodating the South on slavery and ending the war—but he played readily into their hands.[29]

Copperheads in Princeton staged a meeting on June 20 that added to local anxiety. Although they advertised Governor Parker as one of the featured speakers, he couldn't attend, so they had to settle for his letter of support. Instead, the most noteworthy speaker turned out to be one R. S. Tharin, an Alabamian who claimed to be a Unionist, but who spoke venomously about what he saw as the "sneaking, contemptible look in Abe Lincoln" and his "felonious Administration." He laced his speech with racist language, insisting that "he would put his foot down, and swear by the Eternal that no negro shall be freed, but all shall continue slaves." The *Princeton Standard* dismissed the meeting as "the best demonstration which the Copperhead organization in this place could make," noting that Tharin "actually disgusted many of his Democratic hearers." Still, the *Standard* decried those Democrats who would put party first: "Our Country is in its struggle for its life. A gigantic rebellion threatens to divide and degrade the nation." With worrisome war news from Pennsylvania printed on the same page—"The rebels are advancing toward Carlisle 10,000 strong, and the Union troops have evacuated it"—the newspaper showed its own disgust with the Democrats' gathering: "Shame on such meetings. Shame on such speakers. Shame on those who preside over such assemblies. Shame on those who attend them."[30]

At least one of those who attended knew no shame, however, and "he distinguished himself after the meeting, by an attempt to capture Nassau Hall." Claiming to be a graduate of the college, he mobilized a handful of fellow Democrats and cried "Charge on Nassau Hall!" When the attackers got into a scuffle with a group of students, President Maclean and members of the faculty intervened, but the professors again proved impotent. More student reinforcements showed up, and finally "the bully band were driven out into the Street by the young defenders of Nassau." The *Standard* wrote mockingly that "Democratic blood, fresh from the Peace Meeting, now lies on the sacred battlefield crying for vengeance," but it chided President Maclean, who "has not fulfilled his promise to have the leader of this riot arrested."[31] This small skirmish might have seemed petty amid the larger military and political conflict, but it did reveal the underlying presence of dissent—and disloyalty—that ran through Princeton, even as the Confederates were coming so close.

Two weeks later, by July 3, that larger threat lessened when Union troops repulsed the Confederate invasion in the battle of Gettysburg, but Black people in Princeton still had reason to be uneasy. On July 17, the *Princeton Standard* carried a two-paragraph report on "Our Colored People," noting the "fear among the colored people in this place that they will be assaulted and mistreated as their race in other places are, by lawless men." The town's African Americans had to look no further than the other pages of that day's paper to see the immediate source of that fear: "RIOT IN NEW YORK!" read one headline, "Riots and the Rebellion" another. The articles told of the violence in the city that had begun on July 13, triggered by working-class white people, many of them Irish, "under the pretext of resisting the draft," but stemming more deeply from fundamental opposition to the larger aims of the war. "The rebellion is a war for Slavery," the *Standard* explained, and the riots "being in sympathy with the rebellion, are more like a war of races, and of classes." Below the subheadline "Great Destruction of Property," readers could easily see the extent of the attacks on small shops and dwellings on the first day, but perhaps the most disturbing act of damage, certainly to Black people, was the burning of the "colored Orphan Asylum." The story continued with the report that "Every negro who has been seen by the mob has been either murdered or horribly beaten. Some twenty have thus far been killed." News of more killing came on July 15: "The mob roamed about hanging negroes." The following day, the riot "broke out towards evening worse perhaps than at any time." No Black person in Princeton could read that chilling account of anti-Black violence taken out on buildings and bodies by white people who rampaged through New York without thinking that it could happen here, too.[32]

It almost did. Anxieties escalated the next day, with rumors of riot in Princeton itself. A group of Irish workingmen planned to take a stand against the draft and, in the process, also appeared poised to attack the town's Black community. According to the *Standard*, these Irishmen had been "breathing out threatenings of a fiendish character, and had sworn that every negro should be killed or driven out of town, and that those who should be drafted would die here rather than in the army." The Irish were not an inconsequential part of Princeton—Eli Stonaker had counted 391 in the 1860 census, about two-thirds the size of the Black population—and they feared that they would bear an unfair share of the military burden while Black men would not. It made little difference to point out, as the *Standard* later tried to do, that since the total quota for conscription in Princeton was only twenty-seven, and since the Irish accounted for only one-sixth of the town's population, only four or five Irishmen would likely be drafted, and of those, probably only two would actually "be required to go forth from this place to defend the nation to which they have sworn allegiance, and under whose laws they vote." Neither did it seem to matter, as the *Standard* suggested, that Copperhead draft dodgers, "who are in sympathy with the rebellion," might have been trying to stir up Irish antipathy to the war to further their own goals.[33] Instead, the Irishmen saw Black people as easy and immediate targets for deadly violence like that which had ripped New York a few days earlier.

Some white people offered Black people well-meaning words of peace and support, but that would not have been much comfort. On July 15, himself fearful of the New York riots crossing over into New Jersey, Joel Parker issued a gubernatorial proclamation declaring that "Acts of violence do not restore individual rights, nor remedy real or fancied wrongs." Warning that "Mobs often originate without preconcert, in the accidental gathering crowd," Parker called upon everyone "to avoid angry discussions, to discourage large assemblies of people, to counsel moderation, and use every effort to preserve the peace." But a message from this governor would have carried little credibility among African Americans. The *Princeton Standard* seemed hardly more reassuring in its self-serving approach to the town's Black residents: "There has never yet been a quarrel between them and the whites here"—a statement that seemed more than a bit forgetful. "We advise them to conduct themselves properly and avoid collisions: and if they should be attacked, they will find the people of Princeton will defend them if they need help, both in the courts and out of them." James Collins Johnson and the people who fought for the fugitive's freedom in 1843 would find that a surprising assertion. But in the end, the *Standard* implied that the ultimate injury would be to the town: "Princeton will not suffer her fair name to become ignoble, and her institutions disgraced."[34] To any Black reader, that last sentence no doubt showed that the Princeton's reputation mattered more to the white community than the racism that underlay the crisis in the first place.

As it turned out, two men—one white, one Black—spoke more forcefully and directly in bringing the incident to an end. Father James P. O'Donnell, the Irish priest of Princeton's Catholic church, took to the pulpit to scold his parishioners "on the subject of resisting the draft, and fomenting riots." Irishmen in Princeton owed their loyalty to their new nation, he reminded them, and "if they are not content with the laws and government of the United States they had better return to Ireland." They had also better rethink rioting against the town's Black people, because the consequences would be devastating: "he said his own property would be destroyed, and theirs would be destroyed, and they would be utterly cut off, so that there would not be one of them left." The *Standard* praised Father O'Donnell for his "patriotic and christian principle in the matter, notwithstanding the very special interests of his people," particularly for eradicating the "poison that was infused into them" by the Copperheads.[35]

Father O'Donnell was not the only one to tell the Irishmen of the threat they faced. According to a later account, "a well known and courageous colored man" told some of the Irishmen that "as soon as there was a riotous attack made upon them, or on their dwellings, they, the colored people, by concert of action, had resolved to set fire to every Irish habitation in the town."[36] That man was neither named nor noticed in the *Standard's* report, but O'Donnell no doubt had in mind those words of warning.

Given the palpable threat of violence, there might have been another reasonable approach to easing the racial and class tensions in Princeton, not to mention in the rest of the state. Governor Parker could have promoted military service for Black men, which would have had a twofold benefit: it would have enabled more Black men to fight in a war that mattered to them, and it would have reduced the sense of resentment on the part of those white, and particularly Irish, men who faced conscription. Parker certainly had precedent and permission for making that choice. On May 22, 1863, Lincoln's War Department had issued General Order Number 143, which called for organizing Black men into separate regiments, designated US Colored Troops (USCT). On May 29, Parker could have read in his Trenton newspaper a glowing report about a Black state regiment that had been formed even before the War Department order, the Massachusetts Fifty-Fourth. "The ranks of the regiment were entirely full," the newspaper reported on the occasion of its departure for South Carolina. "The men were dressed in the regular United States uniform, and splendidly equipped, and headed by a full band of colored musicians. The regiment made a magnificent appearance."[37] Less than two months later, on July 18—the very day the Irish and Black communities in Princeton stood on the verge of attacking each other—the Massachusetts Fifty-Fourth made a gallant, if ultimately unsuccessful, attack on Fort Wagner in South Carolina, earning the military respect that had long been denied Black soldiers.

In Joel Parker's New Jersey, it would be denied still: he refused to organize a USCT regiment or authorize Black enlistment. Instead, Black men looking to join the fight left New Jersey. "Thirty negroes from Cumberland County went to Philadelphia last week," the *West Jersey Press* reported. "They were a healthy looking set of fellows, and seemed to have a fair appreciation of the work before them. Others have declared their intentions to follow." And others did, some going to New York and Connecticut—"A Recruiting Agent from Connecticut was arrested at Jersey City the other day for attempting to enlist colored men in this state," the *Trenton State Gazette* wrote with apparent surprise—but most to Pennsylvania. The same newspaper later noted that "a considerable number of colored men have been recruited in this city, in Princeton and other parts of the county, for the regiments at Camp William Penn, near

Philadelphia." Princeton's local chronicler of the Civil War, John Hageman, estimated that about fifty men from Princeton joined USCT regiments, most of them serving in the Pennsylvania Sixth.[38]

Betsey Stockton knew many of them—sons of her friends, members of her church, students in her school and Sunday school. She could appreciate their courage and commitment, the sacrifice they were making in fighting for freedom and equality in a war that had been late to embrace those principles, or even to accept them as soldiers. She might hope that they had learned some of those values from her. She certainly knew the odds they faced, and as she and other members of the church came together to make bandages and other hospital supplies for the soldiers, she could imagine the men who might need them. Not all of them would survive the war.

She would, but not by much.

TWO TRAINS TO THE NORTH

Princeton erupted in celebration when news of the fall of Richmond arrived in the first week of April 1865. People filled the streets, and "bells were rung, flags were displayed from many houses and the utmost enthusiasm prevailed." As a neighboring newspaper caustically reported, "Princeton, lethargic Princeton, is at last awakened." But the mood became quite different just over two weeks later, on the morning of April 24, 1865, when a train carrying Abraham Lincoln crept along the tracks near Princeton a little before 7 a.m., slowly making its way north. Like the southbound train that had brought Lincoln through the state in 1861, this one was decorated in patriotic red, white, and blue, but also somber black, with heavy silver fringe and tassels attached. Lincoln was dead, slain by John Wilkes Booth ten days before, and the funeral train was ultimately taking his remains home to Illinois. It had left Philadelphia just after 4 a.m., pulling nine cars of civilian and military dignitaries, and at daybreak, it took on some additional politicians from New Jersey—including Governor Joel Parker, who knew enough to put political appearances before personal antipathy. By 5:30, the train reached Trenton, where it paused for a half hour while a crowd estimated at five thousand paid respect to the late president. From Trenton, it went on, slowing but not stopping in Princeton, reversing the route of 1861, through New Brunswick, Rahway, Elizabeth, Newark, and finally arriving in Jersey City, where eight soldiers removed the coffin, "covered with the American flag, and with flowers not entirely withered," for its trip by ferryboat to New York City.[39]

All along the way through New Jersey, the train passed thousands of mourners. But as had been the case four years earlier, the state had not been altogether friendly toward him in the recent presidential election. Lincoln had again lost New Jersey in 1864, getting only 47.1 percent of the popular vote—1 percent less than in 1860—and none of the state's seven electoral votes. They had gone to New Jersey–born General George B. McClellan, the man who had graduated second behind Charles Seaforth Stewart in the West Point class of 1846 and who had gone on to become a leading general in the Union army during the first two years of the Civil War—until Lincoln relieved him of command in November 1862, following the battle of Antietam. Still in the military but with nothing of substance to do, McClellan ran for president in 1864 as the candidate of the Democrats, a party uneasily divided between the still-committed War Democrats and the concession-oriented Copperheads. McClellan tried to distance himself from the Copperheads' call for peace with the South, but that did him little good in the North—except in his native New Jersey. It was the only northern state to go for McClellan (he also won Delaware and Tennessee), once again making it the most notable outlier in a Lincoln victory.[40]

But this time, Princeton had gone with the president—just barely. It gave Lincoln a razor-thin margin, less than one-half of 1 percent, and the educational institutions may have made the difference. "The votes of the students in the Seminary and College carried the day," reported a Boston newspaper, and all but one of the faculty members also voted for Lincoln. The shift may have signaled a kind of redemption: "Henceforth let it not be said that disloyal and pro-slavery principles are inculcated at Princeton." A Presbyterian publication remained skeptical, however, reminding its readers that the seminary had remained reluctant to support any plan "for turning slaves loose without preparation for freedom." But perhaps the embrace of gradual abolition had finally loosened, and the seminary "may be ready for immediate emancipation by this time."[41]

Immediate emancipation still faced an uphill battle in New Jersey, though. By mid-March 1865, the state assembly and senate had refused, on a straight party-line vote, to endorse the Thirteenth Amendment, which would outlaw slavery and involuntary servitude. The Democrats' intransigence made New Jersey, yet again, the slowest state in the North to embrace emancipation. Since the state's 1804 law providing for gradual abolition, abolition had been gradual, indeed: by the time of the Civil War, slavery had almost been eradicated in the state—almost. The 1860 census counted eighteen Black people in New Jersey still bound as apprentices for life, a condition of near enslavement; the state's Democrats seemed content to let them remain so. New Jersey would not ratify the Thirteenth Amendment until January 1866, but by that time, it had already become the law of the land: the last vote needed for ratification had come from Georgia, on December 6, 1865. And with that, some sixty-one years after New Jersey had passed its original gradual abolition law, slavery finally came to an end in the state.[42]

Betsey Stockton didn't live to see that. She died on October 24, 1865, six months to the day that Lincoln's funeral train had passed by Princeton. She probably hadn't seen that train, either, because it came through most likely too early for an elderly woman in poor health to get herself down to the tracks. Three months earlier, she probably couldn't have made it to Trenton, either, for a convention of the Equal Rights League, a Black-white coalition organized "to endeavor to secure equal political rights and immunities" for the African American population. But one of the action items to come from that meeting would have gratified Betsey Stockton: a separate census of Black people, including the "number of colored children in the free schools" and the "intellectual status of the colored people."[43]

For years, she had made a considerable contribution to both in

Princeton, and she apparently kept at it as long as she could. By the fall of 1865, though, she could no longer continue. The superintendent of the Witherspoon Sunday school reported that she was "unable to meet with me & seems fast declining." A few lines later, he recorded her final decline, adding that "judging from her life, we all feel that Heaven has gained another trophy of redeeming grace."[44]

Betsey Stockton's death proved "a public loss to the community in which she lived," read her obituary, the passing of a woman who had been both a pillar in the Black community and a bridge to the white. "Proof of this was furnished by her funeral, at which, in addition to a highly respectable congregation of her own color, were found representatives from many of the most distinguished families of Princeton, with clergymen and other friends, male and female, from the neighboring cities of New York and Philadelphia." Indeed, it seemed almost as if white people took possession of the ceremony, with President John Maclean presiding and preaching the funeral sermon and Professors John T. Duffield and Charles Hodge also having speaking parts. There was no indication of a formal role for anyone from Stockton's own church or school. Still, her work in both schools served as the main point of her legacy: "As a teacher, whether of children or adults full grown, she was not inferior to the best," her obituary stated, and observers "found no school better trained, better instructed, or with evidences of greater success than hers." Working toward that had been her persistent path through adult life, from her experience in Hawai'i, with "the first school ever established among the common people of the Islands," on to the infant school in Philadelphia, "where her labors were so satisfactory and successful," and eventually to Princeton, where she "held an important position of usefulness as teacher . . . of a large school for people of her own color, in her native town."[45]

But having lived, worked, and died in that native town, Betsey Stockton wanted to spend eternity somewhere else: "It was her desire to repose after death near the graves of the family with which she had been most closely associated in life." Soon after her funeral, then, a train took her body northward, following the track that Lincoln's body had traveled through New Jersey, then going on into upstate New York to the home of the Stewarts: "Her remains now rest with many of theirs amid the groves of the beautiful cemetery of Lakewood, Cooperstown, N.Y."[46] And there she was buried, with a headstone that told the outlines of her story:

The grave of
BETSEY STOCKTON,
a native of Princeton N.J.
WHERE SHE DIED
Oct. 24, 1865.
AGED 67 YEARS

Of African blood and born in
slavery, she became fitted by
education and divine grace,
for a life of great usefulness,
for many years was a
valued missionary at the
Sandwich Islands in the
Family of Rev. C. S. Stewart,
and afterwards till her
death, a popular and able
Principal of Public schools
in Philadelphia & Princeton
honored and beloved by a
large circle of Christian
Friends.

"A life of great usefulness"—a remarkable understatement, but the sort of modest memorial Betsey Stockton might have written for herself.

Epilogue

SOME TIME AGO, Betsey Stockton's tombstone fell over, its back flat in the dirt, the carved words of her life story facing the Cooperstown sky. The stone lay there for years, baked by summer sun, covered by fall leaves, buried under winter snow, splashed by spring rain, still visible but sinking ever slowly into the ground, with grass and weeds creeping over the top. Recently, though, a small group of citizens began an effort to set the tombstone upright again. The task is a challenging one—"The stone is large and will undoubtedly require a tripod and hoist," one of the local supporters said, "a bit more than a few warm bodies can safely handle"—but the trustees of the Lakewood Cemetery have secured funding as part of a larger Monument Repair Project.[1] The anticipated raising of the tombstone suggests a metaphor for the memorials to Betsey Stockton, often fallen into obscurity, sometimes hidden in plain sight, but now being restored to greater visibility.

ONE OF MANY AT THAT TIME

One of those memorials had ups and downs of a different sort. In October 1899, Charles Seaforth Stewart, living in quiet retirement in Cooperstown, wrote to the Hawaiian Mission Children's

Society in Honolulu that "it has been suggested at Princeton that a tablet to her services and memory be cast and sent to the islands & placed there." The man driving that idea was the Reverend Lewis W. Mudge, who had first worked with Stockton as superintendent of the Sunday school at the Witherspoon Street Presbyterian Church, in 1859; now, forty years later, Mudge was a Presbyterian pastor in Princeton, and he proposed remembering Stockton with a permanent marker. Charles Seaforth Stewart followed the Princeton-to-the-Pacific process from Cooperstown with impatience: "How far progress has been made I have not heard recently but it was supposed by this time some action would be had."[2]

But there would be no progress, no action in Hawai'i. As an official of the Hawaiian Mission Children's Society later explained, "it was thought best not to erect a tablet here." Betsey Stockton had indeed done "loyal service" as a missionary in Hawai'i, but so had others: "she was but one of many at that time."[3]

Betsey Stockton was not simply "one of many," but the first of a very few. She had been the first Black person, the first former enslaved person, the first single woman to serve as a missionary in Hawai'i, and the first missionary to start a school for the common people of the islands. When she returned to the United States, she was the first person to run an infant school for Black children in Philadelphia, the first name on the list of Black people leaving the main Presbyterian Church in Princeton to form a separate congregation, the first teacher in the only school for Black children in Princeton. Betsey Stockton lived a life of firsts, all of them in service to people of color.

Charles Seaforth Stewart didn't live to see it—he died in 1904—but there would soon be "a tablet to her services and memory," but in Princeton, not Hawai'i.

A PLAQUE IN PRINCETON

On April 1, 1906, the people of the Witherspoon Street Presbyterian Church gathered in the sanctuary for a Sunday afternoon ceremony in Betsey Stockton's honor. One of the featured speakers, Alfred Alexander Woodhull, who had known Stockton in his college days, gave a brief overview of her life. Noting that she had been born into slavery—which he far too easily dismissed as "that mild servitude that then prevailed in New Jersey"—Woodhull talked of her childhood in the household of Ashbel Green, her missionary experience in Hawai'i, and her enduring role in Princeton, where "her daily work was that of a teacher of the colored youth and her example and counsel were efficient among the colored adults as well." He also spoke of her lifelong relationship with Charles Seaforth Stewart, who now lay near Stockton in the Stewart family plot in Cooperstown, an extension in death of the affectionate connection the two had known in life.[4]

Lewis Mudge couldn't attend the ceremony, but he sent a copy of the 1863 photograph showing Betsey Stockton "with her turban . . . her strong but placid face and her portly form," along with a letter praising the power of her character in Princeton's Black community. "Her opinion was sought on all matters of personal and family concern and her judgment, always thoughtfully given and with great dignity, was regarded with the greatest respect." Recalling her long tenure as a teacher, Mudge reminded the audience that "the scholars were well taught," and among her students "she was both loved and feared."[5]

A good number of those former students were in the church that afternoon, seated in a special section reserved for her "surviving resident scholars." Toward the end of the service, one of them, Alexander Webber of Trenton, unveiled a fifteen-by-twenty-five-inch brass plaque, "set up in recognition of her faithful Christian character and most useful life by friends who honored and loved her." The text on the tablet, "very legibly inscribed with black capital letters," noted her service in Princeton, where "she was for many years a valuable member of this congregation, a teacher of its youth and a powerful influence for good in the community." After the unveiling, the attendees "thanked the speaker as representing the donors for the permanent and beautiful record of this good woman," and then, with a hymn and a benediction, the service ended. The older people who had known Betsey Stockton in their younger days no doubt remembered her imposing presence, while the young people must have wondered what they had missed. As they made their way out, they could all stop to gaze on the brass plaque, in which the memory of Betsey Stockton's life and labors "should be a perpetual inspiration."[6]

PASTOR ROBESON'S SON

One of the young people almost certainly at the ceremony was Paul Robeson, just eight days shy of his eighth birthday. He knew something about Betsey Stockton already: he was a grade-school student at the Witherspoon Street School, and he also attended the Witherspoon Street Presbyterian Church. His father, the Reverend William Drew Robeson, had been pastor of the church from 1880 to 1901, and he remained in Princeton until 1907; both father and son were no doubt part of the overflow crowd at the 1906 event. When young Paul sat in the sanctuary and looked at the stained-glass windows, he could see one dedicated "In Loving Memory of Sabra Robeson," his grandmother who had lived in slavery in North Carolina. Two windows back on the same side, he could see the one "Presented by the Scholars of Elizabeth Stockton."[7]

By the time of the memorial service, though, Paul Robeson already had memories of his own, feelings of pain and bitterness that stayed with him for life. His mother had died as the result of a tragic accident in 1904, suffering horrible burns when her dress caught fire from a coal falling out of the kitchen stove. His father endured injuries of a different sort, inflicted on purpose, and seared in the son's memory.[8]

For years, William Drew Robeson had been a much-respected Black pastor with strong ties to Princeton's white community, his son later explained, "a sort of bridge between the Have-nots and the Haves, and he served his flock in many worldly ways—seeking work for the jobless, money for the needy, mercy from the Law." But by

1900, some of the white Haves apparently determined to bring Reverend Robeson down, charging him with mismanagement, if not actual malfeasance, in the church's financial affairs. The accusations went to the Presbytery of New Brunswick, which opened an investigation that found little more than "great carelessness" in Robeson's attention to financial details, some inconsistency in the quality of Sunday services, and a slight decline in church membership, none of them really reasons for terminating his pastorate. But the presbytery's report also alluded to the "general unrest and dissatisfaction of others who have been the Church's friends and helpers"—some of the powerful white Presbyterians in Princeton.

Reverend Robeson and some of his allies suspected that he was being persecuted for being a Black pastor speaking to a Black congregation about racism and social injustice, but the presbytery denied it, saying he received the same treatment a white pastor would have. Still, the presbytery called for the "dissolution of the Pastoral Relation existing between Rev. William D. Robeson and said Church," and Robeson saw he had no chance: he offered his resignation, effective February 1, 1901. He lost his house and his salary, moving out of the parsonage into a run-down house nearby, making a meager living as an ash collector for Princeton's more prosperous families. "Ash-man, coachman, he was still the dignified Reverend Robeson to the community," Paul Robeson would recall, "and no man carried himself with greater pride." But for Paul, the experience of having to live in a dilapidated shack, where his father had to pile other people's ashes outside the windows, made a powerful impression. He had seen what Princeton's white community could do to a leader of the Black community, and he would never forget all that—or forgive Princeton.[9]

The Princeton of his boyhood, Robeson later wrote, "was for all the world like any small town in the deep South . . . Princeton was spiritually located in Dixie. . . . Rich Princeton was white." Black people were there to serve whites, "restricted to menial jobs at low pay and lacking any semblance of political rights or bargaining power, [they] could hope not for justice but for charity." He found neither, but instead what he called a "caste system" built on racism: "The grade school that I attended was segregated and Negroes were not permitted in any high school," much less any level beyond that: "No Negro students were admitted to the university." In 1913, a book about Princeton's Black community offered a brief but upbeat note about Paul Robeson's academic progress, reporting that he was "a member of the baseball, football and basketball teams and the Glee Club" at the integrated high school in Somerville, New Jersey, where Reverend Robeson had taken up a new pastorate in 1910. But that was Somerville High, not Princeton High, and the athletic and artistic talents he had already begun to develop there would come into greater display as a college student at nearby Rutgers, New Jersey's public university, not Princeton University. Paul Robeson's reflection on the town of his birth was straightforward: "Princeton was Jim Crow."[10]

Still, the best thing Paul Robeson could say about his Princeton days was the "abiding sense of comfort and security" he derived from his extended family and "our close-knit community . . . all the aunts and uncles and cousins—including some who were not actual relatives at all."[11] From them he would have heard about the impressive woman of an earlier era, Betsey Stockton, and he became aware of her legacy at the Witherspoon Street Presbyterian Church. Robeson's father began his pastorate there just fifteen years after she died, and her memory remained alive during the two decades he served. By 1906, as Paul listened to the tributes to Betsey Stockton, he could also begin to appreciate her importance in creating the "close-knit community" Princeton's Black people still managed to preserve.

Paul Robeson left Princeton, though, and went on to become an internationally celebrated actor and singer, not to mention a committed political activist. Although he looked back at white Princeton with disdain, the town later reclaimed him, renaming a street Paul Robeson Place in 1976 and creating the Paul Robeson Center for the Arts in 2008. He is now remembered as the most prominent Princeton-born Black person of the twentieth century.

Betsey Stockton deserves that status for the nineteenth century. She, too, traveled around the world, something people always seemed to take note of: throughout her life, she carried some version of the sobriquet "late missionary to the Sandwich Islands." But hers was a life of service, not celebrity. From Lahaina to Philadelphia to Princeton, she worked at the grass roots, educating ordinary people of color who would otherwise have been ignored. Particularly in Princeton, she demonstrated remarkable commitment to a Black community that had a strong identity but limited opportunity. If Betsey Stockton had been able to read Paul Robeson's later description of Jim Crow Princeton, she would have recognized the reasons for his resentment and known what he meant.

We need to know what she means now. The stained-glass window in the Witherspoon Street Presbyterian Church has been in place for over a century, and the people who worship there have been able to see her name every week. The plaque unveiled in 1906 has had a somewhat rockier history, being removed at times during renovations but most recently reinstalled several years ago. Walking tours of the town, sponsored by the Historical Society of Princeton and the Witherspoon-Jackson Historical and Cultural Society, have brought visitors to Witherspoon Street, where they can pause at the Paul Robeson Center before going two blocks further to the church. Out in front, they can read the New Jersey Women's Heritage Trail sign about Betsey Stockton and get a brief outline of her life.[12]

Back down Witherspoon and on the far side of Nassau Street, the town's two main academic institutions have installed newer memorials to Betsey Stockton. On the second floor of the library at the Princeton Theological Seminary, there's a 1990 painting based on the only known photograph of her, when she was in her sixties, but depicting her in her Hawaiian days, when she was in her twenties, holding a Bible in her hands, flowers tucked into her turban, palm trees and the ocean in the background. Its label highlights her life in education: "Missionary teacher in Hawaii, a founder of the

Witherspoon Presbyterian Church in Princeton in 1840, and an educator of Princeton's African-American youth." In further recognition of those contributions to people of color, the seminary has now named its Center for Black Church Studies in Stockton's honor.[13]

The campus of Princeton University has two Betsey Stockton sites, both installed in 2018, both informed by the research of the Princeton & Slavery Project. At the Maclean House, which had been the President's House from 1756 to 1878, a plaque out front commemorates "at least sixteen enslaved men, women, and children" who lived there as "the personal property of the Presbyterian ministers who served as presidents of this institution"—one of them Betsey Stockton. A couple of blocks away, at the far corner of the campus in front of Firestone Library and near the Nassau Street sidewalk, the Elizabeth "Betsey" Stockton Garden provides a quiet place to sit and perhaps contemplate the university's historical role in promoting both education and exclusion, the two sides of Princeton symbolized by Stockton's life. (The university has also named an arch in honor of James Collins Johnson, the fugitive from slavery who gained his freedom in 1843 and worked on campus until his death, in 1902.) A *New York Times* article about the campus memorials gave the last word to Professor Martha Sandweiss, the founder and director of the Princeton & Slavery Project: "We can have one conversation about what to do with sites named for people connected for slaveholding," she said. "But a positive way to move forward is to also think about who and what is not represented, and how to make Princeton a richer commemorative environment."[14]

And so the work continues in Princeton, and so it should in other communities. Even if Betsey Stockton was "but one of many at that time," her commitment to her community invites us to recognize other people like her, in other places, who worked equally diligently, and usually in obscurity, to challenge the status quo of injustice and inequality in American society. At a time when monuments and memorials to purveyors of racism in America's past are beginning to be taken down, there's an opportunity to put up new ones to better figures in history. There are plenty of possibilities, the thousands of people like Betsey Stockton, who did not stand out at the front of the movement on the national stage, but instead carried on the struggle behind the scenes on the local level, engaging in grassroots resistance to the powers around them. Their stories matter, because they tell us about ordinary people doing extraordinary work, taking on the hard task of seeking justice in the face of challenging, even hostile circumstances. Their stories matter, perhaps precisely because these people were not famous, not familiar—at least not yet. Their stories, like Stockton's, need to be told, remembered, and commemorated. They can give us a better knowledge of who makes history, and how.

Acknowledgments

THIS BOOK BEGAN with Anne Harper, who used her remarkable ability to make intellectual connections to see a link between the Stockton bench on the Princeton campus and the Stockton plaque in the Witherspoon-Jackson neighborhood. She suggested I look into it, and that's what I've been doing for the past few years. During that time, Anne has listened to my questions, raised quite a few others, read drafts, edited out adverbs, and done her own research and writing about Betsey Stockton. My book is for her.

While I was researching this book, I had the very good fortune to enjoy two long-term fellowships, at the American Antiquarian Society and at the Huntington Library, both of them favorite places to work. Paul Erickson initially invited me to AAS, and Jim Moran, in his new role as vice president for programs and outreach, welcomed me, smoothing the way, sharing food and talk, and becoming a good friend. Steve Hindle did the same as director of research at the Huntington, starting in my first week with a challenging hike in the San Gabriels and continuing throughout the year with similar energy and good cheer to make me part of an outstanding intellectual environment. I am grateful for the institutional generosity and, above all, the personal relationships.

At AAS, people talk, only half-jokingly, about "The Miracle of the Dome," and I had at least two miraculous experiences. The first came when AAS president Ellen Dunlap mentioned that an AAS member in Princeton, Joseph Felcone, a rare book collector with a specialization in early New Jerseyana, owned a volume with Betsey Stockton's signature on the flyleaf. The next time I went to Princeton, Joe invited me up to his book-packed third-floor office, where I got to hold Betsey Stockton's book in my hands and take a picture of her autograph—a remarkable moment in my research. The second miracle occurred when, without my even asking, Ashley Cataldo parked a cartload of books and pamphlets beside my work table, telling me there were some uncataloged materials about New Jersey schools in the mix. Indeed there were, and I never would have found them without Ashley's initiative. The most miraculous aspect of AAS, of course, is the collection of staff members, fellows, and other scholars who make the Reading Room such a lively and friendly place. I am enormously grateful to the professionals at AAS—Nan Wolverton, Molly Hardy, Marie Lamoureux, Lauren Hewes, Laura Wasowicz, Vince Golden, and Elizabeth Pope—for sharing their expertise with me, giving me more good ideas and suggestions than I could ever fully absorb. I also appreciated the administrative support of Cheryl McRell and the daily greetings of the four at the door—David Cohen, Joe Haebler, the late Ed Koury, and Sally Talbot—whom I could always count on for talk about matters of mutual interest, from baseball to Worcester weather. I could likewise count on the intellectual energy and good advice of my fellow long-term fellows and potluck-dinner pals—Abby Cooper, Brendan Gillis, Ezra Greenspan, and Chris Phillips—all of whom were models of collegiality and collaboration. I enjoyed lunchtime company and conversation with other researchers throughout the year—above all, Susannah Blumenthal, Denise Miller, and Johanna Siebert—and with longtime AAS friends Steve Bullock, John Hench, and Caroline Sloat. While I was at AAS, another longtime friend, Chris Clark, chair of the History Department at the University of Connecticut, joined with Helen Rozwadowski and Nancy Shoemaker to host me for a talk about my project, and I had particularly good questions from Dick and Irene Brown.

At the Huntington, the professional staff, fellows, and friends were just as numerous and engaging. Juan Gomez, Catherine Wehrey-Miller, and Natalie Serrano had everything organized before I even arrived, and they continued to be a great source of support throughout my tenure. I not only had the honor of holding a fellowship named for the recently retired Robert C. Ritchie, but I also had the pleasure of having the ever-active and ever-generous Roy Ritchie himself in the office next to mine. At the other end of Mahogany Row, I was delighted to find my friend Marni Sandweiss, the founder and director of the Princeton & Slavery Project, who was always a good ally and smart sounding board, ready to listen to my questions and pose her own. Other inhabitants of our hallway included fellow American historians Gary Gallagher, Marjoleine Kars, Rachel St. John, Mike Vorenberg, and Louis Warren, all of whom provided good cheer and good feedback. I could always expect a warm welcome from my office neighbor and fellow baseball fan Kate Adams, but I also got a firm warning about the dangers of historical ventriloquism, about which I try to remain ever attentive. When I presented an overview of my project to these and other colleagues in the Long-Term Fellows Working Group, they gave it a good working-over, with plenty of skeptical questions but also helpful expressions of support, particularly from Lori Anne Ferrell and Danielle Terrazas-Williams, which came at just the right time. I also had the opportunity to present a draft chapter to the American Origins seminar of the USC-Huntington Early Modern Studies Institute; my thanks to Peter Mancall, Lindsey O'Neill, and Carole Shammas for arranging a stimulating session. The Huntington attracts a regular collection of shorter-term fellows, scholars from the Los Angeles area, and snowbirds from the East, and I had wonderful lunch conversations about my work with Edward Armston-Sheret, Eoin Carter, Hal Baron, Bill Deverell, David Igler, Steve Hackel,

Jenny Pulsipher, Barbara Oberg, and Tim Breen. The signature meal of the year came at the home of Wendy Munger and Len Gumport, who hosted a Huntington Salon dinner, where they, Steve Hindle, and a handful of other diners engaged me in a delightful discussion about Betsey Stockton's voyage to the Pacific. Finally, my stay at the Huntington wouldn't have been as much fun without old friends Sara Austin, instigator of the weekly *pétanque* games, and Dan Lewis, my birding buddy and in-house go-to source for all things Hawaiian.

I made shorter visits to other research institutions, and I am grateful to the people who helped me: Izzy Kasdin and Stephanie Schwartz at the Historical Society of Princeton; Brianna Cregle in Rare Books and Special Collections at the Firestone Library, Princeton University; Kenneth Henke and Kate Skrebutenas at the Princeton Theological Seminary Library; Peter Accardo at the Houghton Library, Harvard University; Patrick Spero at the American Philosophical Society; David Koch at the Presbyterian Historical Society; Frances Skelton and Jim Campbell at the Whitney Library, New Haven Museum; Maribeth Bielinski and Carol Mowrey at the Mystic Seaport Collections Research Center; and John Barker, Mike Smole, and Kelsey Karsin at the Hawaiian Children's Mission Society Library and the Mission House Museum Historic Site.

A number of fellow historians gave me good feedback and sometimes a close reading of a particular section or of complete chapters. Shane White offered a very valuable and positive overview of the entire project, both at the outset and in the later stages, and I've much appreciated his enthusiasm. Lois Horton was a wonderful source for both Hawaiian and African American history, and she gave me sensitive and supportive responses to several chapters. So did Seth Archer and Christopher Cook, who reviewed the chapters on the missionaries in Hawai'i and offered helpful suggestions for improvement. Billy G. Smith, Paul Sivitz, Carol Lasser, Carolyn Eastman, Susan Branson, and George Boudreau were reliable resources on Philadelphia, and James G. Gigantino II offered perceptive responses to my inquiries about New Jersey. As I was wrapping up the writing, I took part in a workshop titled "Imagining Lost Lives: Archival Silences and the Challenge of Writing Histories of the Enslaved," sponsored by the Omohundro Institute for Early American History and Culture, and I am grateful to Simon Newman and Frances Bell for their leadership and to my fellow participants for their wise words.

One special note of thanks: I knew I could get a good read from my longtime ally Gary Nash, whose scholarship on slavery and racism, particularly in nineteenth-century Philadelphia, was unmatched, as was his imagination in pondering possible outcomes in my narrative. Gary died just as this book was going to press, and while I mourn the loss, I cherish his memory as a model scholar, an activist historian, a gifted writer, and a good-natured and intellectually generous friend.

People outside academia have also given me good help. Shirley Satterfield, whose family connection with the Witherspoon Street Presbyterian Church extends back to its founding, offered me very valuable insights and saved me from at least one egregious error about the church's history. Alison Green and Abbie McMillen, descendants of Ashbel Green and Robert Stockton, respectively, reached out to me with their thoughts about their ancestor's possible identity as Betsey Stockton's biological father. Lois Leveen also provided useful information about Mary Henly, the young girl who lived with Stockton in 1850. On the subject of Betsey Stockton's burial in Cooperstown's Lakewood Cemetery, C. R. Jones, Merrilyn R. O'Connell, and Richard Fox Young kept me up to date on the current status of her gravestone.

Lisa Adams deserves my great gratitude for helping shape the book proposal and then finding it a good home at the University of Chicago Press. The manuscript came under the careful attention of Tim Mennel, an excellent editor who turned a sharp eye to every line, even every word (including the many thousands that don't appear here), but who also had a smart grasp of the big picture, asking the right questions and making the right suggestions. He was the editor I needed for this project. Others at the press—Susannah Engstrom, Mark Reschke, and Tyler McGaughey—helped turn the manuscript into a book. At some point you have to let your work go, and it's reassuring to know it went into good hands.

Notes

PROLOGUE

1. Ms. Shirley Satterfield, a sixth-generation member of the Witherspoon Street Presbyterian Church and the president of the Witherspoon-Jackson Historical and Cultural Society, has been a central figure in preserving and promoting the history of Princeton's Black community, and I am grateful for her contributions to this book.
2. I first wrote about Betsey Stockton in an essay for the Princeton & Slavery Project, https://slavery.princeton.edu/stories/betsey-stockton, and I commend Dr. Martha Sandweiss of the Princeton History Department for her work as the founder of that initiative. There are, I should note, a number of other journal articles and encyclopedia entries about Betsey Stockton, and I have benefited from many of them. Rather than cite, much less critique, all of them here, I will refer to them as needed in the notes.
3. "How does an ordinary person win a place in history?" Alfred Young asked more than two decades ago, and his pathbreaking work in answering that question has guided my own approach. Alfred F. Young, *The Shoemaker and the Tea Party: Memory and the American Revolution* (Boston, 1999), 1; see also his *Masquerade: The Life and Times of Deborah Sampson, Continental Soldier* (New York, 2005). Young's scholarship, along with his friendship, has long been a touchstone for me. Among the more recent works that have influenced my approach are, most notably, Erica Armstrong Dunbar, *Never Caught: The Washingtons' Relentless Pursuit of Their Runaway Slave, Ona Judge* (New York, 2017); Lolita Buckner Inniss, *The Princeton Fugitive Slave: The Trials of James Collins Johnson* (New York, 2019); Shane White, *Prince of Darkness: The Untold Story of Jeremiah G. Hamilton, Wall Street's First Black Millionaire* (New York, 2015); and Craig Thompson Friend, "Lunsford Lane and Me: Life-Writings

and Public Histories of the Enslaved Other," *Journal of the Early Republic* 39, no. 1 (2019): 1-26.

The biases and silences inherent in the historical archive, particularly as they pertain to Black women, have most recently been highlighted in Saidiya Hartman, *Wayward Lives, Beautiful Experiments: Intimate Histories of Wayward Black Girls, Troublesome Women, and Queer Radicals* (New York, 2019), in which she writes of the need "to grapple with the power and authority of the archive and the limits it sets on what can be known, whose perspective matters, and whom is endowed with the gravity and authority of historical actor" (viii). For a valuable review of Hartman's book, raising a question about the historian's commitment to documentary evidence and the use of "speculative nonfiction," see Annette Gordon-Reed, "Rebellious History," *New York Review of Books*, 22 October 2020. In 2021, I was fortunate to be a member of a weekly writing workshop, "Imagining Lost Lives: Archival Silences and the Challenge of Writing Histories of the Enslaved," sponsored by the Omohundro Institute for Early American History and Culture, and I am grateful to my fellow participants for the quality of our conversations.

4. Craig Steven Wilder, *Ebony & Ivy: Race, Slavery, and the Troubled History of America's Universities* (New York, 2013). The essays and documents of the Princeton & Slavery Project can be found at https://slavery.princeton.edu.
5. Nell Irvin Painter, *Sojourner Truth: A Life, a Legend* (New York, 1996), 281–85. An important work that employs the stories of ordinary Black women to engage a larger national narrative is Daina Ramey Berry and Kali Nicole Gross, *A Black Women's History of the United States* (Boston, 2020).

CHAPTER ONE

1. Ashbel Green Diary, 20–21 September 1804, Ashbel Green Papers, Princeton University Archives, Department of Rare Books and Special Collections, Princeton University Library; hereafter cited as Green Diary.

Like most diary-keepers, Ashbel Green intended his own personal writings "principally for myself . . . [and] to make it useful I must be thoroughly honest." Yet also like most diary-keepers, he worried that his personal revelations might be seen by other eyes, particularly after he died: "Let me realize likewise that whenever what I write shall be read by others (if it be read at all) I shall be in eternity, for in this life I do not intend to show it." To resolve the dilemma, Green began keeping his diary in shorthand, and he kept that up for decades. Happily, a twentieth-century transcriber turned the original shorthand diary back into standard English, in a very readable, double-spaced, typescript copy.

Green's discussion of his early diary-keeping is in Green Diary, 14 June 1790, 29–31 January 1793. See also Ashbel Green, *The Life of Ashbel Green,*

V.D.M., Begun to Be Written by Himself in His Eighty-Second Year and Continued to His Eighty-Fourth. Prepared for the Press by Joseph H. Jones (Philadelphia, 1849), 119, 203.

2. Ashbel Green to Jeremiah Evarts, 3 September 1821, American Board of Commissioners for Foreign Missions Archives, 1810–1961 (ABC 1–91) Houghton Library, Harvard University; hereafter cited as ABCFM Archives. For the larger context of children born into slavery being given as gifts within a slaveholding family, see Jennifer L. Morgan, *Laboring Women: Reproduction and Gender in New World Slavery* (Philadelphia, 2004), in which she writes of "children who survived infancy only to be identified as tokens of affection bestowed by slaveowners upon their kin," 9; esp. chapter 4.
3. For a sketch of Ashbel Green's early life, see Richard A. Harrison, *Princetonians, 1776–1783: A Biographical Dictionary* (Princeton, NJ, 1981), 404–6; and Green, *Life of Ashbel Green*, 19–20. For the political positions of his father, the Reverend Jacob Green, see S. Scott Rohrer, *Jacob Green's Revolution: Radical Religion and Reform in a Revolutionary Age* (University Park, PA, 2014), 128–37, 210–18.
4. Green, *Life of Ashbel Green*, 107, 119–24.
5. For the background of Congress's removal from Philadelphia to Princeton, see Kenneth R. Bowling, "New Light on the Philadelphia Mutiny of 1783: Federal-State Confrontation at the Close of the War for Independence," *Pennsylvania Magazine of History and Biography* 101 (1977): 419–50; *Congress at Princeton, Being the Letters of Charles Thomson to Hannah Thomson, June–October 1783*, ed. Eugene R. Sheridan and John M. Murrin (Princeton, NJ, 1985), xl–xliv; and Benjamin H. Irvin, *Clothed in the Robes of Sovereignty: The Continental Congress and the People Out of Doors* (New York and Oxford, 2014), 268–72.
6. For a description of the 1783 commencement exercises, see Harrison, *Princetonians*, 406; John Freylinghuysen Hageman, *A History of Princeton and Its Institutions*, 2 vols. (Philadelphia, 1879), 1:169–70. Green's own account of the event is in Green, *Life of Ashbel Green*, 143–44. The extract from Green's valedictory address is quoted in Thomas Jefferson Wertenbaker, *Princeton, 1746–1896* (Princeton, NJ, 1946), 65.
7. Green, *Life of Ashbel Green*, 144–45.
8. The overview of the early Stockton family comes from several genealogical and local history sources: J. W. Stockton, *A History of the Stockton Family* (Philadelphia, 1881); Thomas Coates Stockton, *The Stockton Family of New Jersey and Other Stocktons* (Washington, DC, 1911); *Genealogical and Personal Memorial of Mercer County, New Jersey*, ed. Francis Bazley Lee, 2 vols. (New York and Chicago, 1907); and Hageman, *History of Princeton*, 1:33–40, with the reference to the legacy of slavery on 37.
9. Stockton, *A History of the Stockton Family*, 34–35. For Richard Stockton's will, see *New Jersey Abstract of Wills, 1670–1817*, https://ancestry.com/search/collections/2793.

10. Hageman, *History of Princeton*, 1:77–78. Ashbel Green's father, the Reverend Jacob Green, was one of the framers of the New Jersey Constitution; see Rohrer, *Jacob Green's Revolution*, 156–63; and Green, *Life of Ashbel Green*, 56
11. William Paterson, "The Belle of Princeton, Betsey Stockton: A Poem Written at Nassau Hall, 1772" and "A Satire on Betsey's College Suitors," in *Glimpses of Colonial Society and the Life at Princeton College, 1766–1773*, ed. W. Jay Mills (Philadelphia, 1903), 109–25. It is unclear exactly which Betsey Stockton is being celebrated here, perhaps Elizabeth (1729–?), the daughter of Joseph Stockton, or more likely Elizabeth (1739–77), the daughter of John Stockton, who would be closer to the appropriate age range for Paterson's poem.
12. Green, *Life of Ashbel Green*, 144–48.
13. For the early years of Philadelphia's Second Presbyterian Church, see E. R. Beadle, *The Old and the New. 1743–1876. The Second Presbyterian Church of Philadelphia. Its Beginning and Increase* (Philadelphia, 1876), 21–28, 43, 88–89.
14. This summary of Green's achievements comes from Harrison, *Princetonians*, 407–8; John Maclean, *History of the College of New Jersey, from Its Origin in 1746 to the Commencement of 1854* (Philadelphia, 1877), 212–15; and Green, *Life of Ashbel Green*, 260–71.
15. The most recent book-length study of the yellow fever epidemic is Billy G. Smith, *Ship of Death: A Voyage That Changed the Atlantic World* (New Haven, CT, 2013). For a shorter summary of the situation, see Erica Armstrong Dunbar, *Never Caught: The Washingtons' Relentless Pursuit of Their Runaway Slave, Ona Judge* (New York, 2017), 82–84. The larger cultural implications of the crisis are discussed in Sari Altschuler, *The Medical Imagination: Literature and Health in the Early United States* (Philadelphia, 2018), chapter 2. A contemporary account of the epidemic and debates about its origins is in James R. Manley, *An Inaugural Dissertation on the Yellow Fever* (New York, 1803). The prevalence of the fever among the lower classes, white and Black, is reflected in the number of burials in Philadelphia's potter's field: 301 in 1792, 1,757 in 1793; see *Henry Wansey and His American Journal, 1794*, ed. David John Jeremy (Philadelphia, 1979) 107–8.
16. Green's account of the 1793 yellow fever epidemic and its effect on his church is in Green, *Life of Ashbel Green*, 272–76. For the criticism of Green's taking refuge in Princeton, see Benjamin Rush to Mrs. (Julia) Rush, 30 October 1793: "I have done him ample justice whenever I have heard his conduct blamed for leaving the city, and have openly declared that I advised him not to come to town at the time he proposed it." *Letters of Benjamin Rush*, ed. L. H. Butterfield, 2 vols. (Princeton, NJ, 1951), 2:733. For various references to Green's going back and forth between Philadelphia and Princeton in 1797, see Green Diary, 13–20 August 1797; his notes on the daily death toll in Philadelphia are 27–30 September 1798. For his communication to his congregation, see Ashbel Green, *Pastoral Letter, from a Minister in the Country, to Those of his Flock Who Remained in the City of Philadelphia During the Pestilence of 1798* (Philadelphia, 1798), 5–7.

17. Paul first entered the Green household in mid-July 1797, just before the yellow fever epidemic for that year broke out; a month later, Green wrote that "I set out in a private carriage with my wife and children and Miss Innes for Princeton." See Green Diary, 12 July, 15 August 1797. The note about Paul's staying behind comes from Green, *Life of Ashbel Green*, 278. The assumption of Black immunity among white people is discussed in Rana A. Hogarth, *Medicalizing Blackness: Making Racial Difference in the Atlantic World, 1780–1840* (Chapel Hill, NC, 2017), 17–47.

18. For Green's estimate about Stockton's age, see "Sandwich Islands," *Christian Advocate* 2 (May 1824): 232. The New York Index to Passenger Lists, 1820–46, and the 1850 and 1860 US Censuses can be found at FamilySearch .org, https://www.familysearch.org. For the inscription on her tombstone, see chapter 8.

19. In *Rape and Sexual Power in Early America* (Chapel Hill, NC, 2006), 2–4, Sharon Block makes a historically contingent distinction between the definition of *rape* as "legal judgments (whether in terms of indictment or conviction) of forced heterosexual intercourse" and *coerced sex* as "acts not necessarily identified as rape in early America that nonetheless contained some degree of extorted or forced sexual relations." The point is not to limit rape to its technical legal terms as understood at the time, but to understand the ways men's racial and class identities defined the power dynamics of sexual encounters, particularly with enslaved Black women: "Elite white masculinity did not just allow powerful men to possibly avoid criminal prosecution for rape; it also helped men reshape coercion into the appearance of consent before, during, and after a sexual attack."

20. Frederick Douglass, *Narrative of the Life of Frederick Douglass, an American Slave* (Boston, 1845), 2.

21. The published suggestion that Ashbel Green was Betsey's birth father comes from Constance K. Escher, "She Calls Herself Betsey Stockton," *Princeton History*, no. 10 (1991), 71–101, esp. 97. The note about the "conjecture" of direct descendants of Ashbel Green comes from Alison Green, email communication to author, 23 March 2019. Subsequent email communications from Abbie McMillen to author, 11 and 13 November 2020, raise a similar conjecture about her Stockton ancestors, tilting toward one of the sons: "My money's on Job," who "never married, and seems to have stayed pretty close to home," and about whom "letters between nieces seem to imply that he was a little odd." She understandably concludes that the question of paternity remains unanswerable. "If Betsey had only had children, DNA could help!"

22. Robert Stockton to Ashbel Green, 24 April 1797, in Ashbel Green Papers, Box 10, Folder 28, Ashbel Green Papers, Princeton RBSC. Almost two weeks before getting the demanding letter from Robert Stockton, Green noted that he had "received a letter from Major Rodgers relative to Celia," so he must have been aware of the situation, although he doesn't say exactly what that situation was; see Green Diary, 11 April 1797.

23. Stockton to Green, 24 April 1797. For the Fugitive Slave Act of 1793, see *Proceedings and Debates of the House of Representatives of the United States at the Second Session of the Second Congress, Begun at the City of Philadelphia, November 5, 1792*, "Annals of Congress, 2nd Congress, 2nd Session (November 5, 1792 to March 2, 1793)," 1414–15.
24. Green Diary, 25 April, 4 June 1797.
25. *New Jersey, U.S., Wills and Probate Records, 1739–1991*, https://www.ancestry.com/search/collections.
26. Betsey Stockton to Ashbel Green, 15 June 1823, *Christian Advocate* 2 (May 1824): 232.
27. "A slave always had to be prepared for anything," Erica Armstrong Dunbar has written about the experience of Ona Judge; *Dunbar, Never Caught*, chapter 3, quotation on 36. During a year at the American Antiquarian Society, in 2016–17, I also had the good fortune to see Gwendolyn Quezaire-Presutti's riveting one-woman performance about Ona Judge, "If I Am Not for Myself Who Will Be for Me," which did a remarkable job of describing the many intimate aspects of the day-to-day relationship between Judge and Martha Washington.
28. Green to Jeremiah Evarts, 3 September 1821, ABCFM Archives.
29. Green Diary, 10 May 1797, 16 August, 22 December 1798.
30. For the general history of gradual abolition, see Arthur Zilversmit, *The First Emancipation: The Abolition of Slavery in the North* (Chicago, 1967); Joanne Pope Melish, *Disowning Slavery: Gradual Emancipation and "Race" in New England, 1780–1860* (Ithaca, NY, 1998); and James Oliver Horton and Lois E. Horton, *In Hope of Liberty: Culture, Community and Protest among Northern Free Blacks, 1700–1860* (New York, 1997), chapter 3. The "hodgepodge" phrase comes from James G. Gigantino II, *The Ragged Road to Abolition: Slavery and Freedom in New Jersey, 1775–1865* (Philadelphia, 2015), 102.
31. This summary of the Pennsylvania law in this paragraph stems largely from Gary B. Nash and Jean R. Soderlund, *Freedom by Degrees: Emancipation in Pennsylvania and Its Aftermath* (New York, 1991), which I consider still to be the best source on the issue; see 4–9, 99–113, 137–41.
32. In 1780, New Jersey had an estimated 10,600 enslaved people, and by 1800, that number would reach 12,422; see Nash and Soderlund, *Freedom by Degrees*, 7. For the creation of the state's gradual abolition law, see Gigantino, *Ragged Road to Abolition*, 82–94.
33. The notion of negotiation in the gradual abolition period stems from Gigantino, *Ragged Road to Abolition*, 116–48. See also Graham Russell Hodges, *Slavery and Freedom in the Rural North: African Americans in Monmouth County, New Jersey, 1665–1865* (Madison, WI, 1997), esp. chapter 5.
34. Green Diary, 3 August 1803, 2 September, 26 September 1806, 24 March 1807. It's also not clear how old George was, and his age could have been a factor in his freedom. "Instead of a benevolent gift to slaves," Gigantino points out in *Ragged Road to Abolition*, 131, "many owners executed manumission

agreements after their slaves had reached middle age and their productivity declined."

35. Green Diary, 2 April 1803, 18–23 February 1805, 22–27 April 1805, 9–14 December 1806, (n.d.) February 1807. Green wrote the epitaph for her tombstone and considered it "among the best things in verse that I have ever written." Green, *Life of Ashbel Green*, 24, 297.

36. Erica Armstrong Dunbar makes the significant point that "African Americans were often released from enslavement and shuffled into temporary contracts of servitude. The transition was not from slavery to freedom but from slavery to forced servitude. . . . Indentured servitude represented the end of enslavement, but it was a far cry from freedom." Dunbar, *A Fragile Freedom: African American Women and Emancipation in the Antebellum City* (New Haven, CT, 2016), 3–4.

Green writes of Elizabeth's "concurrence" in *Life of Ashbel Green*, 341. The records of the Pennsylvania Abolition Society are on microfilm at the Historical Society of Pennsylvania, where a search of Reels 20–23, Manumissions, Indentures, and Other Legal Papers, turned up no references to either Ashbel Green or Betsey Stockton. Green's reference to giving Betsey her freedom at age twenty comes from Green to Jeremiah Evarts, 3 September 1821, ABCFM Archives.

37. The record of Green's household in 1810 is in Third Census of the United States, National Archives and Records Administration; Year: 1810; Census Place: Philadelphia South Mulberry Ward, Philadelphia Pennsylvania; Series M252, Roll 55; Page: 327; Image: 00014; Family History Library Film: 0193681; Ancestry.com. 1800, 1810 United States Federal Census (database online), Provo, UT. For the number of enslaved people in Philadelphia as a whole, see Nash and Soderlund, *Freedom by Degrees*, 4.

38. Green Diary, 29 December 1807, 17 March 1808.

39. Population figures come from Gary B. Nash, *Forging Freedom: The Formation of Philadelphia's Black Community, 1720–1840* (Cambridge, MA, 1988), 143. For the description of Philadelphia, see S. S. Moore and T. W. Jones, *Traveler's Directory, or a Pocket Companion: Shewing the Course of the Main Road from Philadelphia to New York, and from Philadelphia to Washington* (Philadelphia, 1802), 1–2. The image of "Arch Street, with the Second Presbyterian Church" was drawn and engraved by William Birch and Thomas Birch, part of a series of twenty-seven Philadelphia scenes collected in *The City of Philadelphia, in the State of Pennsylvania North America; as it appeared in the Year 1800* (Philadelphia, 1800).

40. Ashbel Green's Mulberry/Arch Street address comes from James Robinson, *The Philadelphia Directory, for 1810* (Philadelphia, 1810), 118. For a sample of the occupational identities of African American residents who lived nearby, on Sixth Street, see *Census Directory for 1811. Containing the Names, Occupations, & Residence of the Inhabitants of the City, Southwark & Northern Liberties, a Separate Division Being Allotted to Persons of Colour* (Philadelphia, 1811), 367–85.

For the threat of kidnapping in Philadelphia, see Richard Bell, *Stolen: Five Free Boys Kidnapped into Slavery and Their Astonishing Odyssey Home* (New York, 2019), esp. 11–46; and Eric Foner, *Gateway to Freedom: The Hidden History of the Underground Railroad* (New York, 2015), 50–51.

41. Green's various interactions with John Gloucester are in Green Diary, 17 May 1807; 14 June, 10 September 1809; 8 October 1810; and 4 November 1811. The positive estimate of Gloucester by the Presbyterian General Assembly comes from *Minutes of the General Assembly of the Presbyterian Church in the United States from Its Organization A.D. 1789 to A.D. 1820 Inclusive* (Philadelphia, 1847), 387. For useful sketches of Gloucester's life, see Barry Waugh, "The Reverend John Gloucester and America's First Presbyterian Church for Africans," *This Day in Presbyterian History*, http://www.thisday.pcahistory.org/2017/05/may-2-death-of-rev-john-gloucester/; and Harry Reed, *Platform for Change: The Foundations of the Northern Free Black Community, 1775–1865* (East Lansing, MI, 1994), 38–39.
42. The reference to the seating of Black people in Green's Second Presbyterian Church comes from Beadle, *The Old and the New*, 34.
43. Green Diary, 14, 19 August 1811, 18 April 1812, 25 July 1812.
44. For the steps in Betsey Stockton's self-education, see "Betsey Stockton," *Maui News*, 5 May 1906; Ashbel Green, *Life of Ashbel Green*, 341; and Michael Osborn to Jeremiah Evarts, 5 September 1821, ABCFM Archives.
45. Green Diary, 14 August 1812. Green claimed to have been surprised to be chosen president—an "unexpected call," he told the trustees—but he had been an insider for years. He had served on the board of trustees since 1790, and in 1802, when the sitting president, Samuel Stanhope Smith, took a fund-raising trip to the South, Green had filled in as interim president. See Harrison, *Princetonians*, 408–9.
46. Green Diary, 1–31 October 1812. For the evidence of slaveholding among Green's seven predecessors, see R. Isabela Morales, "Slavery at the President's House," Princeton & Slavery Project, https://slavery.princeton.edu/stories/presidents-house.
47. For the sale of enslaved people following Finley's death, see Morales, "Slavery at the President's House."

CHAPTER TWO

1. Ashbel Green Diary, 24 June 1813, Ashbel Green Papers, Princeton University Archives, Department of Rare Books and Special Collections, Princeton University Library; hereafter cited as Green Diary.

   For a larger exploration of the monetary value assigned to enslaved Black people, see Daina Ramey Berry, *The Price for Their Pound of Flesh: The Value of the Enslaved, from Womb to Grave, in the Building of a Nation* (Boston, 2017), in which she notes that the prices paid for women were subject to a number of variables—physical appearance, health, labor skills, location, among others—but one critical factor was age, particularly for women as "breeders," in the prime childbearing years between fifteen and thirty-five; see esp. chapters 1–3. In the case of Green's purchase of Phoebe's time, from age seventeen to twenty-four or twenty-five, childbearing seems to have been less a consideration. Unfortunately, there is no way to account for her subsequent years.

2. Ashbel Green to Jeremiah Evarts, 3 September 1821, American Board of Commissioners for Foreign Missions Archives, 1810–1961 (ABC 1–91) Houghton Library, Harvard University; hereafter cited as ABCFM Archives.
3. On binding out Black children as indentured servants, see Gary B. Nash, *Forging Freedom: The Formation of Philadelphia's Black Community, 1720–1840* (Cambridge, MA, 1988), 77–79; and James J. Gigantino II, *The Ragged Road to Abolition: Slavery and Freedom in New Jersey, 1775–1865* (Philadelphia, 2015), 98–104. In response to my query about Ashbel Green's sale of Betsey's time, Gigantino helpfully writes that "It seems that Green is selling Betsey for just a three year period, so hiring her out. It might be that if she is being troublesome or that in this three year period his labor needs have changed." Email correspondence from James J. Gigantino II to author, 27 March 2017. Green's note about Betsey's departure is in Green Diary, 12 July 1813.
4. The figures for Gloucester County in 1790 and 1800 come from Gigantino, *Ragged Road to Abolition*, 68; for 1820, from Thomas F. Gordon, *A Gazetteer of the State of New Jersey: Comprehending a General View of Its Physical and Moral Condition, Together with a Topographical and Statistical Account of Its Counties, Towns, Villages, Canals, Rail Road* (Philadelphia, 1834), 30. Betsey had been there once before, in 1811, when Green noted that "she left us and went with Dr. Bradford to Woodbury," apparently for a short visit, as recorded in Green Diary, 30 July 1811.
5. Basic biographical information on Nathaniel Todd comes from Joseph M. Wilson, *Presbyterian Historical Almanac and Annual Remembrancer of the Church*, vol. 10 (Philadelphia, 1868), 152–54; and *A History of the Schenectady Patent in the Dutch and English Times; Being a Contribution toward a History of the Lower Mohawk Valley*, ed. J. W. MacMurray (Albany, NY, 1883), 399–408. For Ashbel Green's early assessment of Todd, see Green to Jedediah Morse, 28 August 1804, Box 10, Folder 18, Ashbel Green Papers, Princeton RBSC. Green did, however, attend Todd's installation in Woodbury in May 1809; see Green Diary, 10 May 1809. The pastoral and personal visits, along with occasional correspondence between Green and the Todds are noted on 2 May, 22 July, 2 September, 10 September, 26 September, and 2 December 1812; Betsey's visit to Woodbury appears on 30 July 1811.
6. Information on the Todd family comes from *Index to Marriages in Massachusetts Centinel and Columbian Centinel, 1784 to 1840, Vol. 1, A–D* (Boston, 1961) and *New Jersey, Births and Christenings Index, 1660–1931* (Provo, UT, 2011); the latter lists two girls, Elizabeth Green Todd and Mary Cleveland Todd, born

on the same day, 15 August 1813. The notice about Todd's taking boarders for Woodbury Academy is in the *Trenton Federalist*, 8 May 1812.

7. For the range of Todd's teaching, see *Trenton Federalist*, 8 May 1812.
8. Todd's departure from the Woodbury church is briefly noted in *The Presbyterian Church at Woodbury: Two Hundred Fifty Years, 1721–1971* (Woodbury, NJ, 1971), 8. The most thorough discussion of his subsequent career is in Wilson, *Presbyterian Historical Almanac*, 153.
9. *True American* (Trenton, NJ), 15 July 1816, *Fredonian* (New Brunswick, NJ), 18 August 1816; the ads are dated 12 July and 18 July, respectively.
10. 20 September 1816, Church Book, 1792–1822, Minutes of the Session, Princeton N.J. First Presbyterian Church, Synod of New Jersey Collection, Princeton Theological Seminary Library.
11. 20 September 1816, Church Book, 1792–1822. Presbyterian Church records also help put the chronology of Ashbel Green's later recollections of Betsey in better perspective. When he wrote his narrative account of her life, in 1821, he was in his sixtieth year, old enough to be fuzzy on a few dates and details. He noted that she came back in "the summer of 1816" and joined the church "in the winter of 1816–1817"—a little late on the latter date, but close enough. He also gave incorrect information about her time with the Todds, writing that she had lived with them "between four and five years," which would have been until 1817 or 1818. See Green to Jeremiah Evarts, 3 September 1821, ABCFM Archives.
12. Green to Jeremiah Evarts, 3 September 1821, ABCFM Archives.
13. Green's unhappiness with the intellectual condition of the college is discussed in Richard A. Harrison, *Princetonians, 1776–1783: A Biographical Dictionary* (Princeton, NJ, 1981), 412–13. Green showed that unhappiness, in part, by sending two of his three sons elsewhere: Jacob went to Queen's College (Rutgers) and James to Dickinson. The assessment of the nature of the curricular changes under Green comes from Thomas Jefferson Wertenbaker, *Princeton, 1746–1896* (Princeton, NJ, 1946), 159–62.
14. On the difficult early days of Green's presidency, see Green, *Life of Ashbel Green*, 344–46; and Green Diary, 8–24 December 1812, 24 February 1813.
15. For Green's complaint about college and family troubles, see Green Diary, 16 July 1816. The deaths of his son and his second wife are discussed in Green, *Life of Ashbel Green*, 350–53 and 359–60. As he had done at the death of Elizabeth, Green again calculated the duration of his marriage to Christiana, "4 years and about five months."
16. Green's initial reference to the revival is in Green Diary, 16 January 1815. His general description of the revival comes from Ashbel Green, *A Report to the Trustees of the College of New Jersey Relative to a Revival of Religion among the Students of Said College, in the Winter and Spring of the Year 1815* (Philadelphia, 1815), 6–16.
17. Green Diary, 16–17 July 1816.
18. Green's marriage to Mary McCulloch came after a dogged but ultimately

unsuccessful courtship of a Miss Maskell, to whom he proposed marriage at the end of October 1814. Despite a good deal of letter writing and longing on Green's part, the romance was over by April 1815. Disappointed but undaunted, he then entertained the hope of introductions to a Miss Caldwell and a Miss McCulloch. Miss Caldwell never appeared, but Miss McCulloch did, and Green "was struck and pleased with her appearance and indeed I felt my affections a good deal drawn to her." See Green Diary, 31 October, 4, 6, 11, 15, 24 November, 7–9, 15 December 1814, 15 April, 26–28 May 1815; for the demise and death of Mary McCulloch, see 18, 23 November 1817.

19. Green to Jeremiah Evarts, 3 September 1821, ABCFM Archives; Green Diary, 16 December 1817.
20. Green to Jeremiah Evarts, 3 September 1821, ABCFM Archives.
21. There is an extensive literature on the significance of naming practices among the enslavers and the enslaved, most of it focusing on the Caribbean and the American South. See, for instance, Sarah Abel, George F. Tyson, and Gisli Palsson, "From Enslavement to Emancipation: Naming Practices in the Danish West Indies," *Comparative Studies in Society and History* 61 (April 2019): 332–65; Margaret Williamson, "Africa or Old Rome? Jamaican Slave Naming Revisited," *Slavery & Abolition: A Journal of Slave and Post-Slave Studies* 38 (2017): 117–34; and Susan Benson, "Injurious Names: Naming, Disavowal, and Recuperation in Contexts of Slavery and Emancipation," in *The Anthropology of Names and Naming*, ed. by Gabriele vom Bruck and Barbara Bodenhorn (Cambridge, 2006), 178–99. In a study that focuses on the American North, "The Allure of the Advertisement: Slave Runaways in and around New York City," *Journal of the Early Republic* 40 (Winter 2020): 611–33, Shane White observes that "The passive 'named' followed by the active 'calls himself' gives a fair indication of the tension between owner and slave's differing perspectives on the world," 616.
22. I am very grateful to the current owner of Stockton's volume, Joseph Felcone of Princeton, for generously inviting me to see the book and photograph the flyleaf.
23. Thomas Branagan, *The Flowers of Literature; Being an Exhibition of the Most Interesting Geographical, Historical, Miscellaneous and Theological Subjects, in Miniature. To Which Are Prefixed, Preliminary Addresses, to Parents, Teachers and Their Pupils* (Philadelphia, 1806); the copy Betsey Stockton owned was a subsequent edition published in Trenton, NJ, in 1810. On Branagan's background, see Christopher Phillips, "Epic, Anti-Eloquence, and Abolitionism: Thomas Branagan's *Avenia* and *The Penitential Tyrant*," *Early American Literature* 44 (3): 605–37.
24. Branagan, *The Flowers of Literature*, 318.
25. Branagan, 14–16, 22.
26. Michael Osborn to Jeremiah Evarts, 5 September 1821, ABCFM Archives
27. Branagan, *The Flowers of Literature*, 20–21.
28. Osborn to Jeremiah Evarts, 5 September 1821, ABCFM Archives.

29. Green to Jeremiah Evarts, 3 September 1821, ABCFM Archives.
30. For the positive assessments of Ashbel Green's attitudes toward Black people, see Robert E. Lewis, "Ashbel Green, 1762–1848—Preacher, Educator, Editor," *Journal of Presbyterian History* 35, no. 3 (September 1957): 150; Eileen F. Moffatt, "Betsey Stockton: Pioneer American Missionary," *International Bulletin of Missionary Research* (April 1995), 71–76; Constance K. Escher, "She Calls Herself Betsey Stockton," *Princeton History*, no. 10 (1991), 71–101; and Barbara Bennett Peterson, "Betsey Stockton," in *American National Biography*, 24 Vols. (New York, 1999), 20:808–9; essentially the same entry appears in *African American Lives*, ed. Henry Louis Gates Jr. and Evelyn Brooks Higginbotham (Oxford, 2004), 792–94.
31. The two whippings of John are recorded in Green Diary, 2 May 1815 and 9 December 1816. For a comparison, see Green's diary entry from June 1819 about disciplining his youngest son: "Corrected Ashbel for telling lies. He requested me to pray with him before I corrected him which I did. . . . I endeavoured to instruct him." What form the correction or instruction took Green does not say. Green Diary, 28 June 1819, 17 January 1821.
32. Green Diary, 1 May 1818. In his 1848 autobiography, he noted that "I penned the minute on the subject of slavery, which is yet often referred to by those who are hostile to African slavery." See Green, *Life of Ashbel Green*, 417.
33. This summary discussion of George Bourne's battles stems from the detailed study by John W. Christie and Dwight L. Dumond, *George Bourne and the Book and Slavery Irreconcilable* (Wilmington, DE, 1969), 22–64. In 1816, in fact, Green had been part of a committee of the General Assembly that recommended omitting a reference to slavery as a form of man-stealing, and hence a violation of the eighth commandment, from the Constitution of the Presbyterian Church. But for all its good talk about slavery as a "mournful evil," the statement amounted to little more than a position of appeasement to slaveholding Presbyterians. See *Minutes of the General Assembly of the Presbyterian Church in the United States of America from Its Organization A.D. 1789 to A.D. 1820 Inclusive* (Philadelphia, 1820), 629–30.
34. On Green's role, see Christie and Dumond, *George Bourne*, 59.
35. *Minutes of the General Assembly of the Presbyterian Church*, 688. The other two members of the 1818 committee were George Baxter of Virginia, the opponent of Bourne, and the more sympathetic Dyer Burgess of Ohio. See Christie and Dumond, *George Bourne*, 59.
36. *Minutes of the General Assembly of the Presbyterian Church*, 692.
37. *Minutes of the General Assembly of the Presbyterian Church*, 692.
38. *Minutes of the General Assembly of the Presbyterian Church*, 692.
39. *Minutes of the General Assembly of the Presbyterian Church*, 693. For the founding of the American Colonization Society, see Manisha Sinha, *The Slave's Cause: A History of Abolition* (New Haven, CT, 2016), 160–71. Even before the ACS came into existence, the notion of colonization had already gained con-

siderable traction as a solution to the challenge of slavery. Thomas Branagan, for instance, had argued as early as 1805 for creating a separate territory for free Blacks in the lands just acquired in the Louisiana Purchase. Although he had been a staunch antislavery polemicist just a year before, Branagan's call for colonization stemmed from an anxious-seeming fear of Black people, including the specter of mixed-race sexuality and the prospect that the expanding population of Black people would soon overwhelm white society. Branagan would by no means be the last proponent of colonization as a means of geographic segregation, but he was the first to promote removal to the far reaches of the United States. For Branagan's shift from opposition to slavery to racist removal and segregation, see Gary Nash, "Race and Citizenship in the Early Republic," in *Antislavery and Abolition in Philadelphia: Emancipation and the Long Struggle for Racial Justice in the City of Brotherly Love*, ed. Richard Newman and James Mueller (Baton Rouge, LA, 2011), 98–99; and Sinha, *The Slave's Cause*, 112. The two Thomas Branagan works in question are *Preliminary Essay on the Oppression of the Exiled Sons of Africa* (Philadelphia, 1804) and *Serious Remonstrances to Citizens of the Northern States* (Philadelphia, 1805). The Branagan book Betsey Stockton owned, *The Flowers of Literature*, did not deal with either abolition or colonization.

40. Isaac V. Brown, *Biography of the Rev. Robert Finley. D.D., of Basking Ridge, N.J.; With an Account of His Agency as the Author of the American Colonization Society; also a Sketch of the Slave Trade; a View of Our National Policy and That of Great Britain towards Liberia and Africa* (Philadelphia, 1857), 20, 164–66. From 1797 on, Finley had also been an occasional member of the General Assembly of the Presbyterian Church, and in 1816 he became one of the fund-raisers for the Princeton Theological Seminary, the institutional cause closest to Ashbel Green's heart. Finley's role as founder, however, has been questioned in a study that emphasizes that of Charles Fenton Mercer of Virginia; see Douglas R. Egerton, "'Its Origin Is Not a Little Curious': A New Look at the American Colonization Society," *Journal of the Early Republic* 5, no. 4 (1985): 463–80.

41. Green to Jeremiah Evarts, 3 September 1821; Osborn to Jeremiah Evarts, 5 September 1821, ABCFM Archives.

42. In his letter of recommendation for Betsey Stockton, Michael Osborn opened by noting that Stewart had "ask[ed] permission of the Board to take out with him, in the capacity of domestic servant, and assistant to the mission, Betsey Stockton, a young mulattoe woman of this place." Osborn to Jeremiah Evarts, 5 September 1821, ABCFM Archive. Stockton's status as "domestic servant" would later become the subject of some concern, but at the outset, the important point is that Stewart had her in his plans as early as September 1821.

43. Charles Samuel Stewart to the Prudential Committee of the American Board of Commissioners for Foreign Missions, 1 November 1821, ABCFM Archives.

44. Green to Jeremiah Evarts, 3 September 1821, ABCFM Archives. Stewart's fond characterizations of Green come from a letter he wrote to Green, which Green transcribed; Green Diary, 17 September 1821.
45. Stewart's fund-raising efforts and his marriage are noted in his letters to Jeremiah Evarts, 14 July, 14 August 1822; Harriet Bradford Stewart's statement comes from her own letter to Evarts, 16 July 1822; and Stewart's reference to the help from Nathan Whiting is in his last letter to Evarts, 5 November 1822, ABCFM Archives.
46. The meeting with Stewart and Stockton is recorded in Green Diary, undated entry, October 1822. The document from Ashbel Green, Charles Samuel Stewart, and Betsey Stockton to Jeremiah Evarts, 24 October 1822, is in ABCFM Archives. If Green were not the sole author of the document, it certainly bears the imprint of his authority.
47. The continuing troubles with the College of New Jersey students are recorded in Green Diary, 5 January 1819, and 1–5 February 1822, 27 March 1827; his suspicion of the hostile members of the board on 11 April 1822; and his resignation on 25 September 1822. The context of his difficulties with the trustees is in John Maclean, *History of the College of New Jersey, from Its Origin in 1746 to the Commencement of 1864*, 2 vols., (Philadelphia, 1877), 2:169–97, quotations 196–97; and from Wertenbaker, *Princeton*, 170–72, in a chapter titled "Princeton's Nadir."
48. Green Diary, undated entry, October 1822.

CHAPTER THREE

1. The list of *Thames* missionaries appeared in the *Religious Intelligencer*, 23 November 1822, and was widely reprinted:

> Rev. William Richards, ordained missionary. Married to Clarissa Lyman of Northampton.
>
> Rev. Charles Samuel Stewart, ordained missionary. Married to Harriet B. Tiffany.
>
> Rev. Artemas Bishop, ordained missionary. Married to Elizabeth Edwards.
>
> Dr. Abraham Blatchley, Physician, acquainted also with various mechanical employments. Married to Miss Marvin.
>
> Mr. Joseph Goodrich, Licensed Preacher, acquainted with various mechanical employments. Married to Martha Barns of Southington.
>
> Mr. James Ely, Licensed Preacher, teacher, and mechanic. Married to Miss Everest.
>
> Mr. Levi Chamberlain, teacher and superintendent of secular concerns.
>
> Betsey Stockton, a pious colored woman, qualified to teach a school and take charge of domestic concerns.
>
> Stephen Popohe, a native of the Society Islands.

William Kummo-oo-lah, a native of the Sandwich Islands.
Richard Kriouloo, a native of the Sandwich Islands.
Cooperee, a native man of the Sandwich Islands.

Only four were over thirty: the Blatchleys, Levi Chamberlain, and Cooperee, who may have been as old as fifty; see Thomas French, *The Missionary Whaleship* (New York, 1961), 67–70; and "Private Journal of Chas. Saml. Stewart of His Voyage to the Sandwich Islands," 4 December 1822, Rev. Charles S. Stewart papers, New York Historical Association—Research Library; hereafter cited as Charles Stewart Journal.

The captain of the *Thames*, Reuben Clasby, was thirty-one, and the twenty-two young men in his command ranged in age from eighteen to twenty-eight; all but four came from New England, and most from Connecticut. For Clasby and the crew, see New Haven Register of Seaman's Protection Certificates, National Archives and Records Administration, Waltham, MA.

2. The account of Charles Stewart's struggle to book the ship comes from Betsey Stockton to Ashbel Green, 7 November 1822, *Christian Advocate* 1 (February 1823): 88–89.
3. Betsey Stockton to Ashbel Green, 7 November 1822, *Christian Advocate* 1 (February 1823): 89.
4. For the origins of the *Thames*, see Harry D. Sleight, *The Whale Fishery on Long Island* (Bridgehampton, NY, 1931), 92; and Thomas R. Trowbridge Jr., "History of the Ancient Maritime Interests of New Haven," *Papers of the New Haven Historical Society* 3 (1882): 161. The only remaining part of the *Thames*, the ninety-two-foot-long keel, now rests on display at Mystic Seaport, a little over fifty miles east of New Haven. Betsey Stockton's description of the ship's interior is in her letter to Ashbel Green, 7 November 1822, *Christian Advocate* 1 (February 1823): 89.
5. For the general comparison of the two towns, see Henry D. Gilpin, *A Northern Tour: Being a Guide to Saratoga, Lake George, Niagara, Canada, Boston, &c. &c.* (Philadelphia, 1825), 9, 276.
6. The characterization of New Haven's Black people comes from *A Statistical Account of the Towns and Parishes in the State of Connecticut, Published by the Connecticut Academy of Arts and Sciences* (New Haven, CT, 1811), 57–58.
7. *Statistical Account . . . of Connecticut*, 39–40. See also Timothy Dwight, *Travels; in New-England and New-York*, 4 vols. (New Haven, CT, 1821), 1:187.
8. *Statistical Account . . . of Connecticut*, 66–68, 83; and Dwight, *Travels*, 1:188–89.
9. John Demos offers a very useful overview of the China trade in *The Heathen School: A Story of Hope and Betrayal in the Age of the Early Republic* (New York, 2014), 9–15. For a briefer description, see Jennifer Fish Kashay, "Agents of Imperialism: Missionaries and Merchants in Early-Nineteenth-Century Hawaii," *New England Quarterly* 80 (June 2007): 280–98. The particular place of the Sandwich Islands in the sandalwood trade is discussed in considerable

detail in Noelani Arista, *The Kingdom and the Republic: Sovereign Hawai'i and the Early United States* (Philadelphia, 2019), 18–51.

10. For the origins of the whale-fishery business in New Haven, see Trowbridge, "History of the Ancient Maritime Interests of New Haven," 161–62. The more general history of New England whaling is Alexander Starbuck, *History of the American Whale Fishery from Its Earliest Inception to the Year 1876* (Waltham, MA, 1878), 4–95; quotation, 10.
11. Starbuck, *History of the American Whale Fishery*, 90, 96; and Rhys Richards, *Honolulu: Centre of Trans-Pacific Trade; Shipping Arrivals and Departures, 1820 to 1840* (Honolulu, 2000), 12.
12. Starbuck, *History of the American Whale Fishery*, 3.
13. For the origins of the ABCFM, see Arista, *The Kingdom and the Republic*, 56–57; and Demos, *Heathen School*, 64–65.
14. The estimate for the Yale library comes from Gilpin, *A Northern Tour*, 277. For the volumes related to "Geography, Voyages and Travel," see *Catalogue of Books in the Library of Yale College* (New Haven, CT, 1823), 92–96, which lists "Cook (Js.) Voyages, 2 vol. 8vo. Lond.," presumably James Cook, *A Voyage Towards the South Pole and Round the World: Performed in His Majesty's Ships the Resolution and Adventure, in the Years 1772, 1773, 1774 and 1775*, 2 vols. (London, 1777). The Yale catalog also includes several works on geography by Jedediah Morse, the latest being the seventh edition of *The American Universal Geography; or, A View of the Present State of All the Kingdoms, States, and Colonies in the Known World*, 2 vols. (Boston, 1819); the section on the Sandwich Isles is in 2:714–15.
15. The letter from "Mrs. ——" is reprinted in *Religious Intelligencer* 6, no. 1 (June 2, 1821): 3–4; the letter from "S.M." to the Reverend G. Bourne, 2 September 1822, appears in *Religious Intelligencer* 7, no. 17 (September 21, 1822): 225–26. Neither correspondent noted the larger context of political and religious transformation that followed the death of the great chief Kamehameha I, in 1819, which will be discussed in chapter 4.
16. John Demos, in *Heathen School*, has provided a thorough history of the Foreign Mission School in Cornwall; for the account of the school's origins in 1817, see 66–79.
17. The *Memoirs of Henry Obookiah, a Native of Owhyhee, and a Member of the Foreign Mission School; Who Died at Cornwall, Conn. Feb. 17 1818. Aged 26 Years* (New Haven, CT, 1818). Demos has found evidence that Ōpūkaha'ia was actually thirty, perhaps thirty-one, at the time of his death; see Demos, *Heathen School*, 282n7. For a full-length modern biography of Ōpūkaha'ia, see Christopher L. Cook, *The Providential Life & Heritage of Henry Obookiah: Why Did Missionaries Come to Hawai'i from New England and Tahiti?* (Waimea, Kaua'i, HI, 2015).
18. Demos, *Heathen School*, 20–22.
19. *Memoirs of Henry Obookiah*, 19–25; Demos, *Heathen School*, 16–18; Cook, *Providential Life & Heritage of Henry Obookiah*, 47.

20. Demos, *Heathen School*, 22–29.
21. The first edition of *Memoirs of Henry Obookiah* was published anonymously, but a subsequent edition (Philadelphia, 1830) revealed the author to have been Edwin W. Dwight; see Demos, *Heathen School*, 84. For a discussion of the importance of the book to the missionary movement, see Jeffrey K. Lyons, "Memoirs of Henry Obookiah: A Rhetorical History," *Hawaiian Journal of History* 38 (2004): 35–37.
22. After the original edition (New Haven, CT, 1818), a subsequent one was published in Elizabethtown, New Jersey, in 1819, while Stockton still lived in Princeton. I am grateful to Joseph Felcone for information about that edition.
23. Ashbel Green and Timothy Dwight were two of the most prominent Protestant intellectuals of the time, but they had another point in common: both had held enslaved females—Betsey Stockton in Green's case, a woman named Naomi in Dwight's. Like Green, Dwight could on one hand deprecate the fundamental sinfulness of slavery as an institution but still take an indulgent view of those Americans who benefited most from slavery, southern planters. Both Dwight and Green, as northern college presidents who relied on tuition-paying students from the South, could set aside whatever ethical qualms they may have had about slavery in the interest of keeping in the good graces of the slaveholding class. See "Naomi, Slave of T. Dwight," http://www.yaleslavery.org/WhoYaleHonors/dwight2.html.
24. The accounts of the two church services are in the *Connecticut Courant* (Hartford), 26 November 1822. Jeremiah Evarts's sermon is in American Board of Commissioners for Foreign Missions, *Instructions to the Missionaries about to Embark for the Sandwich Islands; and to the Rev. Messrs. William Goddell, & Isaac Bird, Attached to the Palestine Mission* (Boston, 1823), quotations on 7 and 13.
25. *Connecticut Mirror*, 25 November 1822, 3; *Christian Advocate* 1 (February 1823): 89.
26. For the list of possessions, see Hawaiian Mission Children's Society, *Missionary Album: Portraits and Biographical Sketches of the American Protestant Missionaries to the Hawaiian Islands* (Honolulu, 1969), 2. Betsey Stockton Journal, 22 November 1820, *Christian Advocate* 1 (May 1824), 237.
27. Herman Melville, *Moby-Dick; or, The Whale* (New York, 1851), chapter 20. For an extensive list of necessary items, see A. Hyatt Verrill, *The Real Story of the Whaler: Whaling, Past and Present* (New York and London, 1916), 60–67.
28. For Clasby's previous voyages, see *Whaling Masters*, compiled by the Federal Writers Project of the Works Progress Administration of Massachusetts (New Bedford, MA, 1938; repr. San Bernardino, CA, 1975), 80. Betsey Stockton's initial appraisal of Clasby comes from her letter to Ashbel Green, 19 December 1822, in *Christian Advocate* 1 (September 1823): 423. Charles Stewart's observations are in *Christian Advocate* 1 (February 1823): 90.
29. For the various roles of the men, see New Haven Register of Seaman's Protection Certificates, National Archives and Records Administration,

Waltham, MA. See also Margaret S. Creighton, *Rites and Passages: The Experience of American Whaling, 1830–1870* (New York, 1995), 28–31; and Lance E. Davis, Robert E. Gallman, and Karin Gleiter, *In Pursuit of Leviathan: Technology, Institutions, Productivity, and Profits in American Whaling, 1816–1906* (Chicago, 1997), 47–48.

30. Different sources give slightly different information about the return of the *Thames* to New Haven: French, in *Missionary Whaleship*, 123–24, says 4 November 1825, with "1900 barrels of whale oil." Sleight, in *The Whale Fishery on Long Island*, 93, puts it at "1826, with 1800 barrels of sperm oil."

31. Charles Samuel Stewart's note about the initial burst of writing comes from his shipboard journal, 26 November 1822. Stewart filled five small notebooks with intermittent entries while on the *Thames*, edited and revised those volumes in another manuscript notebook, then published yet a final revised version in his *Private Journal of a Voyage to the Pacific Ocean, and Residence at the Sandwich Islands, in the Years 1822, 1823, 1824, and 1825* (New York, 1828); hereafter cited as *Private Journal*. To reflect Stewart's onboard observations at the time, I have chosen to use the manuscript version; hereafter cited as Stewart Journal.

32. Stockton's initial shipboard correspondence with Green, dated 19 December 1822 and 2 February 1823, was published in *Christian Advocate* 1 (1 September 1823): 423–25. Her second letter, dated 15 June 1823, appeared in *Christian Advocate* 2 (May 1824): 232–33, followed immediately by the first installment of her journal.

    There is no surviving manuscript version of Stockton's journal, so the passages cited come from the published version in the *Christian Advocate* 1 (May 1824): 233–35; 2 (December 1824): 563–66, and 3 (January 1825): 36–41. References to her journal will be identified as Stockton Journal, by date, followed by the page numbers in the *Christian Advocate*. For her account of trying to send mail, see Stockton Journal, 26 November 1822, *Christian Advocate* 2 (May 1824): 233.

33. For Green's editorial comments, see *Christian Advocate* 2 (May 1824): 232; and Ashbel Green, *The Life of Ashbel Green, V.D.M., Begun to Be Written by Himself in His Eighty-Second Year and Continued to His Eighty-Fourth. Prepared for the Press by Joseph H. Jones* (Philadelphia, 1849), 326. Green did write in his diary about editing Stockton's work: "I labored hard on . . . Betty's journal on public affairs," he noted in November 1824, and then again in December, "Spent the day in reviewing and correcting Betsy Stockton's journal for Advocate." See Green Diary, 2–6 November 1824, 31 December 1824, Box 6, Folder 8, Ashbel Green Papers, Princeton University Archives, Department of Rare Books and Special Collections, Princeton University Library. Since every published work goes through at least some degree of editing, it still makes sense to accept Betsey Stockton's published journal as a legitimate reflection of her experiences on board the *Thames*.

34. Charles Stewart clearly anticipated future publication of his own *Thames*

journal, and he no doubt hoped to see Betsey Stockton's published as well: the more missionary writings in print, the better to promote the work of their mission. The unpublished missionary journals from the *Thames* voyage are the Levi Chamberlain Journal, in the collections of the Hawaiian Mission Houses Historic Site and Archives, also available as Levi Chamberlain Journals, 1822–49, typed transcripts, at the University of California, Berkeley; hereafter cited as Chamberlain Journal; and the Louisa Everett Ely Diary, 1822–23, in the Connecticut Historical Society Library, Historical Manuscripts (77547); hereafter cited as Ely Diary.

35. The sentence ending with "bid the American shores a long adieu" does not appear in the published version of Stewart's *Private Journal*. The "long adieu" language did appear again in a published letter of appreciation from the missionaries to Reuben Clasby, which noted that the missionaries had a "desire to be engaged in the work for which we have bid our native Country a long adieu." See Artemas Bishop et al. to Captain Reuben Clasby, 2 May 1824, published in New Haven's *Connecticut Courant*, 18 May 1824, 2.
36. Stockton Journal, 21 November 1822, *Christian Advocate* 2 (May 1824): 233.
37. Stewart Journal, 30 November 1822.
38. Stockton Journal, 23 November 1822, 3 January 1823, *Christian Advocate* 2 (May 1824): 233, 234. Stockton may not have been able to employ Milton's words here, but she did occasionally quote other literary sources, apparently from memory; the *Thames* did not have a reference library on board. For subsequent literary references, see 8 February and 26 March 1823, *Christian Advocate* 2 (December 1824): 564; and 4 (January 1825): 38, when she quotes two lines from William Falconer, "The Shipwreck," Canto III, and a phrase from the Book of Revelations.
39. Stockton Journal, 9 February 1823, *Christian Advocate* (December 1824): 564.
40. Betsey Stockton to Ashbel Green, 19 December 1822, *Christian Advocate* 1 (September 1823): 424–25.
41. Stockton Journal, 23, 25, 30 December 1822; 8 January 1823, *Christian Advocate* 2 (May 1824): 233–35; 25 March 1823, *Christian Advocate* 3 (January 1825): 37–38. Stockton's reference to a "bonetta" fish no doubt refers to a bonito. Her characterization of the cook comes from Betsey Stockton to Ashbel Green, 19 December 1822, *Christian Advocate* 1 (September 1823): 424. Other notes about food come from Chamberlain Journal, 5 December 1822; and Ely Diary, 22 April 1823.
42. Stockton Journal, 8 February 1823, *Christian Advocate* 2 (December 1824): 564.
43. Stockton Journal, 2 April 1823, *Christian Advocate* 3 (January 1825): 38–39.
44. Stewart Journal, 4 December 1822. Where Stewart's spelling of a name differs from that of another source, I have included the latter in parentheses.
45. Stockton Journal, 5 December 1822, *Christian Advocate* 2 (May 1824): 233; Stewart Journal, 25 November 1822; Chamberlain Journal, 24 December 1822; 19 January, 2 February 1823.
46. Chamberlain Journal, 24 December 1822; 19, 31 January 1823.
47. Chamberlain Journal, 15, 29 December 1822; 9, 16 February; 30 March 1823.

48. Chamberlain Journal, 26 January; 1, 12 February; 3 March 1823.
49. Stewart Journal, 4 December 1822. The ordeal of the *Essex* crew was first told in Owen Chase, *Narrative of the Most Extraordinary and Distressing Shipwreck of the Whale-Ship* Essex (New York, 1821). Stewart knew the story, referring in his journal to "a narrative of the shipwreck of the Essex, sunk by a whale in the Pacific . . . He is the one whose hard lot it was to shoot his comrade Coffin (on whom the lot to die for the sustenance of the remaining two fell) & who was picked up with the Capt. after having been 93 [days] at sea in an open whale boat."
50. Stewart Journal, 4 December 1822.
51. Stewart Journal, 25 January, 6, 31 March 1823; Chamberlain Journal, 5 February 1823.
52. Stockton Journal, 5 December 1822, *Christian Advocate* 2 (May 1824): 233; 9 February 1823, *Christian Advocate* 2 (December 1824): 565–66; 10, 30 March 1823, *Christian Advocate* 3 (January 1825): 37, 38. For an extensive description of the rough language of mariners, see Paul Gilje, *To Swear Like a Sailor: Maritime Culture in America, 1750–1850* (New York, 2016), esp. chapters 1 and 2.
53. Stockton Journal, 9 February 1823, *Christian Advocate* 2 (December 1824): 565–66.
54. Stockton Journal, 4 January 1823, *Christian Advocate* 2 (May 1824): 234. See also Chamberlain Journal, 4 January 1823.
55. Stewart Journal, 6 January 1823. Louisa Ely also took note of the ship—"Spoke a Portuguese Brig bound to the West Coast of Africa. It is thought they are in pursuit of slaves"—but made no further comment; Ely Diary, 9 January 1823. Levi Chamberlain wrote, "Did not understand where she was from, not how long she had been out; but learned that she was bound to the coast of Africa." Chamberlain Journal, 9 January 1823. It is unclear why the entries by Ely and Chamberlain have a later date than Stewart's.
56. Stockton Journal, 6 January 1823, *Christian Advocate* 2 (May 1824): 235.
57. Stockton Journal, 6 January 1823, *Christian Advocate* 2 (May 1824): 235.
58. Stockton Journal, 23 November, 25, 30 December 1822, *Christian Advocate* 2 (May 1824): 233, 234.
59. Chamberlain Journal, 14 January 1823.
60. Stockton Journal, 6, 8, 9 February 1823, *Christian Advocate* 2 (December 1824): 564–66; 25 March 1823, *Christian Advocate* 3 (January 1825): 37–38.
61. Stockton Journal, 30 March 1823, *Christian Advocate* 3 (January 1825): 38.
62. Stockton Journal, 4–24 April 1823, *Christian Advocate* 3 (January 1825): 39; events from several dates appear in this entry because, as Stockton explained, "you must excuse me if my journal is now weekly instead of daily." For the birth of the baby, see also Ely Diary, 11, 19 April 1823; on the latter date she wrote, "He is called Charles Clasby Stewart," and so he was for a while, until his parents changed his middle name to "Seaforth."
63. Stockton Journal, 4–24 April 1823, *Christian Advocate* 3 (January 1825): 39.

64. Stockton Journal, 4–24 April 1823, *Christian Advocate* 3 (January 1825): 39; Chamberlain Journal, 24 April 1823; Ely Journal, 24 April 1823.
65. All five verses of the hymn are quoted in Ely Diary, 24 April 1823.
66. Stockton Journal, 4–24 April 1823, *Christian Advocate* 3 (January 1825): 39.
67. Stockton Journal, 4–24 April 1823, *Christian Advocate* 3 (January 1825): 39.

CHAPTER FOUR

1. Levi Chamberlain Journal, 27 April 1823, Hawaiian Mission Houses Historic Site and Archives, also available as Levi Chamberlain Journals, 1822–1849 typed transcripts, University of California, Berkeley; hereafter cited as Chamberlain Journal; Charles Stewart Journal, 26 April 1823, *Christian Advocate* 2 (June 1824): 278; hereafter cited as Stewart Journal; Louisa Everett Ely Diary, 27 April 1823, Connecticut Historical Society Library, Historical Manuscripts (77547); and Betsey Stockton Journal, 27 April 1823, *Christian Advocate* 4 (January 1825): 41; hereafter cited as Stockton Journal.

   Upon his arrival in Hawai'i, Charles Stewart began to keep his "private" journal, which was published in Ashbel Green's *Christian Advocate*; and an "official" journal, prepared with William Richards, which appeared in the *Missionary Herald*, published by the American Board of Commissioners for Foreign Missions (ABCFM). Because of the intermittent pace and sometimes inconsistent order of the appearance in the two sources, I cite both with the date of the entry and the date of publication, which could be well over a year apart.
2. Stewart Journal, 29 April 1823, *Christian Advocate* 2 (July 1824): 320–21.
3. Herman Melville, *Typee: A Peep at Polynesian Life* (London, 1846), 251; Mark Twain, *Roughing It* (Hartford, CT, 1872), 462. As David Zmijewski points out, however, Twain could also have positive things to say about the role American missionaries played in the cultural transformation of Hawai'i; see "Mark Twain's Dual Visions of Hawai'i: Censoring the Creative Self," *Hawaiian Journal of History* 38 (2004): 99–119.

   For the most recent critique of the American missionary effort as a contribution to American imperialism, see Emily Conroy-Krutz, *Christian Imperialism: Converting the World in the Early American Republic* (Ithaca, NY), esp. 6–13; Conroy-Krutz, "The Vast Kingdom of God," *William and Mary Quarterly* 78, no. 2 (April 2021): 223–28; and Jennifer Fish Kashay, "Agents of Imperialism: Missionaries and Merchants in Early-Nineteenth-Century Hawaii," *New England Quarterly* 80 (June 2007): 280–98. The connection between Christian missionaries and imperialism was by no means an American phenomenon alone, of course, nor was it limited to the Pacific. See, for instance, Andrew Porter, *Religion versus Empire? British Protestant Missionaries and Overseas Expansion, 1700–1914* (Manchester, 2004). As Chinua Achebe observed in his classic work on British colonialism in Africa, *Things Fall*

Apart (Oxford, 1958), 124, "The white man is very clever. He came quietly and peaceably with his religion. We were amused at his foolishness and allowed him to stay."

4. Stewart Journal, 3 May 1823, *Christian Advocate* 2 (July 1824): 322; Betsey Stockton to Ashbel Green, 15 June 1823, *Christian Advocate* 2 (May 1824): 232; Charles Stewart to Ashbel Green, 24 May 1823, *Christian Advocate* 2 (May 1824): 255.
5. Stewart Journal, 29 April 1823, *Christian Advocate* 2 (July 1824): 321.
6. Stewart Journal, 3 May 1823, *Christian Advocate* 2 (July 1824): 322.
7. Stewart Journal, 7 May 1823, *Christian Advocate* 2 (July 1824): 323.
8. Stewart Journal, 11, 14 May 1823, *Christian Advocate* 2 (July 1824): 324.
9. Stockton Journal, 10 May 1823, *Christian Advocate* 3 (January 1825): 40. For a similar description of the accommodations, see Stewart Journal, 10 May 1823, *Christian Advocate* 2 (July 1824): 323–24.
10. Stockton Journal, 10 May 1823, *Christian Advocate* 3 (January 1825): 40.
11. For a valuable overview of Allen's life, from which this paragraph is drawn, see Marc Scruggs, "Anthony D. Allen: A Prosperous American of African Descent in Early 19th Century Hawai'i," *Hawaiian Journal of History* 26 (1992): 55–93; for Charles Stewart's description of Allen's compound, see 64–65.
12. *Connecticut Mirror*, 30 July 1821.
13. *Connecticut Mirror*, 30 July 1821.
14. Scruggs, "Anthony D. Allen," 92–93.
15. Stockton Journal, 31 May 1823, *Christian Advocate* 3 (January 1825): 40; "Journal of Messrs. Richards and Stewart at Lahainah," 31 May 1823, *Missionary Herald* (February 1825), 39. On the origins of *Cleopatra's Barge*, which had been built in Salem, Massachusetts, sailed to Hawai'i, and sold to Liholiho, see Hiram Bingham, *A Residence of Twenty-One Years in the Sandwich Islands* (Hartford, CT, 1848), 126.
16. "Journal of Messrs. Richards and Stewart at Lahainah," 31 May 1823, *Missionary Herald* (February 1825), 39. That source puts the permanent population of Lahaina at 2,500, but Elisha Loomis noted that Richards estimated the number to be five thousand; see *Copy of the Journal of E. Loomis* (Honolulu, 1937), 4. Betsey Stockton Journal, 31 May 1823, *Christian Advocate* 3 (January 1825): 40.
17. Stewart Journal, 20, 24 May 1823, *Christian Advocate* 3 (May 1825): 217.
18. The impact of foreign contact in Hawai'i, including the nature of disease and the pre-1850 population decline, comes from Seth Archer, *Sharks upon the Land: Colonialism, Indigenous Health, and Culture in Hawai'i, 1778–1855* (New York, 2018), 2–3, 135–39. David E. Stannard, in *Before the Horror: The Population of Hawai'i on the Eve of Western Contact* (Honolulu, 1989), argues that the common estimates for the precontact population have been too low, and he puts that population at eight hundred thousand to one million. For the nineteenth-century observation, see Francis Allyn Olmsted, *Incidents of*

a Whaling Voyage: To Which Are Added Observations on the Scenery, Manners and Customs, and Missionary Stations of the Sandwich and Society Islands (New York, 1841), 261.

19. The description of the sandalwood trade, here and below, comes from Noelani Arista, *The Kingdom and the Republic: Sovereign Hawaiʻi and the Early United States* (Philadelphia, 2019), 18–51.
20. For the alignment of the four island chiefdoms, see Ruth Tabrah, *Hawaii: A Bicentennial History* (New York, 1980), 14; the significance of Kamehameha I is summarized in Arista, *The Kingdom and the Republic*, 18–23.
21. For the influence of Kaʻahumanu and Kālaimoku after the death of Kamehameha I, see Arista, *The Kingdom and the Republic*, 26, 42–49.
22. Arista, 29–51. See also Kashay, "Agents of Imperialism," 280–98.
23. Quoted in Arista, *The Kingdom and the Republic*, 47. See also Kashay, "Agents of Imperialism," 282–86. This outburst by John Coffin Jones came barely two months before Betsey Stockton, Charles Stewart, and their shipmates on the *Thames* arrived.
24. Arista, *The Kingdom and the Republic*, 105–9. See also Archer, *Sharks upon the Land*, 139–47; and Jennifer Fish Kashay, "From Kapus to Christianity: The Disestablishment of the Hawaiian Religion and Chiefly Appropriation of Calvinist Christianity," *Western Historical Quarterly* 39 (February 2008): 17–39.
25. Stockton Journal, *Christian Advocate* 3 (January 1825): 40–41.
26. Stewart Journal, 20 May 1823, *Christian Advocate* 3 (May 1825): 219–20.
27. Stewart Journal, 20 May 1823, *Christian Advocate* 3 (May 1825): 219.
28. For the drawn-out process of Keōpūolani's dying, see Stewart Journal, 1–16 September, *Christian Advocate* 3 (July and August 1825): 314–19, 359–60; "Letter from Messrs. Richards and Stewart to the Corresponding Secretary," 1 December 1823, *Missionary Herald* (April 1825), 100–3. William Richards also published a brief book, *Memoir of Keopuolani, Late Queen of the Sandwich Islands* (Boston, 1825).
29. Stewart Journal, 1 September 1823, *Christian Advocate* 3 (July 1825): 359.
30. Stewart Journal, 20 May 1823, *Christian Advocate* 3 (May 1825): 220, 222.
31. Betsey Stockton to Ashbel Green, 15 June 1823, *Christian Advocate* 2 (May 1824): 232; Betsey Stockton to unnamed recipient, 30 December 1823, *Religious Intelligencer* 9 (September 1824): 209.
32. Betsey Stockton to Ashbel Green, 15 June 1823, *Christian Advocate* 2 (May 1824): 232; 15 September 1824, *Christian Advocate* 3 (April 1825): 188.
33. Betsey Stockton to Ashbel Green, 16 September 1824, *Christian Advocate* 3 (April 1825): 188. Green's note about receiving the trunkful of specimens comes from *Christian Advocate* 3 (May 1825): 234.
34. Betsey Stockton to unnamed recipient, 30 December 1823, *Religious Intelligencer* 9 (September 1824): 210.
35. Stockton Journal, 29 June 1823, *Christian Advocate* 3 (January 1825): 41.
36. For the list of the initial ABCFM missionaries and their approach to teaching, see Bingham, *A Residence . . . in the Sandwich Islands*, 60–61, 101–3.

37. Bingham, 153–56. Bingham's reference to pupils teaching other pupils offers an insight into the missionaries' pedagogical approach, the Lancastrian, or monitorial, method, in which slightly more advanced student "monitors" would instruct others. This system relied largely on learning by rote, not the most imaginative form of education, but a reasonably effective means of promoting literacy. See Larry Prochner, "Betsey Stockton, Pioneer Early Childhood Teacher," *Young Children* 73 (July 2019), https://www.naeyc.org/resources/pubs/yc/jul2019/betsey-stockton-early-childhood-teacher.
38. Bingham, *A Residence . . . in the Sandwich Islands*, 162, 163; Arista, *The Kingdom and the Republic*, 123–24.
39. "Journal of the Mission at Honoruru," 19 April 1824, *Missionary Herald* (July 1825), 211–12.
40. "Journal of Messrs. Stewart and Richards at Lahainah," 31 January, 2 February 1824, *Missionary Herald* (September 1825), 278.
41. "Sandwich Islands. Maui. Station at Lahaina," 15 November 1824, *Missionary Herald* (February 1826), 38. For additional notes on Stockton's teaching, see also John A. Andrew, "Betsey Stockton: Stranger in a Strange Land," *Journal of Presbyterian History* 52, no. 2 (Summer 1974): 161–62; Constance K. Escher, "She Calls Herself Betsey Stockton," *Princeton History*, no. 10 (1991), 85–86; Barbara Bennett Peterson, "Betsey Stockton," *American National Biography* 20 (New York, 1999): 808–9.
42. Michael Osborn to Jeremiah Evarts, 5 September 1821, American Board of Commissioners for Foreign Missions Archives, 1810–1961 (ABC 1–91) Houghton Library, Harvard University; Ashbel Green, Charles Samuel Stewart, and Betsey Stockton to Jeremiah Evarts, 24 October 1822, ABCFM Archives.
43. Betsey Stockton to Ashbel Green, 15 and 16 September 1824, *Christian Advocate* 3 (April 1825): 188. The prevalence of these problems became clear in the last few entries of her journal, covering late June and early July 1823, just after her arrival in Lahaina. She reported "another attack of the pain in my breast, with a little spitting of blood," which William Richards treated by bleeding her. Stockton Journal, 4 July 1823, *Christian Advocate* 3 (January 1825): 41.
44. Betsey Stockton to Levi Chamberlain, 25 December 1824, Missionary Letters, Hawaiian Mission Children's Society Library.
45. Stewart Journal, 1 September 1823, 1 March 1824, *Christian Advocate* 3 (July, November 1825): 314, 503.
46. Stockton Journal, 4 July 1823, *Christian Advocate* 3 (January 1825): 41; Stewart Journal, 1 September 1823, 1 March 1824, 18 March 1824, *Christian Advocate* 3 (July, November 1825): 314, 503, 506.
47. Charles Stewart Journal, 2–8 April 1824, *Christian Advocate* 3 (December 1825): 552–54.
48. Betsey Stockton to Ashbel Green, 15 September 1824, *Christian Advocate* 3 (April 1825): 188. See also Betsey Stockton to Levi Chamberlain, 25 December 1824. In April 1824, Charles Stewart had noted that young Charles weighed

twenty-two pounds by the time of his first birthday, a gain of fourteen pounds in the year; Stewart Journal, 8 April 1824, *Christian Advocate* 3 (December 1825): 553. On the general poor health among missionary women, see "Sandwich Islands. Joint Letter of the Missionaries," 15 October 1825, *Missionary Herald* (July 1826), 209.

49. Stewart Journal, 9 January, 14 February, 7 March, 17 April 1825, *Christian Advocate* 4 (July, August, December 1826): 311, 317, 365, 415.
50. Stewart Journal, 17 April, 31 May, 11 June 1825, *Christian Advocate* 4 (December 1826): 415, 542–46.
51. On the trip to London, see two articles by J. Susan Corley, "Kamehameha II's Ill-Starred Journey to England Aboard *L'Aigle*, 1823–1824," *Hawaiian Journal of History* 44 (2010): 1–35; and "Queen Kamāmalu's Place in Hawaiian History," *Hawaiian Journal of History* 46 (2012): 37–60.
52. For Elisha Loomis's notes on the deaths of the royal couple, see the entries for 10 March, 5 and 10 May 1825, in *Copy of the Journal of E. Loomis*, 30, 34–35; Stewart's observations of the funeral are in "Journal at Honoruru," 7–11 May 1825, *Missionary Herald* (March 1826), 68–70.
53. Stewart Journal, 5 June 1825, *Christian Advocate* 4 (December 1826): 543.
54. "Sandwich Islands. Joint Letter of the Missionaries," 15 October 1825, *Missionary Herald* (July 1826), 206. For the arrival and departure dates of the *Blonde* and the *Fawn*, see Rhys Richards, *Honolulu Centre of Trans-Pacific Trade: Shipping Arrivals and Departures, 1820 to 1840* (Honolulu, 2000), 71–74.
55. Eliab Grimes to Josiah Marshall, 7 June 1825, quoted in Kashay, "Agents of Imperialism," 285; and in Arista, *The Kingdom and the Republic*, 168–69. The notion of sailors presuming access to sex also comes from Arista, 138.
56. For a very thorough discussion of the *kapu* and its longer-term implications, see Arista, *The Kingdom and the Republic*, 132–74.
57. Arista, 168–73; Charles Stewart to Ashbel Green, n.d., quoted in "Visit of Mr. Stewart at Lahaina, Previous to his Embarkation," *Missionary Herald* (August 1826), 244.
58. "Sandwich Islands. Joint Letter of the Missionaries," 15 October 1825, *Missionary Herald* (July 1826), 207.
59. Different sources give different dates for the *Fawn*'s arrival in London: April 7, in the Cooperstown, New York, *Watch-Tower*, 7 July 1826; April 9, in Richards, *Shipping Arrivals and Departures, 1820 to 1840*, 71; and April 19, in "Sandwich Islands. Joint Letter of the Missionaries," 15 October 1825, *Missionary Herald* (July 1826), 210. For Charles Stewart's connection to the London Missionary Society, see *Report of the Directors to the Thirty-Second Annual Meeting of the Missionary Society, Usually Called the London Missionary Society* (London, 1826), 22.
60. Cooperstown *Watch-Tower*, 7 July 1826.
61. Index to Passenger Lists of Vessels Arriving at New York, New York, 1820–1846, 4 August 1826, https://www.familysearch.org.

CHAPTER FIVE

1. Amelia Davidson to Betsey Stockton, 18 February 1828, Letter Book of the Coloured School Committee; see also the minutes of the Managers of the Infant School Society, 3 March 1828, Board of Managers Letter Book 1827–1830, which noted "a communication from the Rev. Dr. Green intimating that Betsey Stockton would accept the appointment of teacher of the coloured school." Both sources are in the Infant School Society of Philadelphia Records, Historical Society of Pennsylvania; hereafter cited as ISSPR.
2. Amelia Davidson to Betsey Stockton, 18 February 1828, Letter Book of the Coloured School Committee, ISSPR.
3. Amelia Davidson to Betsey Stockton, 1 April 1828, Letter Book of Coloured School Committee, ISSPR.
4. For Charles Stewart's out-of-town speeches, see, for example, "Missionary Sermons," *Poulson's American Daily Advertiser*, 5 May 1827, announcing two talks in Philadelphia. On Betsey Stockton's illness, see Harriett Bradford Stewart to Olivia Murray, 21 March 1827, Rev. Charles S. Stewart Papers, 1822–1862, Coll. No. 263, New York State Historical Association.
5. The village of Cooperstown lay in the town of Otsego, at the borderline of the adjacent town, Middlefield, and in 1830, the Black population of both communities was forty-nine and thirty-one, respectively, out of a total two-town population of 7,686; see African Americans in the Census Otsego County, New York (1790–1930), http://theusgenweb.org/ny/otsego/aacensus/aacensus.htm.
6. For the possible route of travel, see *The Tourist's Map of the State of New York, Compiled from the Latest Authorities in the Surveyor General's Office* (Utica, NY, 1828); for the travel allowance, see *The First Annual Report of the Infant School Society of Philadelphia* (Philadelphia, 1828), 12.
7. Elizabeth Stordeur Pryor, *Colored Travelers: Mobility and the Fight for Citizenship before the Civil War* (Chapel Hill, NC, 2016), esp. chapters 1 and 2. Theodore Wright's speech to the New-York State Anti-Slavery Society is printed in the *New York Evangelist*, 4 November 1837, and the passage about Betsey Stockton also quoted in S. B. Treadwell, *American Slavery: Morally and Politically Illustrated* (Boston, 1838), 211–14.
8. Ashbel Green's address comes from Robert Desilver, *Desilver's Philadelphia Directory, and Stranger's Guide for 1829* (Philadelphia, 1829), 75, which lists him as "DD editor Christian advocate." The likelihood of Betsey Stockton's living with him comes from the 1830 federal census, which lists a free woman of color, aged between twenty-four and thirty-five, in Green's household; Stockton would have been around thirty or thirty-two. See 1830 Federal Census, Philadelphia New Market Ward, Philadelphia, Pennsylvania, www.ancestry.com.
9. On the changing racial composition of the Gaskill Street neighborhood, see

Gary B. Nash, *Forging Freedom: The Formation of Philadelphia's Black Community, 1720–1840* (Cambridge, MA, 1988), 169–71.

10. Population figures for the early decades of the nineteenth century and the shift to the south side come from Nash, 143, 165–69. The "natural gateway" characterization is in W. E. B. Du Bois, *The Philadelphia Negro: A Social Study* (Philadelphia, 1899), 25. On the issue of fugitives, Richard Bell, in *Stolen: Five Free Boys Kidnapped into Slavery and Their Astonishing Odyssey Home* (New York, 2019), 21, notes that "perhaps a thousand . . . found their way to the city in 1825." Emma Jones Lapsansky discusses the larger institutional implications of Black population growth in "'Since They Got Those Separate Churches': Afro-Americans and Racism in Jacksonian Philadelphia," in *African Americans in Pennsylvania: Shifting Historical Perspectives*, ed. Joe William Trotter Jr. and Eric Ledell Smith (State College, PA, 1997), 95–96. On the development of educational institutions for African Americans, see Erica Armstrong Dunbar, *A Fragile Freedom: African American Women and Emancipation in the Antebellum City* (New Haven, CT, 2016), 52–58.

11. For the Gaskill Street location of the Adelphi school, see *Philadelphia in 1824; or, A Brief Account of the Various Institutions and Public Objects in This Metropolis, Being a Complete Guide for Strangers* (Philadelphia, 1824), 131. In 1825, the school relocated to a space belonging to the Pennsylvania Abolition Society, on Cherry Street. See also Bell, *Stolen*, 27–28. For Amelia Davidson's report about finding a place for the infant school, see her letter to Betsey Stockton, 1 April 1828, Letter Book of Coloured School Committee, ISSPR.

12. On the occupational opportunities of Philadelphia's Black people, see Nash, *Forging Freedom*, 146–53, 247–53. The particular situation of women comes from Mathew Carey et al., "Report on Female Wages, Philadelphia March 25, 1829," in Carey, *Miscellaneous Essays* (Philadelphia, 1830), 266–72.

13. Betsey Stockton's salary increase is recorded in the Minute Book of the Board of Managers of the Infant School Society, 3 June 1828. Cobb's salary comes from the same source, 5 May 1828. On the salaries of Ephraim Bacon and his assistant, Caroline Hyde, see E[liza] P. Sparhawk to E. Bacon, 7 August 1827, and to Caroline Hyde, 8 September 1827, Board of Managers Letter Book 1827–1830, ISSPR.

14. *The First Annual Report of the Infant School Society of Philadelphia* (Philadelphia, 1828), 5. For the twenty-five members of the Board of Managers in 1827, see *Poulson's American Daily Advertiser*, 16 June 1827. The Board of Managers also reflected a mix, with twelve married and thirteen unmarried women in 1828; see the meeting minutes for 26 May 1828, Board of Managers Letter Book 1827–1830, ISSPR. To determine their racial identities, I consulted *Desilver's Philadelphia Directory . . . for 1829*, which puts a small cross-mark next to the names of African American heads of household; none of these women came from a household so indicated. For the longer-term background of female philanthropy for the poorer classes in Philadelphia, see Margaret

Morris Haviland, "Beyond Women's Sphere: Young Quaker Women and the Veil of Charity in Philadelphia, 1790–1810," *William and Mary Quarterly* 51, no. 3 (July, 1994): 419–46. For a broader view of Protestant female philanthropy in the antebellum Northeast, see Lori D. Ginzberg, *Women and the Work of Benevolence: Morality, Politics, and Class in the Nineteenth-Century United States* (New Haven, CT, 1990), esp. chapter 2.

15. *The First Annual Report of the Infant School Society of Philadelphia* (Philadelphia, 1828), 5–6; *Second Annual Report of the Infant School Society of Philadelphia* (Philadelphia, 1829), 10–12.

    The prominent women donors listed are Sarah Pettit Bayard, wife of Andrew Bayard, president of the Commercial Bank of Philadelphia; Jane Margaret Craig Biddle, wife of Nicholas Biddle, president of the Second Bank of the United States; Rachel Jackson Strickland, wife of William Strickland, architect of, among other buildings, the Second Bank of the United States; and Margaret Wistar Vaux, wife of Roberts Vaux, "gentleman" and proponent of public education.

16. *The First Annual Report of the Infant School Society of Philadelphia*, 10. The philanthropic support for a segregated school and segregated resources reflects the "benevolent racism" suffusing antebellum reform movements that Susan M. Ryan addresses in *The Grammar of Good Intentions: Race and the Antebellum Culture of Benevolence* (Ithaca, NY, 2003).

17. *The First Annual Report of the Infant School Society of Philadelphia*, 12.

18. *The Second Annual Report of the Infant School Society*, 9, 12. A Philadelphia newspaper, the *National Gazette*, 15 September 1829, reported a lower figure from the subscribers for the "colored school," $103, adding that the fund for that school "is entirely distinct from the general fund." The four life subscribers were Mrs. (Hannah) Chancellor, widow of merchant William Chancellor; Abraham Pennock, merchant; William Short, "gentleman"; and Joseph Watson, Philadelphia's "late mayor," 1824–28. Black people among the two-dollar donors were identified without first names: Mrs. Cassey and Miss Cassey, presumably the wife and daughter of Joseph Cassey; Mrs. Douglass, presumably the wife of Robert Douglass; and Mr. Forten. Both Joseph Cassey and James Douglass were listed in *Desilver's Philadelphia Directory . . . for 1829* as "hairdressers and perfumers"; James Forten, "sailmaker," was the wealthiest African American in Philadelphia. The work of Julie Winch provides the best guide to their prominence; see Winch, *Philadelphia's Black Elite: Activism, Accommodation, and the Struggle for Autonomy* (Philadelphia, 1988); *The Elite of Our People: Joseph Willson's Sketches of Black Upper-Class Life in Antebellum Philadelphia* (University Park, PA, 2000); and *A Gentleman of Color: The Life of James Forten* (New York, 2002).

19. For the extent of Carey's publications, see James N. Green, *Mathew Carey: Publisher and Patriot* (Philadelphia, 1985), 22–29.

20. Samuel Wilderspin, *On the Importance of Educating the Infant Children of the*

Poor . . . Containing an Account of the Spitalfields Infant School (London, 1823), 19–27.

21. Wilderspin, 21, 36.
22. For the spread of infant schools in the Northeast, see Caroline Winterer, "Avoiding a 'Hothouse System of Education': Nineteenth-Century Early Childhood Education from the Infant Schools to the Kindergartens," *History of Education Quarterly* 32, no. 3 (Autumn 1992): 289–314.
23. "Thoughts on Infant Schools" (18 June 1827), in Carey, *Miscellaneous Essays*, 309–12.
24. "Thoughts on Infant Schools" (18 June 1827), 309–12.
25. On the development of public schools in Philadelphia, see John Trevor Custis, *The Public Schools of Philadelphia: Historical, Biographical, Statistical* (Philadelphia, 1897), 9–15. See also Nash, *Forging Freedom*, 269–70.
26. "The Infant School" (28 December 1827), in Carey, *Miscellaneous Essays*, 313–17.
27. Mathew Carey, "A Short Account of the Malignant Fever Which Prevailed in Philadelphia, 1793" (Philadelphia, 1793).
28. Absalom Jones and Richard Allen, "A Narrative of the Proceedings of the Black People, during the Late Awful Calamity in Philadelphia, in the Year 1793: And a Refutation of Some Censures, Thrown upon Them in Some Late Publications" (Philadelphia, 1794).
29. Andrew Shankman, "Capitalism, Slavery, and the New Epoch: Mathew Carey's 1819," in *Slavery's Capitalism: A New History of American Economic Development*, ed. Sven Beckert and Seth Rockman (Philadelphia, 2016), 243–61; Carey quoted on 257.
30. Mathew Carey, "Reflections of the Causes that Led to the Formation of the Colonization Society, with a View to Its Probable Results" (Philadelphia, 1832), 1.
31. "The Emancipation of Slaves in the United States. No. I" (Philadelphia, 1827), in Carey, *Miscellaneous Essays*, 223–26.
32. "The Emancipation of Slaves in the United States. No. II" (Philadelphia, 1827), in Carey, *Miscellaneous Essays*, 228–31.
33. Mathew Carey, "African Colonization, No. I" (Philadelphia, 1829), in Carey, *Miscellaneous Essays*, 215–16.
34. For a discussion of growing African American opposition to African colonization in Philadelphia, see Nash, *Forging Freedom*, 235–45; Winch, *Philadelphia's Black Elite*, 34–37; and Ousmane K. Power-Greene, *Against Wind and Tide: The African American Struggle against the Colonization Movement* (New York, 2014), 11, 23–26. These works make an important distinction between opposition to colonization to West Africa and some measure of support for voluntary emigration to other places, primarily Haiti.
35. Mathew Carey, "Reflections on the Causes That Led to the Formation of the Colonization Society, with a View of Its Probable Results" (Philadelphia, 1832), 16 .

36. On the hostile racial climate in the 1820s, see Nash, *Forging Freedom*, 253–59; for the threat of kidnappers, see Bell, *Stolen*, 33–41.
37. The rules are recorded on 4 September 1827, and the furnishing of the Gaskill Street school on 5 May 1828, Minute Book of the Board of Managers of the Infant School Society, ISSPR. Rosswurm's support no doubt reflected his frustration with the slow pace of creating a similar school for Black children in New York: "while so much time was spent by our friends here in *councils and palavers*, our neighbours were actively engaged in the cause of humanity." *Freedom's Journal*, 9 May 1828.
38. Bacon's *A Manual of the System of Instruction Pursued at the Infant School, Chester Street, Philadelphia*, is attached to J. R. Brown, *An Essay on Infant Cultivation: With a Compendium of the Analytical Method of Instruction and Elliptical Plan of Teaching, Adopted at Spitalfields Infants' School, with General Observations on the System of Infant Tuition &c.* (Philadelphia, 1828), 25–45. The question about learning in Liberia does not appear in his System of Instruction, but is noted in Helen May, Baljit Kaur, and Larry Prochner, *Empire, Education, and Indigenous Childhoods: Nineteenth-Century Missionary Infant Schools in Three British Colonies* (London, 2014), 167–68.
39. Committee for the Coloured School, 5, 26 May 1828, Letter Book of the Coloured School Committee, ISSPR. In an upbeat report on Ephraim Bacon's school for white children, the *American Sunday School Magazine* also noted, with considerably more restraint, that "A school of 66 children has been opened on Gaskill street, under the instruction of a competent teacher"; quoted in the *American Journal of Education* 3, no. 8 (1828), 490.
40. The comments are recorded on 1 December 1828, 5 January and 2 February 1829, in Letter Book of the Coloured School Committee, ISSPR. One other visitor of note was the Reverend Ashbel Green, who one evening recorded in his diary that he had "Visited Betsy's school"—nothing more. See Ashbel Green Diary, 4 December 1828, Box 6, Folder 12, Ashbel Green Papers, Princeton University Archives, Department of Rare Books and Special Collections, Princeton University Library; hereafter cited as Green Diary.
41. Minute Book of the Board of Managers, 4 May 1829.
42. For Green's meeting with William Case, see Green Diary, 18 April 1829, Box 6, Folder 13, Princeton RBSC. Case's comments come from his address to the Methodist Missionary Society of New York, in *Zion's Herald*, 14 May 1828.
43. For the references to Betsey Stockton in Canada, see May, Kaur, and Prochner, *Empire, Education, and Indigenous Childhoods*, 164, 168.
44. On the Ojibwa and Methodist missionaries in Upper Canada, see Hope MacLean, "A Positive Experiment in Aboriginal Education: The Methodist Ojibwa Day Schools in Upper Canada, 1824–1833," *Canadian Journal of Native Studies* 22, no. 1 (2002): 23–63; and "Ojibwa Participation in Methodist Residential Schools in Upper Canada, 1828–1860," *Canadian Journal of Native Studies* 25, no. 1 (2005): 93–137; for the Grape Island mission, see May, Kaur, and Prochner, *Empire, Education, and Indigenous Childhoods*, 153–76.

45. The Reverend William Case to the *Christian Advocate and Journal*, 15 May 1828, published in *Zion's Herald*, 9 July 1828. Betsey Stockton arrived at Grape Island in mid-May, perhaps accompanying William Case; there is no record of her travel to Canada.
46. The available evidence comes from May, Kaur, and Prochner, *Empire, Education, and Indigenous Childhoods*, 170–73.
47. Minute Book of the Infant School Society of Philadelphia, 7 September, 2 November, 7 December 1829, 4 January, 3 May, 24 May 1830; *The Second Annual Report of the Infant School Society of Philadelphia*, 6.
48. Charles Samuel Stewart, *A Visit to the South Seas, in the U.S. Ship* Vincennes, *during the Years 1829 and 1830; with Scenes in Brazil, Peru, Manila, the Cape of Good Hope, and St. Helena*, 2 vols. (New York, 1831), 2:306.
49. Minute Book of the Infant School Society of Philadelphia, 4 October, 1 November 1830, 3 January, 7 February 1831. *The Fourth Annual Report of the Infant School Society of Philadelphia* (Philadelphia, 1831), 4, sought to put the situation in a more positive light. Without mentioning Betsey Stockton by name, it admitted that the "school for coloured children . . . has met with a great loss in the resignation of a valuable teacher, who . . . was called to perform other duties, and was obliged to relinquish an employment, in which she had been eminently successful." On the other hand, the report noted "130 enrolled, and from 80 to 90 attending daily. . . . A qualified teacher has lately been obtained, to take charge of the school, and it is again in a flourishing condition."

CHAPTER SIX

1. *Commercial Advertiser* (New York), 10 July 1835.
2. For the early history of the church, see William Edward Schenck, *An Historical Account of the First Presbyterian Church of Princeton, N.J.* (Princeton, NJ, 1850), 26–33. Membership figures come from Lefferts A. Loetscher, "New Vitality in Church and Nation," in *The First Presbyterian Church of Princeton: Two Centuries of History*, ed. Arthur S. Link (Princeton, NJ, 1967), 43, who notes 391 members in 1835, up from 355 the previous year.
3. For a useful view of Charles Stewart's life in the early 1830s, see Lawrence B. Brennan, "Captain Charles S. Stewart, US Navy (Retired) 1795–1870 and a 158 Year Old Cover," *Journal of the New Jersey Postal History Society* 43, no. 3 (August 2015): 136. A biographical sketch of James Sproat Green appears in John Frelinghuysen Hageman, *Princeton and Its Institutions*, 2 vols. (Philadelphia, 1879), 1:318–20; the early days of the Edgehill School are covered in 2:221–22. Betsey Stockton's return to Princeton Presbyterian, "admitted upon Certificate," is documented in the entry for 1 May 1835 in Minutes of the Proceedings of the Session of the Presbyterian Church of Princeton (N.J.), Vol. 2d, Beginning 1822 (typescript), Synod of New Jersey Collection, Princeton

Theological Seminary Library, Special Collections, 117; hereafter cited as Minutes of the Session. The reason for the apparent delay in the renewal of her membership is unclear.

4. Brennan, "Captain Charles S. Stewart," 136.
5. For the rebuilding of the Presbyterian church, see Hageman, *Princeton and Its Institutions*, 2:135–36.
6. James W. Alexander to John Hall, 17 November 1837, in *Forty Years' Familiar Letters of James W. Alexander, D.D., Constituting, with the Notes, a Memoir of His Life*, ed. John Hall, DD, 2 vols. (New York, 1860), 1:260. See also the summary of the separation in Loetscher, "New Vitality in Church and Nation," 34–35, which contains Alexander's letter and the language regarding the sexton; Hageman, in *Princeton and Its Institutions*, 2:100, cites slightly different wording about the sexton's orders.
7. Albert B. Dod (1805–45) served as an elder from 1836 on; see Schenck, *Historical Account*, 77. His role in reseating the church is in Hageman, *Princeton and Its Institutions*, 2:136–37. Dod's name appears as the contact person in an 1837 advertisement for the sale of pews in the new church; see *Princeton Whig and Somerset & Middlesex Advertiser*, 15 September 1837. For Dod's meeting with the Black members, see Hageman, *Princeton and Its Institutions*, 2:209. The other member of the committee with Dod was Samuel A. Lawrence. Alexander's comment is in James W. Alexander to John Hall, 17 November 1837, in *Forty Years' Familiar Letters* 1:260.
8. 1 August 1832, Minutes of the Session, 88–89; see also Loetscher, "New Vitality in Church and Nation," 41–42.
9. Alexander to John Hall, 17 November 1837, in *Forty Years' Familiar Letters*, 1:260. In 1840, Princeton's free Black population numbered 637, 20.9 percent of the total; see Year: *1840*; Census Place: *Princeton, Mercer, New Jersey*; Roll: *254*; Page: *48*; Family History Library Film: *0016518*.
10. On Lowrey's appointment, see the entry for 24 August 1839, Minutes of the Session, 315; his biographical sketch is in Hageman, *Princeton and Its Institutions*, 1:273–74. John Breckinridge's role in fund-raising is noted in Hageman, *Princeton and Its Institutions*, 2:209, and his biographical sketch in 2:364–66.
11. *Princeton Whig and Somerset & Middlesex Advertiser*, 22 July 1836. The article also mentioned that the "African Methodist Church is also in progress of enclosure"; it later came to be called the Mt. Pisgah AME Church, first organized in 1832 by an AME preacher from Trenton, Samson Peters. In its early years, the congregation met at a house on Witherspoon Street, then moved into the new structure at the corner of Witherspoon and Maclean Streets. See "Mt. Pisgah AME Church," Albert E. Hinds Memorial Walking Tour: African American Life in Princeton, https://www.princetonhistory.org/tour/24.html.
12. On the history of the cemetery, including the segregation of Black bodies, see Hageman, *Princeton and Its Institutions*, 2:179–81, 417–18; and Loetscher, "New Vitality in Church and Nation," 33.

13. Hageman, *Princeton and Its Institutions*, 1:254; 2:14, 10–181. For more recent descriptions of the Witherspoon neighborhood, see Constance M. Greiff, Mary W. Gibbons, and Elizabeth G. C. Menzies, *Princeton Architecture: A Pictorial History of Town and Campus* (Princeton, NJ, 1967), 89; Cynthia Gooding, *A Princeton Guide: Walks, Drives, & Commentary* (Somerset, NJ, 1971), 39; and Historical Society of Princeton, Albert E. Hinds Memorial Walking Tour: African American Life in Princeton, https://www.princetonhistory.org/tour/.
14. Alexander to John Hall, 12 April 1840 ("Monday after Palm Sunday"), *Forty Years' Familiar Letters*, 1:301; Loetscher, "New Vitality in Church and Nation," 35. Alexander's use of "our" stemmed from his position as preacher, a role he began during his time on the Princeton faculty and would continue until 1844, with his departure for a pastorate at the Duane Street Presbyterian Church in New York.
15. Among the notes about the disciplining of Black church members, the three cases cited are from 4, 15, and 29 May 1838; 16 December 1842; 30 December 1842; and 5 January 1843, in Minutes of Session 1822–1844, Presbyterian Church of Princeton vol. 2 (manuscript), Synod of New Jersey Collection, Princeton Theological Seminary Library, Special Collections, 304–5, 384, 388; hereafter cited as Minutes of Session 1822–1844.

    The session records include the names of the people brought before the session, but I have chosen not to do so here.
16. On the meetings in the "African church," see the entries for 22 March 1845 and 24 May 1845 in Minutes of Session 1822–1844, 424, 430.
17. 10 March 1846, Minutes of Session 1822–1844, unpaginated. The notion of a "push-away" congregation here suggests a comparison to the move by Richard Allen and Absalom Jones to lead the Black worshippers in a walkout of St. George's Methodist Church in Philadelphia in 1792 or 1793; see Albert J. Raboteau, "Richard Allen and the African Church Movement," in *Black Leaders of the Nineteenth Century*, ed. Leon Litwack and August Meier (Urbana, IL, 1988), 1–18.
18. The most thorough account of this incident is Yanielli, "Princeton Students Attempt to Lynch an Abolitionist," Princeton & Slavery Project, https://slavery.princeton.edu/stories/attempted-lynching. The details come from a letter from John Witherspoon Woods, class of 1837, to his mother, in John Witherspoon Woods Letters, Student Correspondence and Writings Collection, Folder 10, Box 7, Princeton University Archives, Department of Rare Books and Special Collections, Princeton University Library. For another account, see Lolita Buckner Inniss, *The Princeton Fugitive Slave: The Trials of James Collins Johnson* (New York, 2019), 51–52, which includes extracts from a September 1835 letter from Gilbert Rodman McCoy to his cousin Gilbert Rodman Fox, classes of 1837 and 1835, respectively.
19. *Princeton Whig and Somerset & Middlesex Advertiser*, 4 September 1835, in Yanielli, "Princeton Students Attempt to Lynch an Abolitionist," Princeton & Slavery Project.

20. Theodore Wright's letter is reprinted in the *Liberator*, 5 November 1836. See also Inniss, *The Princeton Fugitive Slave*, 49–51, which notes that the perpetrator was either William Alexander Ancrum (College of New Jersey, class of 1836) or Thomas James Ancrum (College of New Jersey, class of 1838), two brothers from South Carolina, and suggests that it was likely the latter.
21. For a very detailed, book-length study of the James Collins Johnson case, see Inniss, *The Princeton Fugitive Slave*. The trial itself is covered in chapter 4.
22. Hageman's reflection on the outcome of the trial comes from *Princeton and Its Institutions*, 1:267–69. The report about the "fracas" comes from the *Newburyport Herald* (Newburyport, MA), 10 August 1843; for similar reports, see also the *North American* (Philadelphia), 5 August 1843; *Centinel of Freedom* (Newark, NJ), 8 August 1843; *Daily National Intelligencer* (Washington, DC), 8 August 1843; *Philadelphia Public Ledger*, 9 August 1843; *Portsmouth Journal of Literature and Politics* (Portsmouth, NH), 12 August 1843; *Republican Farmer* (Bridgeport, CT), 15 August 1843; *Jamestown Journal* (Jamestown, NY), 17 August 1843; and *Farmer's Cabinet* (Amherst, NH), 28 August 1843.
23. Philip Wallis's account of the Johnson trial appeared in the *Louisville Journal* (Louisville, KY) and was reprinted in the *Newark Daily Advertiser*, 13 November 1843. Severn Teackle Wallis's expression of appreciation appeared in the *Princeton Whig* and was reprinted in the *Daily National Intelligencer* (Washington, DC), 8 August 1843.
24. Inniss, *The Princeton Fugitive Slave*, chapters 5 and 6.
25. For the reactions of northern newspapers to the issues raised in the trial, see *Jamestown Journal*, 17 August 1843; *Philadelphia Gazette*, reprinted in the *North American* (Philadelphia), 5 August 1843; *Expositer* (Bangor, ME), 1 August 1843.
26. For a full account of the two related incidents, see R. Isabella Morales, "The Riot of 1846," Princeton & Slavery Project, https://slavery.princeton.edu/stories/riot-of-1846.
27. The account of the attack was in the *Baltimore Saturday Visiter* [*sic*], 24 October 1846.
28. For the mayor's concerns and the local ordinance and records of prior actions, see Minutes of the Common Council of the Borough of Princeton, 6 April 1830 to 5 August 1848, Borough Hall, Princeton, NJ. The note about the "loose characters" first appeared in the *Princeton Whig* and was reprinted in the *Newark Daily Advertiser*, 5 September 1846.
29. Betsey Stockton to Charles Samuel Stewart, 28 October 1845 and 6 January 1846, Rev. Charles Samuel Stewart Papers, New York Historical Association—Research Library.
30. The records of the Witherspoon Street Presbyterian Church were apparently lost during a twentieth-century renovation. But Rogers and Gardner must have brought a fresh perspective on their preaching. On the nature of Black theology in the antebellum era, see, for instance, Albert J. Raboteau, *The Invisible Institution in the Antebellum South* (New York, 1978) and *African-*

American Religion (New York, 1999); Eddie S. Glaude, *Exodus! Religion, Race, and Nation in Early Nineteenth-Century Black America* (Chicago, 2000); and Raphael G. Warnock, *The Divided Mind of the Black Church: Theology, Piety, and Public Witness* (New York, 2013).

31. This account comes from a profile of Rogers in Joseph M. Wilson, *The Presbyterian Historical Almanac, and Annual Remembrancer* (Philadelphia 1862), 191–95. Rogers served the Plane Street Church throughout the 1850s, writing sermons, hymns, and poems. But he had his sights set on Africa, where he could "proclaim the gospel of peace to his African brethren . . . and thus be useful to the dying and perishing heathen." Joining the African Civilization Society, an African American emigration organization created in 1857—and, significantly, distinct from the American Colonization Society—Rogers sailed in late 1860 to Sierra Leone. He came down with a fever not long after his arrival and died.

32. For Gardner's background, see Harry Reed, *Platform for Change: The Foundations of the Northern Free Black Community, 1775–1865* (East Lansing, MI, 1994), 40–41. As Anna Bustill-Smith recalled in *Reminiscences of Colored People of Princeton, N.J., 1800–1900* (Philadelphia, 1913), 8, "Dr. Ashbel Green was always interested in him and remembered him in his will." Green's will is in the collections of the Historical Society of Pennsylvania.

33. On Gardner's politics, see David McBride, "Black Protest against Racial Politics: Gardner, Hinton and Their Memorial of 1838," *Pennsylvania History: A Journal of Mid-Atlantic Studies* 46, no. 2 (1979): 149–62, esp. 154–58.

34. Organized in 1837, the Vigilant Association of Philadelphia had a successful record of helping fugitives escape from slavery, but internal disagreements and external attacks, including race riots, had caused it to all but cease to function. Gardner led a short-lived effort to revive the committee in late 1843. On Gardner's role in the organization, see Beverly C. Tomek, "Vigilance Committees," in *The Encyclopedia of Greater Philadelphia*, https://philadelphiaencyclopedia.org/archive/vigilance-committees; and Vigilant Committee of Philadelphia Records 1839–1844, Collection 1121, Historical Society of Pennsylvania. For the marriage of James Collins Johnson and Catherine McCray (McCrae), on 23 December 1852, see Inniss, *The Princeton Fugitive Slave*, 105.

35. The reflection on Gardner's intellect comes from Bustill-Smith, *Reminiscences of Colored People of Princeton*, 8.

36. Wilbur Henry Siebert, *The Underground Railroad from Slavery to Freedom* (New York, 1898), 123–24. Modern scholars who suggest taking Siebert's evidence with some skepticism include David W. Blight, *Race and Reunion: The Civil War in American Memory* (Cambridge, MA, 2001), 232–33; and Eric Foner, *Gateway to Freedom: The Hidden History of the Underground Railroad* (New York, 2015) 11–15.

37. Both notices originated in the *Princeton Whig* and were reprinted in the *Newark Daily Advertiser*, 5 September 1846.

38. The notice about the 1830 Temperance Society meeting in New York comes

from the *Christian Watchman* (New York), 20 August 1830. For the account of the Philadelphia Daughters of Temperance meeting, see the *Liberator*, 10 November 1848.

39. *Trenton State Gazette*, 29 August 1849.
40. *North Star*, 27 June 1850. The membership figure and self-congratulatory description come from the original history of the organization, Orlando Lund, *The Order of the Sons of Temperance, Its Origin—Its History—Its Secrets—Its Objections—Its Designs—Its Influence* (Syracuse, NY, 1851), 12.
41. *Burritt's Christian Citizen* (Worcester, MA), 3 August 1850.
42. For the newspaper account, see the *Trenton State Gazette*, 7 September 1850. The Princeton's student's version comes from Charles Colcock Jones Jr. to the Reverend and Mrs. Charles Colcock Jones, 16 September 1850, in Robert Manson Myers, *A Georgian at Princeton* (New York, 1976), 88.
43. In 1850, the top five locations for free Black people were Newark (1,229, or 3 percent), Camden (768, or 8 percent), Mannington (760, or 34.7 percent), Princeton (552, or 18.2 percent), and Trenton (525, or 8 percent); see Seventh Census of the United States, 1850: Statistics of New Jersey, Table II—Population by Subdivisions of Counties, 137–41, https://www.census.gov/library/publications/1853/dec/1850a.html.
44. In 1840 and 1860, the decennial census listed Betsey Stockton as living in her own dwelling, the head of a household of one. In 1850, her household contained a Black eight-year-old named Mary J. Henly, who had been born in Virginia. There is no further evidence about how she came to be there or how long she stayed, but she was not there ten years later. Henly was, according to Lois Leveen, "born into slavery, boarded with Stockton and attended her Sabbath school, then was expatriated to Liberia, where she was miserable, and came back to the US, returning to her birth city of Richmond, Virginia—where she became an espionage agent as part of a pro-Union underground ring, largely run by her former owner, Bet Van Lew." Lois Leveen email to author, 6 December 2018, 26 February, 1 and 4 March, 19 June 2019.
45. The *Trenton State Gazette*, 8 March 1848, reported that Scudder had died "on Monday last," 28 February.
46. For an announcement of Green's death, on 19 May, see the *Newark Daily Advertiser*, 20 May 1848. A longer report on Green's death and funeral appeared in the *Spectator* (New York), 25 May 1848.

CHAPTER SEVEN

1. Town Superintendent's Common School Register of the Township of Princeton, 1 August, 18 September 1847, 2 March, 25 June 1848, Historical Society of Princeton.
2. *Colored American* (New York), 30 September 1837, quoted in Marion Manola

Wright, *The Education of Negroes in New Jersey* (New York, 1941), 113–14; *Colored American* (New York), 11 November 1837.

3. The story of Prudence Crandall's experience has been told most recently and concisely by Manisha Sinha, *The Slave's Cause: A History of Abolition* (New Haven, CT, 2016), 229–30; and Richard D. Brown, *Self-Evident Truths: Contesting Equal Rights from the Revolution to the Civil War* (New Haven, CT, 2017), 159–67.
4. *Princeton Whig and Somerset & Middlesex Advertiser*, 17 February 1837; hereafter cited as *Princeton Whig*.
5. The notices for the various schools are in the *Princeton Whig*, 18 March and 31 October 1836. The local prices for commodities are listed in that newspaper on 23 December 1836, and the ad for the runaway servant on 2 September 1836. For a listing of female academies in Princeton, see John Freylinghuysen Hageman, *History of Princeton and Its Institutions*, 2 vols. (Philadelphia, 1879), 2:224–25. For the larger context of female education, see Mary Kelley, *Learning to Stand and Speak: Women, Education, and Public Life in America's Republic* (Chapel Hill, NC, 2006); and Lucia McMahon, *Mere Equals: The Paradox of Educated Women in the Early American Republic* (Ithaca, NY, 2012).
6. For the Princeton Academy curriculum and prices, see *Princeton Whig*, 22 April 1836; for Alvord's School, 3 June 1836; for the costs of the college, 15 July 1836.
7. *Princeton Whig*, 10 February 1837. For a historical sketch of the Edgehill Academy, see Hageman, *Princeton and Its Institutions*, 2: 221–23.
8. Town Superintendent's Common School Register of the Township of Princeton, 1 August 1847.
9. For the push for public education in New Jersey, see Nelson R. Burr, *Education in New Jersey, 1630–1871* (Princeton, NJ, 1942), 259–67; for Princeton in particular, see *Princeton Whig*, 1 December 1837.
10. Burr, *Education in New Jersey*, 261, 263–64; the note from the *Rahway Herald* is quoted in *Princeton Whig*, 15 December 1837.
11. *Princeton Whig*, 15 December 1837.
12. *Princeton Whig*, 22 December 1837.
13. *Princeton Whig*, 5 April 1839, 21 August 1841.
14. *Princeton Whig*, 29 October 1841.
15. *Princeton Whig*, 24 June 1842, 29 October 1841.
16. Hageman, *Princeton and Its Institutions*, 1: 226; Town Superintendent's Common School Register of the Township of Princeton, 18 September, 2 December 1847, 25 June 1848, 6 April 1849.
17. O. H. Bartine, "Princeton Township," in *Annual Report of the State Superintendent of Public Schools of New Jersey, for the Year 1851* (Trenton, NJ, 1852), 73–76. I am grateful to Ashley Cataldo of the American Antiquarian Society for providing these reports.
18. Bartine, "Princeton Township," in *Annual Report . . . for the Year 1851*; for the financial figures, see Town Superintendent's Common School Register of the Township of Princeton, 1850.

19. O. H. Bartine, "Princeton Township," in *Annual Report of the State Superintendent of Public Schools of New Jersey, for the Year 1855* (Trenton, NJ, 1856), 100. John T. Duffield, "Princeton," in *Annual Report of the State Superintendent of Public Schools of New Jersey, for the Year 1856* (Trenton, NJ, 1857), 96–97.
20. Burr, *Education in New Jersey*, 266–67.
21. H. M. Blodgett, "Princeton," in *Annual Report of the State Superintendent of Public Schools of New Jersey, for the Year 1859* (Trenton, NJ, 1860), 110.
22. Blodgett, "Princeton," 110.
23. A brief biographical sketch of Simmons is in Anna Bustill Smith, *Reminiscences of Colored People of Princeton, N.J., 1800–1900* (Philadelphia, 1913), 2–3; a longer one is Rina Azumi, "John Anthony Simmons," Princeton & Slavery Project, https://slavery.princeton.edu/stories/john-anthony-simmons. Simmons's request for teaching space is in the entry for 13 December 1833, Minutes of the Proceedings of the Session of the Presbyterian Church of Princeton (NJ), Vol. 2d, Beginning 1822 (typescript), Synod of New Jersey Collection, Princeton Theological Seminary Library, Special Collections, 107.
24. Information about the early years of the Sunday school comes from Thomas R. Markham, 3 March 1853, in Colored Presbyterian Church Princeton, NJ, "Records of the Morning Sabbath School of the Presbyterian Church (Colored) in . . ." 1852–1865, General Manuscripts [Bound] CO 199, no. 869, Princeton University Library Department of Rare Books and Special Collections; hereafter cited as Records of the Morning Sabbath School, RBSC.
25. See "List of Superintendents," "List of Teachers, Male," and "Female Teachers," Records of the Morning Sabbath School, RBSC.
26. Erica Armstrong Dunbar, *A Fragile Freedom: African American Women and Emancipation in the Antebellum City* (New Haven, CT, 2016), 55–58.
27. Wright, *Education of Negroes in New Jersey*.
28. 11, 18 September 1852, in "Minutes," Records of the Morning Sabbath School, RBSC.
29. "Order of Exercises," Records of the Morning Sabbath School, RBSC.
30. "Order of Exercises," Records of the Morning Sabbath School, RBSC.
31. 6 September, 5 November in "Minutes," Records of the Morning Sabbath School, RBSC.
32. 28 September 1861, Records of the Morning Sabbath School, RBSC.
33. Records of the Morning Sabbath School, RBSC.
34. Records of the Morning Sabbath School, RBSC.
35. Records of the Morning Sabbath School, RBSC.
36. Records of the Morning Sabbath School, RBSC. For Markham's post-Princeton career, see Edward H. Roberts, *Biographical Catalogue of the Princeton Theological Seminary* (Princeton, NJ, 1933), 177.
37. Archibald Alexander, *History of Colonization on the Western Coast of Africa* (Philadelphia, 1846; 2nd ed. 1849), 80.
38. Wright, *Education of Negroes in New Jersey*, 105. Samuel Cornish and Theodore Sedgwick Wright, *The Colonization Scheme Considered in Its Rejection by*

the Colored People, in Its Tendency to Uphold Caste, in Its Unfitness for Christianizing and Civilizing the Aborigines of Africa, and for Putting a Stop to the African Slave Trade: In a Letter to the Hon. Theodore Frelinghuysen and the Hon. Benjamin F. Butler (Newark, NJ, 1840). For Gardner's role in the remonstrance committee, see David McBride, "Black Protest against Racial Politics: Gardner, Hinton and Their Memorial of 1838," *Pennsylvania History: A Journal of Mid-Atlantic Studies* 46, no. 2 (1979): 156; the other members listed are James Forten, S. H. Gloucester, Robert Douglass, and Bishop Morris Brown.

39. March 1853, Records of the Morning Sabbath School, RBSC. On Eli Botsford's role as supply minister, see Roberts, *Biographical Catalogue of the Princeton Theological Seminary*, 174

40. For Brookes's comment about Betsey Stockton, see David Riddle Williams, *James H. Brookes: A Memoir* (St. Louis, 1897), 57. For Stockton's gift to Giger, see Betsey Stockton to George Musgrave Giger, 20 October 1856, Princeton University Library Collection of Stockton Family Materials, Box 1, Folder 14, Manuscripts Division, Department of Rare Books and Special Collections, Princeton University Library. For a brief sketch of Giger, College of New Jersey, class of 1841, and Princeton Theological Seminary, class of 1844, see Roberts, *Biographical Catalogue of the Princeton Theological Seminary*, 122; Roberts does not note Giger's service as pastor at Witherspoon Street Church. The *Daily True American* (Trenton, NJ), 10 February 1860, reported that "A memorial from the Witherspoon St. (colored) Church, Princeton, asking for the ordination of Mr. G. W. Giger, who has been preaching several years as the stated supply, was presented and their request was granted." For Giger's role as superintendent, see *Annual Report of the State Superintendent of Public Schools of New Jersey, for the Year 1861* (Trenton, NJ, 1862), 123–24.

41. On Lewis Ward Mudge, see *General Catalogue of Princeton University, 1746–1906* (Princeton, NJ, 1908), 210. His role in bringing baseball to the college in the fall of 1858 is discussed in *Athletics at Princeton: A History*, comp. and ed. Frank Presbrey and James Hugh Moffatt (New York, 1901), 20. Mudge's reflections on his time as superintendent come from the *Maui News*, 5 May 1906.

42. Born in New Jersey in 1783, Ann Maria Davison had lived most of her life in Louisiana, most recently as a widow with her daughter and son-in-law on a cotton and rice plantation north of New Orleans. Surrounded by a slaveholding society, she had nonetheless become an opponent of slavery, relying on her belief in Christian principles of human equality to challenge those who argued that enslaved Blacks in the South were better off than free people of color in the North. See R. Isabela Morales, "A Southern Woman in 'Negro Town,'" and a transcript of her diary, "A Visit to the Colored People of Princeton," both in Princeton & Slavery Project, https://slavery.princeton.edu/stories/a-southern-woman-in-princetons-negro-town and https://slavery.princeton.edu/sources/a-visit-to-the-colored-people-of-princeton. See also the note on Davison in the Radcliffe Institute for Advanced Study, Harvard

University, https://www.radcliffe.harvard.edu/inside-collections/ann-maria-davison; the manuscript copy of Davison's diary is in Ann Maria Davison Papers, 1814–1861, MC 234, folder 22, Schlesinger Library, Radcliffe Institute, Harvard University.

43. Davison, "Colored People of Princeton."
44. Davison.

CHAPTER EIGHT

1. Stonaker's instructions came from *Eighth Census of the United States—1860, Instructions to U.S. Marshals, Instructions to Assistants* (Washington, DC, 1860), 2–4, 18 (hereafter cited as *1860 Instructions*); and his count for Princeton from US Census, 1860, database with images, *FamilySearch*, https://familysearch.org/ark:/61903/1:1:MFHG-N87; hereafter cited as 1860 Census, Princeton. Stonaker's election as mayor is noted in John Freylinghuysen Hageman, *History of Princeton and Its Institutions*, 2 vols. (Philadelphia 1879), 2:10.
2. For a discussion of unmarried Black women, see James Oliver Horton, "Freedom's Yoke: Gender Conventions among Antebellum Free Blacks," *Feminist Studies* 12 (Spring 1986): 51–76, esp. 67–69.
3. The definition of "family" comes from *1860 Instructions*, 3.
4. *1860 Instructions*, 3; 1860 Census, Princeton. As James Oliver Horton, in *Free People of Color: Inside the African American Community* (Washington, DC, 1993), 126, has pointed out, "Each census taker was likely to record the race of a person in accordance with his perception of a person's racial group." That being the case, "the census can not be said to have recorded racial heritage . . . [but] apparent skin color."
5. *1860 Instructions*, 12; 1860 Census, Princeton.
6. 1860 Census, Princeton.
7. The revision of the New Jersey State Constitution, in 1844, removed the property requirement and extended the vote to "Every white male citizen of the United States, of the age of twenty-one years, who shall have been a resident of this state one year, and of the county in which he claims his vote five months next before the election, shall be entitled to vote for all officers that now are, or hereafter may be elective by the people." See *Proceedings of the New Jersey State Constitutional Convention of 1844*, compiled and edited by the New Jersey Writer's Project of Works Progress Administration, Sponsored by the New Jersey State House Commission (1942), 92–95, 584.
8. The descriptions of Lincoln's procession come from the *West Jersey Pioneer* (Bridgton, NJ), 2 March 1861; the *Philadelphia Inquirer*, 22 February 1861; William Gillette, *Jersey Blue: Civil War Politics in New Jersey, 1854–1865* (New Brunswick, NJ, 1995), 127; and Ted Widmer, *Lincoln on the Verge: Thirteen Days to Washington* (New York, 2020), 362–67.
9. *West Jersey Pioneer*, 2 March 1861. Gillette, *Jersey Blue*, 102–5.

10. Gillette, *Jersey Blue*, 100–101.
11. *West Jersey Pioneer*, 2 March 1861; see also Widmer, *Lincoln on the Verge*, 369–72.
12. On the politics of the *Princeton Standard*, see Hageman, *Princeton and Its Institutions*, 1:282, 288. For the 1860 election returns in Princeton, see W. Barksdale Maynard, "Princeton and the Civil War," Princeton & Slavery Project, https://slavery.princeton.edu/stories/princeton-and-the-civil-war.
13. Paris Amanda Spies-Gans, "'Let the Southerns Come Here': Letters of a Slaveholding Father and Son," Princeton & Slavery Project, https://slavery.princeton.edu/stories/let-the-southerns-come-here-letters-of-a-slaveholding-father-and-son. For an earlier similar observation about the diversity of political positions, see James Buchanan Henry and Christian Henry Scharff, *College as It Is; or, The Collegian's Manual in 1853*, ed. J. Jefferson Looney (Princeton, NJ, 1996), 246–47: "The Northerner and Southerner, the Abolitionist and free-soiler, the Secessionist and State-rights man, lived in perfect harmony, none endeavouring to intrude their peculiar opinions on the others."
14. For an account of the effigy-burning, see Kimberly Klein, "The Civil War Comes to Princeton in 1861," Princeton & Slavery Project, https://slavery.princeton.edu/stories/the-civil-war-comes-to-princeton-in-1861. The question of college student suffrage had come up during the drafting of the New Jersey Constitution in 1844, with a proposed amendment to prohibit out-of-state students from voting in New Jersey, but after considerable debate, the amendment was withdrawn. The age and residency requirements might have excluded some students, but in 1860, over 60 percent of the College of New Jersey undergraduates were over twenty-one and thus eligible to vote. It is impossible to know exactly how many of them voted in Princeton, but given the political climate of the campus, the presumption has to be that most were not Lincoln supporters.
15. On the role of Robert Field Stockton and other Princeton men in the Peace Commission, see Craig Hollander, "Navigating Slavery: Robert F. Stockton and the Limits of Antislavery Thought," Princeton & Slavery Project, https://slavery.princeton.edu/stories/navigating-slavery. See also Hageman, *Princeton and Its Institutions*, 1: 286.
16. Klein, "Civil War Comes to Princeton"; James Waddel Alexander, *Princeton—Old and New: Recollections of Undergraduate Life* (New York, 1898), 101–3; Hageman, *Princeton and Its Institutions*, 1:292.
17. Klein, "Civil War Comes to Princeton."
18. Klein; *Trenton State Gazette*, 16 September 1861; see also Hageman, *Princeton and Its Institutions*, 1:293, for the quotation from the *Princeton Standard*, 16 September 1861.
19. Hageman, *Princeton and Its Institutions*, 1:289–90.
20. Hageman, 1:295–96.
21. Betsey Stockton's will is in New Jersey, Wills and Probate Records, 1739–1991,

https://www.ancestry.com/search/collections/8796/?name=betsey_stockton; hereafter cited as Betsey Stockton will.

22. For the presence of Brazier and her children, David and Mary, in the Sunday school, see "Female Teachers," "List of Scholars, males" and "Female Scholars," in Colored Presbyterian Church Princeton, NJ, "Records of the Morning Sabbath School of the Presbyterian Church (Colored) in . . ." 1852–1865, General Manuscripts [Bound] CO 199, no. 869, Princeton University Library Department of Rare Books and Special Collections; hereafter cited as Records of the Morning Sabbath School, RBSC.
23. Betsey Stockton will. Unfortunately, there's no indication of what happened to all of that; to date, the only known book Betsey Stockton owned is the volume of Thomas Branagan's *Flowers of Literature*.
24. It is admittedly easier to measure the duration of this friendship than its depth. In *Founding Friendships: Friendships between Men and Women in the Early American Republic* (New York, 2015), Cassandra Good explores male-female friendships among members of the white upper class, describing them as "both a product and a way of demonstrating elite status." But for such friendships "among lower class, black, or native people, evidence is difficult to find." The Stockton-Stewart connection could be an instructive exception.

    The "picture of the landing of the first missionaries at Otahite" Stockton left for Stewart is Francesco Bartolozzi, "To the treasurer & directors of the London Missionary Society. This print representing the cession of the district of Matavai in the island of Taheité to Captain James Wilson for the use of the missionaries sent hither by that Society in the ship Duff." The engraving, after a 1798 painting by Robert Smirke, was reproduced several times in the nineteenth century. I am grateful to Christopher Cook, a member of the Board of Trustees of the Hawaiian Mission Houses in Honolulu, for directing me to the Bartolozzi image.
25. For Stewart's West Point education and subsequent military career, see *Thirty-Sixth Annual Reunion of the Association of the Graduates of the United States Military Academy, West Point, New York, June 13, 1905* (Saginaw, MI, 1905), 63–71. Some of his classmates went on to be much more illustrious officers in the Civil War, including General George McClellan for the North and Generals Thomas "Stonewall" Jackson and George Pickett for the South, but Stewart did his duty with distinction. The reference to Stewart's recuperation under the care of Betsey Stockton comes from his reflection in a Hawaiian newspaper, the *Maui News*, 5 May 1906.
26. Betsey Stockton will.
27. Charles Seaforth Stewart sent the photographs of his father and Betsey Stockton to the Hawaiian Mission Children's Society; see his letter to Martha A. Chamberlain, 27 October 1899, Hawaiian Mission Children's Society Library. The pictures, along with Stockton's *carte de visite*, are now in the HMCS Family Photo Collection, Hawaiian Mission Houses Historic Site and Archives, Honolulu; they also appear in *Portraits of American Protestant*

Missionaries to Hawaii, Hawaiian Mission Children's Society (Honolulu, 1901), 18–19, both with the caption "Photo about 1863." Constance Escher, in "She Calls Herself Betsey Stockton," *Princeton History*, no. 10 (1991), 94–95, suggests the connection between the two photographs came on the occasion of Stewart's honorary degree; for an account of the commencement event, see *New York Times*, 19 June 1863.

28. For examples of Governor Parker's proclamations in the summer of 1863, see *Newark Daily Advertiser*, 18 June, 3 July 1863; *Trenton State Gazette*, 25 June 1863.
29. *Newark Daily Advertiser*, 20 January 1863; Gillette, *Jersey Blue*, 213–15; James. S. Yard, *Joel Parker: "The War Governor of New Jersey"; A Biographical Sketch* (Freehold, NJ, 1888), 19. Black men later remembered Parker's position. In 1871, the first time they could vote in New Jersey election, some seven thousand voted against him. He won, but not with the help of Black voters.
30. For reports of the Copperhead meetings, see *Trenton State Gazette*, 12, 23 June 1863; *Princeton Standard*, 26 June 1863.
31. *Princeton Standard*, 26 June 1863.
32. *Princeton Standard*, 17 July 1863.
33. *Princeton Standard*, 17, 24 July 1863. For the Irish population, see 1860 Census.
34. For Parker's proclamation, see *Egg Harbor Pilot*, 18 July 1863. The brief article about "Our Colored People" in the *Princeton Standard* appeared on 17 July 1863.
35. *Princeton Standard*, 24 July 1863; see also *Trenton State Gazette*, 30 July 1863.
36. Hageman, *Princeton and Its Institutions*, 1:300–301.
37. *Trenton State Gazette*, 29 May 1863.
38. *West Jersey Press*, 29 July 1863; *Trenton State Gazette*, 28 December 1863, 18 January 1864. For the list of Black soldiers from Princeton, see Hageman, *Princeton and Its Institutions*, 1:308.
39. Gillette, *Jersey Blue*, 307–9.
40. Gillette, 290–94.
41. I am grateful to Stephanie Schwartz of the Historical Society of Princeton for information about Lincoln's margin of victory in Princeton. For contemporary reports, see *Boston Recorder*, 12 November 1864, quoted in the *Presbyter* (Cincinnati, OH), 23 November 1864, which is also the source of the skeptical comment.
42. Gillette, *Jersey Blue*, 301–4, 325–26. On New Jersey and the ratification of the Thirteenth Amendment, see Michael Vorenberg, *Final Freedom: The Civil War, the Abolition of Slavery, and the Thirteenth Amendment* (New York, 2001), esp. 231–32.
43. *Trenton State Gazette*, 7 April 1865, 15 July 1865.
44. For the note about Betsey Stockton's death, see the entry for 12 November 1865 in Records of the Morning Sabbath School, RBSC.
45. Betsey Stockton's obituary ran in the Cooperstown, New York, *Freeman's Journal*, 3 November 1865, and in the *New York Observer*, 9 November 1865.
46. *Freeman's Journal*, 3 November 1865.

EPILOGUE

1. Email correspondence from C. R. Jones of Cooperstown to author, 1 May 2018, 14 October 2020. A subsequent email from a member of the Lakewood Cemetery's trustees and project director for the Monument Repair Project, Merrilyn R. O'Connell to author, 22 October 2020, reports that the restoration of Stockton's gravestone will be funded by a grant from the New York State Division of Cemeteries.
2. Charles Seaforth Stewart's letter to the Hawaiian Mission Children's Society, 27 October 1899, is noted in "Information from Mrs. E. C. Cluff, Jr., Librarian, Hawaiian Mission Children's Society, 6 March 1962," in Charles Samuel Stewart Papers, Fenimore Art Museum, Cooperstown, New York. The idea of putting a monument in Lahaina apparently came from Colonel Alfred Alexander Woodhull (College of New Jersey class of 1856), who had known Stockton during his time in Princeton and was then serving as the army's deputy surgeon general in the Philippines. Perhaps he felt he might pass by Hawaiʻi at some point to facilitate the process. (He may also have been working in concert with Stewart's son, Cecil Stewart, also an army officer in the Philippines.) This information comes from an undated newspaper clipping, probably from 1899, also in Charles Samuel Stewart Papers.
3. "Information from Mrs. E. C. Cluff, Jr." As Mrs. Cluff explains, the reference to Betsey Stockton as "but one of many at that time" came from "a note by a secretary of this society many years ago," but she does not give a specific date.
4. Though the plaque never came to Hawaiʻi, the news of the memorial ceremony did. Two Hawaiian newspapers ran verbatim accounts of the event from the *Princeton Press*; see the *Maui News*, 5 May 1906, and the *Pacific Commercial Advertiser*, 12 May 1906, which headlined the story "Hawaii Once Had a Negro Missionary," a fact that may have been news to many of its readers.
5. *Maui News*, 5 May 1906.
6. *Maui News*, 5 May 1906.
7. Paul Robeson was born 9 April 1898; this account of his early childhood in Princeton comes from Martin Bauml Duberman, *Paul Robeson* (New York, 1988), 3–8. For Robeson's recollections of the stained-glass window to Sabra Robeson, "my father's slave mother on the Carolina plantation," see Paul Robeson, *Here I Stand* (Boston, 1958), 7.

   William Drew Robeson had quite an inspirational story of his own. He had been born into slavery in North Carolina in 1844, then escaped at age fifteen. After working as a laborer during and after the Civil War, he earned two degrees at Pennsylvania's all-Black Lincoln University. He and his wife, Maria Louisa Bustill, had seven children, two of whom died in infancy. Paul was the youngest of the surviving five.
8. Duberman, *Paul Robeson*, 8.

9. Duberman, 6–8. For the controversy surrounding Reverend Robeson, see also Sheila Tully Boyle and Andrew Bunie, *Paul Robeson: The Years of Promise and Achievement* (Amherst, MA, 2001), 17–20. Robeson's description of his father's continuing dignity comes from *Here I Stand*, 12.
10. Robeson, *Here I Stand*, 10; Anna Amelia Bustill Smith, *Reminiscences of Colored People of Princeton, N.J., 1800–1900* (Philadelphia, 1913), 12.
11. Duberman, *Paul Robeson*, 6; Robeson, *Here I Stand*, 15.
12. I am grateful to Ms. Shirley Satterfield for sharing her detailed knowledge of the church, including her role in restoring the plaque to its proper place, in a telephone conversation, 29 October 2020.
13. The portrait of Betsey Stockton in the Hawaiian setting was done by Kevin Stanton. I am grateful to Kenneth Henke, former archivist of the Princeton Theological Seminary, for showing me the painting, and to him and PTS reference librarian Kate Skrebutenas for helping me track down the details about it. For the naming of the Center for Black Church Studies, see "A Report of the Historical Audit on Slavery Recommendations Task Force, Adopted by the Princeton Theological Seminary Board of Trustees on October 18, 2019," Princeton Seminary and Slavery, https://slavery.ptsem.edu/action-plan.
14. "Princeton to Name Two Campus Spaces in Honor of Slaves," *New York Times*, 17 April 2017.

Index